PHILOSOPHY AND THE HUMAN SCIENCES

R.J. ANDERSON, J.A. HUGHES AND W.W. SHARROCK

CROOM HELM
London & Sydney

© 1986 R.J. Anderson, J.A. Hughes and W.W. Sharrock
Croom Helm Ltd, Provident House, Burrell Row,
Beckenham, Kent BR3 1AT
Croom Helm Australia Pty Ltd, Suite 4, 6th Floor,
64-76 Kippax Street, Surry Hills, NSW 2010, Australia

British Library Cataloguing in Publication Data

Anderson, R.J. (Robert John)
    Philosophy and the human sciences.
    1. Social sciences — Philosophy
    I. Title   II. Hughes, J.A.   III. Sharrock, W.W.
    300′.1   H61
    ISBN 0-7099-0552-1
    ISBN 0-7099-0578-5 Pbk

Phototypeset by Words & Pictures Ltd, Thornton Heath, Surrey
Printed and bound in Great Britain
by Billing & Sons Limited, Worcester.

CONTENTS

Preface

Acknowledgements

PREFACE

For a number of years, and under a variety of guises, we have tried to introduce our students to what we have felt are important developments taking place in modern philosophy. We have tried to do so by indicating the range of philosophical questions that were at issue and their philosophical locales. Willing though many of our students were to grapple with and try to understand both the philosophical complexities of the cases being made and their implications for their own studies in the social and human sciences, they seemed to be hampered by the lack of a clear, non-specialist exposition of most of the philosophical doctrines that we wanted to discuss. Time and again, having tried and got nowhere with texts written for philosophers, they gave up in dismay and frustration. We found that there was little, other than sympathy, that we could offer. So, we decided to write this book.

First and foremost, then, our intention is to introduce non-specialists to some of the complexities that need to be taken into account when certain philosophical movements and doctrines are under discussion. To put it bluntly but clearly, we want to make it quite plain what they are getting into and what issues they will have to address if they want, first, to understand and, second, to apply particular philosophies. Because we offer an introduction, we have deliberately kept ourselves to exposition and have avoided extensive critiques and evaluations. All too often, we feel, student texts are inclined to rush to criticism without ensuring understanding first. Because we are not writing for philosophy specialists, we have felt free to select for inclusion only those philosophers whom the students we have in mind are likely to have run across in their lectures, reading and so on. It follows from this that our discussions are partial in that we have generally tied to slant them towards the interests of and connections with the human sciences. We make no claim to have given an adequate summary of the whole of recent and not so recent philosophical history. The general historical surveys which we have included are twisted to fit in with our major aims and with the chapters which they accompany. No doubt we have excluded many topics and doctrines which philosophers feel are essential for the understanding of modern philosophy. However, we do feel that we have provided a fair and impartial summary and exposition of all of the philosophies which we have included. It is no part of our intention to use this book as an occasion to promote or defend any individual philosopher or philosophical tenets. We have tried to give a preliminary survey not a collection of final judgements.

There is a second set of considerations which we think ought to be kept in mind. The relationship between philosophy and any of the sciences is, at the moment, extremely unclear. This is particularly true of the sciences of human nature and action. There are many views of what the possibilities are and how they ought to be selected. Our tactic has not been to offer guidelines for decision-making but to sketch in the background and relate the major features so that students could come to see more clearly just what the philosophical issues might be, and just how philosophical questions and techniques differ from those of the human and social sciences. It seems to us that the differences between philosophy and the empirical sciences are just as important as the similarities, and that they have consequences for the sort of use that can be made of philosophical arguments and doctrines when discussing either empirical questions or the nature of an empirical science.

We have written this book as a text. We know that the division between the sections is an artificial one and that other ways of thematising them could be provided. The justification of our way would be two-fold. First, we have taken the line we have because we wanted each chapter to be a self-contained entity. No attempt at cumulation is made or expected. We feel the reader could begin with any chapter in the book. Certainly it was not written to be read all the way through. For this reason, except where the demands of space have been overwhelming, we have not pruned the text of repetitions, reformulations and rephrasings of the same arguments in different chapters. In our view such reiterations help the reader make connections. Second, it would be our claim that anyone who tried to review the philosophers which we cover would come up with the sort of clustering that we have used. The boundaries of the groups might have been drawn differently, have been a little more fuzzy or more defined, but the members would have been much the same.

Finally, a brief word about the segregation of the philosophy of science in a section of its own. There were several reasons for this. First of all, the philosophy of science has had a largely independent life within philosophical discussion in the human sciences. Often it is the first and only contact that students have with any sort of philosophising. Second, and related to this, is the influence which the philosophy of science has had. The questions which occupy the philosophers of science concerning the nature of explanations, the character of method and the like, have occupied centre stage in most philosophical discussions in the human and social sciences. Finally, as things have developed in the philosophy of science, many of the themes which we draw out in the previous sections have come to be prominent of late. The final section provides an opportunity to bring these themes together in one relatively easily defined topic area.

ACKNOWLEDGEMENTS

A number of people have generously given of their time and patience in reading drafts of this book. We would especially like to thank Stuart Shanker for his many, detailed comments, and our friends and colleagues Linda Birbeck, Ilham Dilman, Dave Francis, John Lee, Fred Kersten, Michelina Vaughan, Philip Pettit, Larry Ray, Keith Soothill and Terry Wallace for their help. Needless to say, any shortcomings are our own responsibility.

RJA. JAH. WWS.

PART ONE

1 INTRODUCTION: NATURE AND REASON

Running through the philosophical movements which we discuss in this section is a common set of themes. These were not first addressed in modern philosophy but were given pre-eminence and modern form by the worries which preoccupied philosophy during the Enlightenment period of the seventeenth and eighteenth centuries. Prime among these worries was the significance to be accorded to the growing and developing sciences. With hindsight we know that these constituted a revolution of the utmost importance. They have shaped our lives and ways of thinking in fundamental ways. However, to the Enlightenment philosopher matters were not so clear. One could not be quite so certain about science, nor about what it told us of the natural world. What was at issue can be summarised by a series of interlinked questions. The first, and historically probably the most important, was: 'What is the nature of our knowledge of the world?' which is a question about the character of our knowledge and whether there are any limitations imposed upon what we can know and find out. The second question concerned the structure and content of the world as these are revealed to us by science, mathematics, religion and other forms of knowledge. It is simply 'What sorts of things are there in the world, and how do they relate to one another?' A distinctive edge was given to this second question when it was harnessed to the first by asking about the similarities and differences between our knowledge of human beings and of other objects in the world. Are humans *just* objects in the world like chairs and mountains, or do they have a different mode of existence entirely? Does the fact that we have a mental life, with consciousness, intentionality and subjectivity make any difference to what we are and what we can know of ourselves? In fact, of course, the question was never put in this minimalist way. It was always couched in terms of how far-reaching these differences might be. For example, we have Reason (mental life) which means that our actions are never entirely determined from outside; we do have free will and are moral agents. Reason stands over against Nature in human life. This raises, of course, the character of our mental life. Does what we know about the world derive entirely from our experience of it? Or do we have innate structures which fix our knowledge? If we do, where to these derive from, and does all mankind share them?

To the Enlightenment philosopher, one of the reasons for taking up these matters was to examine the possibility of extending the scope of scientific knowledge and procedure to human life. If it were possible to obtain scientific or, as they would term it, 'objective' knowledge of human life, then it might be possible to frame social and political laws and conventions which would allow for the creation of the well regulated and harmonious society. Today not many of those working within the human and social sciences share this aspiration, nor hold it with the same innocence. Nevertheless, the possibility of a scientific understanding of human life remains an important topic of debate and dissention. Part of this dissent has been over the nature and possibility of any kind of objective knowledge of social life. What is important to notice here is that while our methods of obtaining knowledge about human life are far from being those used in the seventeenth century, our ways of talking about the knowledge we gain and the frameworks we use to organise that knowledge are very much derived from the Enlightenment. When we talk of the 'underlying realities' of social structures, when we insist upon the 'strict dichotomy' of the mental and the physical, when we contrast 'learned' and 'innate' patterns of behaviour, we are talking in terms first laid down in the seventeenth century and are still raising the possibility of a human science modelled on natural science. We should not be unaware, though, that today the character of scientific knowledge is once again under review, and with it the nature of the world which science reveals to us. How does that world relate to the one which we ordinarily inhabit? How is science related to ordinary commonsense knowledge? In many ways modern philosophers of science find themselves back in the position which seventeenth and eighteenth century philosophers were in and are looking anew at the concepts and categories which were used then. They have done so because of developments within philosophy in the intervening period as well as those taking place in science. The old formulae worked out as a consequence of and in response to the Enlightenment no longer seem satisfactory. As we point out, both in the section which follows and that devoted to the philosophy of science itself, this may have profound implications for the debate over the possibility of and putative nature of the human and social sciences. Two central issues are now being discussed again. The first is the character of our knowledge and its objectivity. This is an *epistemological* question. The second concerns the general frame of reference we should adopt towards the world, our *metaphysics*, and the types of things we can say are to be found in it. This classification of types of things which exist is an *ontology*. As in the seventeenth century, epistemology, metaphysics and ontology are intextricably entangled in modern discussions of science and the possibility of human science.

To get a little room for manoeuvre here, let us take one or two steps backwards. Just where does the difficulty over the objectivity of knowledge lie? If we can see how that was posed, then we might be able to see why the philosophical discussions took the form they did. To do this, we will set up a mock argument between two contending positions. While no philosopher has ever argued for either of the positions we will sketch out, many have felt it necessary to refute one or both of them. We will use them, then, as they have often been used in philosophy, as strawmen, in contrast to which other positions are thrown into relief.

Position 1

There is a world of real objects which exists independently of my thinking about it. My knowledge of this world is obtained wholly through my experience of it. The organisation of the world has imposed itself upon my mind, hence ideas are a reflection of the way that the world is. There is, then, some one way that the world is that we could know. Our objective knowledge would be a description of this one way. When our descriptions of how things are change or are at odds with one another, this is simply a product of imperfections in our measurement and other techniques. This position might be called 'naïve realism'.

Position 2

My knowledge of the world, like anyone's knowledge of the world, is gained from a point of view and therefore is determined by how I see things. If this is so, how can we be certain that any knowledge is certain and not simply the reflection of our own opinions? How do we know what is veridical and what is corrigible knowledge? How can I be certain that I am not dreaming, or being deluded when I say that there is an independent world of objects? How do I know that when I say the pen is red and you agree, it does not really look to you as if it were what I would call green? How can I be sure that the methods we use to find out about the independent world really do work? We may agree that the parcel weighs 12lbs, but how do we know that the agreement is about a fact and not an agreement of opinions?

The crucial thing to notice about both positions is that there can be no pointing to the evidence to decide in favour of either side. Calling up the findings of science will not refute position 2, nor will they prove position 1. The argument is about what is to be allowed to stand as evidence and fact. These positions are differences, not over *scientific* questions, where the facts do count, but over philosophical issues concerning the possibility of facts. What is needed to resolve the dispute is an argument, a set of steps leading from agreed premisses to a set of conclusions which would allow either of our positions or a modified version of them to stand. During the Enlightenment effort was largely directed towards finding arguments for the objectivity of certain forms of knowledge in order to ground the sciences properly and to distinguish them from religion and commonsense. So, while very few people wanted to argue for a naïve realism of the sort set out in position 1, most thought they had to fend off the marauding scepticism of position 2, to protect philosophical knowledge itself as well as the knowledge of science. The task, then, was to show that objective knowledge of the world was possible and just what this epistemology would require by way of a metaphysics.

One way of going about this task is to look for the proposition or propositions, not simply that it would be absurd to doubt, but which, in logic, we could not doubt without self-contradiction. We might try to achieve this by setting aside all those propositions which we could so doubt. So we might suspend judgement upon or doubt propositions such as 'It is raining' simply because I might be deluded or dreaming. Similarly, we might have to set aside others like 'Lancaster is an hour's drive from Manchester up the M6'. 'Lancaster' might not be the name of the town I mean, or it might even have moved, which might sound far-fetched but is not a logical impossibility. By setting aside propositions in this way, inch by inch, we ought to get closer and closer to those which it impossible to doubt without logical contradiction. Once we reach them, we can then use this as the fixed point, the foundation on which to build our deductive chain of reasoning back to the objectivity of the world and our knowledge of it. The most famous user of this method of doubt, is the French philosopher, René Descartes. He argued that while it was feasible to doubt anything else, it was self-contradictory to doubt that one is doubting. As doubting is a form of thinking, then for Descartes the indubitable proposition has to be 'I am thinking'. Descartes now makes a further step. If I cannot doubt that I am thinking then I cannot doubt the existence of a thinker, an 'organon' which has the thoughts. This thinking thing Descartes calls the *res cogitans*. From the indubitability of thinking we have deduced the indubitability of a thinking being, a mind. Even if we grant the existence of a mind we do not have to grant the existence of the material world, nor of bodies to go with minds. The mind does not have to be housed in a body (*res extensa*). Although this is a difficult idea for us to grasp and to accept, for Descartes, believing as he did in the doctrine of the soul, it posed no problem at all. He was willing to consider the possibility of two sorts of entities with two sorts of existence; bodies and minds. To deduce the existence of bodies, and with them the existence of the material world, Descartes has recourse to the existence of a benevolent God who is incapable of deceiving us. The tendency we all have to be certain that there is an external world is innate. The idea of an independent real world was placed in our minds by God. If there was not such a world, God would have deliberately planted that idea in us with the intention of deceiving us. Deception is evil; and so God would have to will evil. For Descartes this is impossible, and so he rejects it. We will come back to this argument in a moment since many have found it fatally flawed. However, once Descartes has deduced the existence of the external world — to his own satisfaction at least — then his dualism of body and mind is assured. On the one hand he has matter, given in nature and studied by science, and on the other he has mind, given in reason and studied by philosophy. The objectivity of the two realms is given by the indisputability of the arguments he offers. They are, or so it seems to him, logical entailments of the fact of consciousness. This objectivity allows science, religion and other forms of knowledge to be objective. The world is divisible into two: an outer publicly scrutable part, the domain of science, and an inner, private part, the domain of philosophical introspection.

From its inception, the argument we have just sketched was felt to be inadequate. To begin with, it was soon pointed out that there was no compelling reason to deduce the existence of a thinking agent from the fact of thinking. All that Descartes could say was that there was thinking going on. This might seem bizarre to us, but we have to remember that our commitment to the materialist half of Descartes' dualism is a consequence of later arguments over it. We are all materialists now. The arguments were not so clear-cut then, and Descartes does want to suspend judgement on the existence of the material world. Second, the argument for the existence of an objective world depends upon the existence of a benevolent God. Many have said that Descartes is arguing in a circle here. He wants to use the whole deduction of mind, body and objectivity as part of an argument for the existence of God. It is a version of the medieval First Cause argument in which God is required to be the Prime Mover, the First Cause, of the universe, since everything has a cause. But the idea of a First Cause, that something created us and our ideas, *is* one of our ideas, and what guarantees His existence other than our reasoning? So God is guaranteed by our reasoning, and — in the case of the external world — guarantees our reasoning.

In response to Descartes' dualism, two sorts of arguments were offered. There were those who agreed that our ideas were innate. They did not require any grounding outside of the claim that they were the structure of the mind. Through the use of our reasoning power alone, we are able to grasp the essential character of the universe around us. The correct method for obtaining this knowledge of essences is by logical deduction and mathematical reasoning; the procedures, that is, of Pure Reason. Providing these procedures are adhered to, there will be a correspondence between our ideas and the way that the world in fact is. This correspondence would be between the essential ideas and the 'basic stuff' of the world. The logical structure of our reasoning will match the logical structure of the world.

The second response came from the sceptics not as a contending programme but an allegation that the conditions which the idealists had set out to satisfy were unattainable. They had failed to show by reasoning alone that there must be an external world of mind-independent objects. The argument did not ground the possibility of objectivity. This scepticism was based on three intertwined components:

1. There is no reason to suppose that any of our ideas are innate. Our ideas are, in fact, 'faded impressions' we have of the perceptions we have of things, people and events we see. Because our ideas are derived from experience, they are corrigible in the light of experience. We can never be certain that we will experience things exactly the same way tomorrow, nor that others are experiencing exactly what we are. That we trust our sense and generalise our impressions is a fact about our psychology, the way we are, not the world. This being so, essential knowledge of reality cannot be guaranteed.

2. Given (1), all attempts to build metaphysical systems are

pointless. None can be better grounded than any other and so all are open to the charge of being self-deluding.

3. The regularities that we do see in nature — for example, that there are certain irreducible substances which stand in causal relation to one another — are the outcome of our habits of mind. We cannot assert that they are independent of our ways of thinking.

The conclusion which Hume and other sceptics drew from their arguments was not that we know nothing. We might, for all we can say, have stumbled upon the truth about the world. But if we do have such knowledge, then it is a purely adventitious and contingent fact of our intellectual history. The truthful and factual character of our knowledge is not guaranteed.

We have here two opposing views of our ideas, and the inferences that lead from these views go in diametrically opposing directions. In the one view, ideas are innate and the experience we have of the world is fixed by these innate principles. In the other, our view of natural order is simply the result of habits of mind. In seeking a middle road between innatism and empiricism, Kant brought about what he thought of as a Copernican revolution in philosophy. Certainly, the solutions that he offered have preoccupied philosophers ever since. The question, as Kant saw it, was quite straightforward, though his answer was circuitous and obscure in the extreme. The question was how to provide for the possibility of objective knowledge of an independent reality from within our experience of that reality; such an argument could not be had simply by relying on our experience of reality, but had to proceed from our experience back to the character of reality which enabled us to experience it in the ways that we do. If we could have a sound argument which did that, then we would have a metaphysics which was indubitable, and hence the possibility of objective knowledge. This metaphysics Kant called 'transcendental idealism'.

Kant begins by accepting as foundational a set of distinctions which, in one way or another, have recurred again and again in modern philosophy. The first is the one we have already met, that between appearance and reality. It is expressed in a distinction between two aspects of objects, how they appear to us (phenomena) and how they are in themselves (noumena). Though it is never really clear what this distinction is supposed to capture, one thing is evident: Kant wants us to agree that because our experience of the world is mediated by our concepts, we can never have direct knowledge of things in themselves. All we can ever gain is knowledge through appearances. The second distinction relates to the propositions we can offer about the world. The truth of some propositions is apprehended directly by reason, they are *a priori*. Other propositions we hold to be true because of our experience of the world. These are *a posteriori*. The proposition $(a+b)^2 = a^2+2ab+b^2$ is seen to be true — given the nature of our algebra — by reason alone. We do not check it out by testing it with 2, 4 and so on to see if $(2+4)^2$ does equal $2^2 + (2\times2\times4)+4^2$. It is, we might say, a formal truth. However, the proposition 'some snakes have vestigial legs' is not like this. We know this is true because it is something we have found out by examining snakes of many different types. Its truth depends upon what we have found out. This second distinction is used in tandem with a third, that between analytic statements and synthetic ones. An analytic statement is true simply in virtue of the meanings of the terms which make it up. So the statement 'husbands are married men' is true simply because being a married man is what we mean by the term 'husband'. However, the proposition 'married men are happy' is true, if it is, because of how marital relationships turned out, not because part of the meaning of 'husband' is that such people are happy. It is necessarily true that husbands are married men. If it is true, it is contingent that they are happy. The distinctions between a priori and a posteriori truths and analytic and synthetic statements can be used to discriminate knowledge. Kant proposes that they can be schematised in the following way.

	A priori	A posteriori
Analytic	Logic	ϕ
Synthetic	Mathematics Metaphysics	Science Commonsense

We will not go into the reasons Kant offers for categorising mathematics and metaphysics as synthetic a priori. All we need to see is that having done so, he has allowed that they can make discoveries about how things are in fact in the world, but do so by the application of reason alone. This co-ordination offers the possibility of a synthesis of Nature and Reason. This possibility was to be taken up by Hegel in an entirely different way and was to form the basis of his dialectical logic. The fourth distinction Kant makes use of is that between empirical and transcendental arguments. An argument such as slow-worms are not snakes but lizards is empirical because it rests upon a body of facts concerning the similarity of anatomy between slow-worms and lizards. Slow-worms are lizards without legs. On the other hand a transcendental argument does not rest upon empirical evidence, but tries to show how such evidence is possible. It goes beyond the limits of experience to show how this experience is possible at all. How do we come to see forms such as snakes and lizards as similar and different? What makes something an instance of this or that? This transcendental-empirical dichotomy became central in Husserl's phenomenology, since his technique was designed to enable the philosopher to go back to things in themselves through a transcendental deduction (cf. Chapter 6). There is one other distinction relevant here, one which we have already introduced *en passant* — between a deductive form of argument and an inductive one — when we suggested that Descartes wanted a deductive chain of reasoning from agreed premises about experience to entailed conclusions about the world. An inductive argument is one based upon our experience. From the facts that we have assembled so far we induce or generalise other facts; from what we know about some members of the class of phenomena, we generalise to all members. Kant's objective is a deductive argument, that is one that is independent of experience, which shows the possibility of synthetic a priori knowledge. If he can demonstrate this, then he will have shown that it is possible to gain knowledge of the independent world which is both objective and based upon the use of Reason. He would have synthesised the noumenal-phenomenal distinction and so used Reason to get an ordered and objective view of the world or nature.

Kant attacks on both fronts at once. Against the innatists he asserts that knowledge is not simply reducible to innate principles. Against the empiricists he argues that knowledge is not the reflex of experience. The world is independent of but known through our concepts. His strategy is to try to reach back beyond our experience to propositions about the conditions for or premises of experience; what are often called the grounds of experience. If he can do this, Kant presumes that such propositions would state ideas which correspond with how reality must be for us to have any experience of it at all. Once we know what the a priori grounds of experience are, we will be able to see how we organise the world as a world of objective experience. The steps back to the grounds of experience are carried out by reflecting upon the nature of our experience of the world, our subjectivity. Kant calls this the subjective deduction. The steps to the independent world comprise the objective deduction.

For Kant, both innatists and empiricists are wrong. Experience is constituted by both cognition and sensation. We have sensibility and understanding. As the famous aphorism has it, 'Thoughts without content are empty; intuitions without concepts are blind'. Kant reasons his way back to the categories we use to organise experience by means of abstraction. If I see rain running down the window pane, what I see is an instance of a natural object, rain, which is in turn a manifestation of a general category, substance. The action of running downwards is an example of causal process. Cause and substance are two of the primordial categories of our mental life. Others he lists are quantity, quality, mutual interaction and many more. These categories are what I bring to experience to organise it. They correspond to features which reality must necessarily have if we are to experience it at all in the ways we do. If the argument Kant puts forward is valid, then he will have shown that, working from our experience of the world as conscious beings, it is possible to deduce what reality is like. Nature and reason would be connected. The spectre of the sceptic still hovers though. Even if Kant is right, and the categories are the principles we use to organise our experience, how do we know that these correspond to reality?

At this point Kant's argument becomes more than a little obscure. The gist of it seems to be something like this. Sensations can derive from outside as well as inside our consciousness. I can feel the heat, but I can also imagine the pain of toothache. This possibility is integral to Descartes' version of dualism. This distinction between inner and outer (the public and the private) is a spatial one. Similarly, all sensations are located in time. The dimensions of space and time are the axes of our experience. They stand outside experience and so put limits upon it. We cannot experience outside of space and time. These two are not categories of experience but give our experience its form. The objectivity of space and time, their independence of any particular experience, is the foundation on which experience rests. Space and time give us the co-ordinates, as it were, of our experience, our subjectivity. The next question is how to get from the co-ordinate constitution of subjectivity to that of objectivity.

Kant makes a set of deductions. Consciousness is always intentional; it is consciousness of something. I am conscious of things in time and over time. These experiences have continuity in time. I can see the same red patch I saw before. I can recall the redness of the curtains and see if it is the same as the bedspread. Kant argues that to have temporal continuity — that is to be the same experience — is to exist. He then argues to exist is to be substantial. He takes this to mean that whatever exists — that is, is substantial — stands in a network of causal relations. Thus a condition of our consciousness has to be that there is something to be conscious of. None the less our consciousness, our experience is bounded by time and space. To try to go beyond these bounds is to step outside the possibilities of experience, and hence understanding, and so is to subvert Reason. It can only be self-defeating.

While Kant's arguments have been the source of much discussion, not to say disagreement, they provided the three major themes which occupy the philosophical movements and arguments we review in Section One — Themes which can be summarised as follows:

(1) There are clear and definite limits to knowledge. We cannot know how things are in themselves, nor can we adopt an Archemedean position outside the framework of our concepts in space and time. The dichotomies of analytic/synthetic, subject/object, reality/appearance, inner/outer have all been questioned in one way or another. Hegel, whose influence today is, as we shall see, largely mediated through Marxism, sought to develop a whole new set of logical relations to capture the antinomies that Kant stipulates. Husserl and the founders of Hermeneutics sought in their different ways to begin the objective study of subjectivity and so dissove that distinction.

(2) The character of experience is constituted by sensibility and understanding. Husserl took this and the opposition of appearance and reality and sought to reach back beyond Kant's transcendental idealism to the essence of experience. What are the constitutive elements of all experience? What is the evidence beyond which reduction cannot go? How is this evidence made available to consciousness? Phenomenology tried to show that all our knowledge of the world had to be derived through the adoption of various 'attitudes' from such apodictic evidence — that is, evidence of the essence of a phenomenon which could be gained through pure reflection.

(3) The organising principles of the mind are fixed and given. They are the a priori categories. Such ideas were the guiding concepts of the development of structuralism in linguistics. The diversity of linguistic

forms is the expression of an underlying unity of mental structure. The application of structuralism elsewhere took the deep and surface structure dichotomy and mapped it on to the appearance/reality and subject/object ones. The deep structure provided the underlying real forces which determine the surface forms, the objective forces determining subjectivity. Here again, of late, the antinomies have been questioned.

In addition to these major themes, there is a fourth, more subsidiary one. Kant's philosophy was critical in character. In Hegel this theme was taken over and extended not just to knowledge and reason but to all forms of thought. In turn, Marx developed this into a fundamental critique of all social relations in contemporary society. Husserl, beginning from very different sets of predispositions, in his later years developed a swingeing critique not just of the idolatry and mystification of modern scientific knowledge but of the cultural forms which give rise to this process. The same critical commitment can be seen being carried forward in the work of Foucault, Heidegger, Sartre, Wittgenstein and many others.

In the following chapters each of these themes is addressed. We have not tried to set the arguments out as a unilinear, unfolding story which goes from error to truth, or from confusion to clarity. Things are much more tangled than that. The point of each chapter is to try to bring out just how tangled the positions and arguments are, and why, therefore, the questions which pre-occupied Kant and his contemporaries turn out to be still relevant to us today.

Recommended Reading

Introductions to the history of philosophy abound. M. Walsh's *The History of Philosophy* (Chapman, 1985) is comprehensive while Roger Scruton's *A Short History of Modern Philosophy*, (Ark, 1984) is both readable and covers all of the standard philosophical themes. His little book on *Kant* (Oxford University Press, 1982), is excellent. Bernard Williams' *Descartes*, although the object of some technical criticism, is clear and systematic. A very useful collection of expositions and commentaries can be found in Ted Honderich (ed.), *Philosophy Through its Past*, (Penguin, 1984). In general, we can recommend two series which contain volumes on particular philosophers. They are the *Past Masters* series published by Oxford

University Press and the *Modern Masters* series by Fontana. For the more philosophically inclined there is also the *Arguments of the Philosophers* series published by Routledge and Kegan Paul. The *International Encylopaedia of Philosophy* is also a very useful reference work.

2 MARXIST PHILOSOPHY

This chapter is about some of the leading strands in Marxist philosophy. It will not deal in any depth with Marx's economic or political theories even though, as Marx himself well knew, they are intimately connected with his philosophy. The distinction we have drawn is an artificial one and the decision to hold to it must provide a peculiarly unMarxist view of Marxism. Be that as it may, our reasons for doing so are twofold. First, we could not possibly cover the whole range of Marxist theory in the space allotted. Second, our intention is to provide an introduction to Marxist philosophy as both continuous with and distinct from other philosophies. It is, we think, fair to say that although Marx remained interested in philosophical matters all his life, he had settled his own philosophical framework in a collection of work written prior to 1850. This framework did not alter throughout the rest of his life. As a consequence, we have felt free to concentrate on those writings. Because of this, our discussion will tend to highlight the extent to which Marx's philosophy is both a response to and a recasting of Hegel's philosophical system. In itself, this is a common enough suggestion. However, we will go a little further. When looked at as a species of philosophy, Marxism is Hegelian through and through.

Given this emphasis, we have sought to redress the balance in the direction of the more conventional view, and certainly the orthodoxy within Marxism, by means of the philosophers we have selected for coverage in the second half of the chapter. Two of these, Althusser and Cohen, want to underplay if not eradicate what they regard as the anti-materialist humanism which is often meant by Hegelian Marxism. Alongside them, we will look at the predominant Marxist philosophy of the twentieth century, Critical Theory, through one of its most famous luminaries, Herbert Marcuse. Marcuse wants to rework Marx's argument with Hegel within the modern context. Since Hegel is, then, the *eminence grise* of this chapter, it is only fair that we should begin by setting our briefly what he thought he was up to.

Hegel

Hegel has suffered the fate of becoming known to non-philosophers largely through the rejection of his system by Marx. In this sense, unlike many of the great philosophers of the Enlightenment and post-Enlightenment period, Hegel's fame is not confined to a small group of technically minded specialists. Every student in the social sciences, for example, learns early on that Marx overthrew Hegel's idealism and replaced it with his own brand of materialism. The trouble is that if we approach Hegel from the point Marx reached after he rejected the system, we are not likely to be all that sympathetic towards it. This is particularly so if, as is usually the case, we address Hegel by first examining Marx's rejection of his metaphysics and ontology. How can anyone take seriously the contention that the universe was designed by, set in motion by, and is the emanation of a Universal Mind? From the vantage point of post-Marxian, anthropocentric materialism, such a suggestion can only seem bizarre. However, if we try not to read philosophical history backwards in quite this way, we may be able to situate Hegel with regard to matters which were of direct importance to him, and not simply those that occupied his later critics. Second, in the case of Marx anyway, the importance of the philosophy could well be heightened by stressing not the break with Hegel but the continuity. In turn, this will give us a way of grasping many of the contemporary quarrels in Marxism. The tension between continuity with and separation from Hegel remains as dynamic as ever. Third, and perhaps most important of all, we may be able to understand Hegel better and glimpse some of the fascination which he continues to exert over many philosophers. Because we are primarily interested in the influence that Hegel had on Marx, we will take up three general areas for discussion: the idea of a philosophy of history; the philosophic understanding of particular events in history through one instance, the Jacobin Terror; and finally the modern dilemma and the cunning of Reason as the unfolding of a new moral and ethical community — a *Sittlichkeit*.

A Philosophy for History

If we think of the compass of history at all, we are likely to think of it, in Henry Ford's immortal phrase, as 'one damn thing after another', a view which expresses rather neatly one of the general philosophies of history current in Hegel's day. This philosophy marked historical time-off by breaking the linear continuous flow into discrete, contingent, 'accidental' events. While one might talk of the 'march of history' or even of 'historical progress', it was stressed that such images were images. History was not going anywhere, nor likely to achieve some definable goal. If we see a pattern to history, that is because we are set by our habits of mind to do so. There is no essential order and progress for us to discover.

As we saw in the Introduction to this Section, empiricism was one of the dominant approaches to the philosophy of mind and human nature in the Enlightenment. We contrasted it with a rationalism that saw ideas and Pure Reason as innate. In the post-Enlightenment period there was a reaction against both of these. Romanticism, as it was called, sought a different kind of connection between Nature and Reason: a connection that was based upon expressivism and spirituality. Against the empiricists, the Romantics argued that matter and mind were definable in terms of their essences. But against the rationalists, they argued that this essence was not formal reasoning but Spirit. For the Romantics, then, history was of prime philosophical importance. The essence of human nature is spirituality expressed in the capacity to reason which achieves its fulfilment in the historical development of philosophy. What the Romantics offered was a new definition of both philosophy and human nature. In Hegel, this emerged as the definition of philosophy as the unfolding of Reason (defined in terms of spirituality) in history. While empiricism could see no sense to the question 'What is the meaning of history?', for the Romantic, the most important philosophical task was to discover the logic inherent in historical processes. The pattern of history would reveal itself to those who knew how to look. Philosophy had to learn the technique for looking.

Hegel felt that his approach provided the definitive rebuttal of empiricism. In common with Romanticism, he proposed a normative and prescriptive philosophy of history. It outlined the necessary stages that history had to pass through. It was this pattern of progress and the manner by which it was achieved which gave meaning to historical events. Such meaning could not be grasped simply by looking at the particulars of each case, but by placing each in the broad context, the total sweep of history. Such a context is given once we see history as the realisation of Reason in the world. This is the central idea in Hegel and, from our point of view today, the most difficult to grasp. The major thrust of empiricism had been in the direction of materialism; all there are are material objects standing in causal relations. The image of clockwork constantly reappears in explanations, much as micro-processors and computer languages do today. Spirituality had been banished to the dark corners, so to speak. In opposition to this view of matter and hence of mankind,

Hegel insists that the essence of human nature is reasoning and that our Reason is an expression, an emanation of Universal Reason (*Geist*) which underlies the universe. The logic of history is no more than the unfolding of *Geist* through its embodiment in our reasoning power. One way of understanding just how Hegel offers a distinctive synthesising of the Kantian distinctions we set out in the introduction is to see the unfolding of *Geist* as the development of human institutions of thought. The development of art, religion and philosophy are expressions of human spiritual development as a universal, abstract phenomenon. Hegel is not saying anything about the evolution of psychological capacities and processes, but of categories of thinking. The socially constructed institutions of thought replace one another in history as they move towards the essence of thought, society's self-understanding. Put in this way, Hegel's ontology of material objects, human beings and *Geist* becomes more comprehensible. The existence of human beings as both material and spiritual objects is a necessary condition of the actualisation of *Geist* in the world in the various institutions of thought which require the use of Reason for their construction. In this way, Hegel could argue that history was not a contingent and causal matter but the necessary manifestation of Reason.

It is crucial to remember at this point just what is and what is not being claimed. This is not an empirical historical hypothesis, a claim that could be tested against the facts. It is a metaphysical speculation which defines what is and what is not a fact, what is real, and how appearance and reality are related. Just as there are orders of being, so too there are orders of reality. There is what we take to be the immediate reality of ordinary events and the deeper reality of world history. The meaning of events is their world-historical significance in the process of Reason's self-fulfilment. This notion of different orders of reality becomes crucial in Marx's thought.

One of the things which makes Hegel appear to be very difficult to understand is his proclivity for treating particulars as instances of universals and thereby trying to overcome the duality between the particular and the universal. The tree's existence, the rabbit in the garden's existence, my existence are all instances, or 'objectifications', of Being. One way of clarifying this obscurity has been to talk of *Geist* as God, and hence turn the whole system into a theodicy. This is fine, and it rightly brings out an important theme in Romanticism, as long as it is not an Old Testament Jehovah that we have in mind. Jehovah was the Prime Mover; He did not require the world to exist in order that His being be realised. *Geist* is a principle, a force, a motivation, not a super-human omniscient old man. It has to be embodied in the world in order to be realised. Embodiment in human reasoning overcomes the limitations of actualisation. As we said a little earlier, philosophy's role is to act as the midwife in this process by formulating the logic of history. Once it has done so, it will have expressed the actuality of *Geist* in the world; *Geist* will be actualised in the world in the institution of philosophy. At that point history, as the unfolding of *Geist*, will stop. Because *Geist* is a universal, and not a particular reasoning being, Hegel denies that the process can be a consciously designed or planned one. The events which lead to the ultimate realisation of history's progress cannot be planned for and created by individuals. The inevitable process will be accomplished because individuals freely follow their own inclinations which, because of the cunning of Reason, lead to one end. What is being offered is a non-determinist determinism, a non-designed pattern, and therefore a way of resolving the age old dichotomy of freedom and determinism in human action. We will see the same vision in Marx.

The Terror

Hegel's philosophy instructs how to understand history, how to fathom its meaning. It requires that every particular event be located in the flow of the embodiment of Reason. To philosophers of Hegel's generation, the French Revolution and its culmination in the Terror presented moral and political theory with its most pressing problem. How was it possible for a movement dedicated to personal freedom and the liberty and dignity of all to end in tyranny and mass murder? — A question with more than passing contemporary relevance. How could these things happen? Hegel answers this question by locating the revolution of 1789 in the broad sweep of history. Its origins are traced back to the break-up of the *polis* of the Greek city states. It does not matter that Hegel's view of the polis as the last working instance of a unified ethical community (a *Sittlichkeit*) is a romantic idealisation, because we are not being offered a verifiable historical thesis but a way of looking at and theorising history. To Hegel, Greek society was the last time that individuals submerged themselves in the community of which they were a part by accepting and submitting to the obligations imposed upon them by their participation in the community and its decision-making. By losing themselves in the community, they achieved freedom. This conception of freedom is very different to that embedded in the modern notion of radical individual autonomy. As we shall see, it is the emergence of the modern notion that Hegel feels accounts for the Terror. The Greek submission to the community was a rational choice whereby freedom was achieved in the pursuit of Reason. At its height, the political dimension of the *Sittlichkeit* matched its philosophical dimension. However, the pursuit of Reason in philosophy soon led to the downfall of the polis. The ideas that philosophy was creating could not be contained within the existing framework. One of these ideas, in fact the most important, was that of the primacy of human subjectivity and human consciousness. This ran counter to the notion of the submission of the individual to the institutions of public decision-making. Individuals could refuse, in conscience, to submit. Within the philosophical reading of history, Hegel gives Socrates a world historical role. As a philosopher, Socrates understands the tension between the ideas which he advocates and the society in which he lives. He resolves the tension by sacrificing himself, and yet in doing so he expresses the freedom of individual conscience. Christianity took this theme over and particularised it in the emphasis it gave to individual conscience in salvation. Philosophical history since the Greeks was, for Hegel, a story of two separating themes; the gradual emergence and fulfilment of radical autonomy and absolute freedom, and the alienation of this freedom in the political organisation of the state apart from civil society as a means of regulating and thus limiting this freedom. Radical freedom is the antithesis of the ethical community of the *Sittlichkeit* and requires the development of the institutions of the state.

We ought to stress at this point that the concept of alienation is somewhat ambivalent in Hegel's writing. On the one hand it refers to the processes by which certain sorts of social practices, and hence the social facts associated with them, correspond to the stages in the development of thought. The nature of the social world as that is given within a particular society is defined through the alienation of Thought. Alienation is the 'objectifying' of the social world; it is social world building. Thus, for example, with the notion of freedom as radical autonomy and creativity goes the *fact* that every man has the right to be treated equally. This fact is expressed or alienated in the social institutions of participatory democracy and hence in elections, parliaments and the like. However, alienation also refers to the separation of such institutions and the *Sittlichkeit* they are supposed to express. When such a separation occurs, the social institutions become oppressive fetters and are, eventually, overthrown. As will become apparent, the Marxist theory of alienation is simply a materialised version of this connection between social forms (alienations) and society. In the place of the *Sittlichkeit*, Marx puts the actual ways of ensuring the means of life, the labour process.

The philosophy of absolute freedom reached its apotheosis in the empiricism of utilitarianism. At the same time, it led to the search for a set of regulatory principles which would guarantee individual freedom while not subverting it. In Hegel's view, utilitarianism's application of rational calculation to ethical questions sought to do just that. Once the general principles of the calculus had been worked out, everyone would submit to them. The basic line was to be a conformity with human desires and the best interests of all. However, Hegel argued that this definition of subjectivity is, so to speak, this-worldly. Human subjectivity is looked at from the point of view of individuals. It is not viewed from the standpoint of *Geist*, Universal Subjectivity. In trying to treat all individual subjectivities as equivalent, utilitarianism ends up by homogenising them. All distinctions are broken down; all constraints on liberty are abolished. In Hegel's view, this makes utilitarianism empty as an ethical theory. It has nothing to put in place of the regulations it destroys. If a political movement gains its energy solely from a destructive philosophy, sooner or later it must destroy itself. This is what happened in the French Revolution. The pursuit of freedom led to the Terror; that was the inevitable consequence of the attempt to actualise absolute freedom. The institutions and procedures set up to free individuals become in themselves constraining as individual participation in collective decision-making becomes mandatory. In Rousseau's phrase, people are forced to be free. The idea of freedom is alienated in the 'collective line' and objectified in 'decision-making by committee'.

The failure of the French Revolution was inevitable because it could not recapture the *Sittlichkeit* of the polis. Two factors above all else militated against it. The functional complexity and size of modern societies mean that full participation in community decision-making would be impossible. At the same time, the ideology of radical autonomy breaks down all forms of social differentiation and atomises society. It creates the mass society: a collection of unregulated, self-determining individuals.

The Recovery of Community

Against this gloomy prognostication, Hegel does offer some hope.

Through the pursuit of Reason, philosophy provides a way of breaking out of the descent into barbarism. Once philosophy comes to see history as the unfolding of Reason, it will see that the Terror was a necessary consequence of radical individualism. That being so, we will be forced back, not to the particular freedom of the individual, but to universal freedom. This would be the next-world historical shift and involves the abandoning of absolute freedom. In its place we would have not collective decision-making as in the polis, but meaningful differentiation. This would re-create *Sittlichkeit* upon the membership of social orders. This new collectivity would be the dialectical transformation of the fragmentation inspired by the ethos of the Enlightenment and the conception of moral and social life as the product of social engineering. The regulatory principle of the new ethical community would be submission to the collectivity at large. Such voluntary submission *is* freedom; the sets of social arrangements which would facilitate it are the embodiment of Reason.

Hegel does not suppose that any particular state actually provides the conditions for such a community. Rather, he sees the stages in the development of history from the collapse of the polis leading to an inexorable fulfilment in Western Europe and its satellites. The socio-economic and political changes that had been set in train after 1815 seemed, to him, to lay the foundation for a reunification of the state and civil society, the differentiation of which had its origins, as we saw, in the break up of the polis. A society which fused these two would be one which embodied Reason. Once it was attained, history, and hence philosophy, would be at an end.

To summarise, then, in Hegel's philosophy we have a view of history as an unfolding process which is only now reaching its culmination. This process is marked by several stages, each of which was necessary for the development of those which followed. The inner logic, the reality, of the process is the actualising of *Geist*. Philosophy's task is to understand this. Once it has done so, and has laid the foundations for the achievement of Reason in society, historical development will be at an end. The form of theory, its vision, is what Marx *took* from Hegel; what he *changed* was its content.

Marx

Probably the two most famous observations made about Marx's

relationship to Hegelian philosophy are these: first that Marx found Hegel standing on his head and turned him the right way up; second, the one summarised in the twelfth thesis on Feuerbach: 'The philosophers have only interpreted history: the point is to change it.' These two are famous because they do encapsulate both the continuity and disjunction between Hegel and Marx. They show that Marx did indeed see himself as taking over and surpassing Hegel's understanding of history, and also why and how such an understanding overcame the limitations of Hegel. Hegelian philosophy was passive; Marx's was to be active. The key to this transformation is to be found in what could be termed the 'philosophical anthropology' which Marx develops when defining the nature of human life and its significance. This anthropology has two main elements: a transformation in the nature of philosophy to that of the philosophy of praxis and its corollary; and the transformation of Hegel's philosophy of history by setting it in its historical context, thereby revealing its real character, its material basis. This anthropology hardly altered at all from the time of its final formulation before 1850 to Marx's death, although it did regress in importance as he became more and more occupied with political matters and the nature of Political Economy. We will concentrate on the early formulations. We are very well aware that, of late, there has been much debate over the claim that Marx's thought displays a fundamental unity. Some have argued that there is a distinct 'epistemological break' around 1845-50, when he broke with speculative philosophy and laid the grounds for the science of history. We will take this up again when we discuss Althusser. However, it is our view that even if this thesis could be substantiated, Marx's scientific theorising did not take place in a metaphysical vacuum. His philosophical anthropology provides the backdrop against which the science is to be understood.

The Philosophy of Praxis

Part of Hegel's account of the development of alienation in the modern world was that Chrisianity had implanted the sanctity of the individual conscience within ethical and moral matters. This occurred with the absorption of Greek philosophy into Christianity by Aquinas. The doctrine of the cunning of Reason held that the unanticipated consequences of actions lead towards fixed historical goals. The essence of Christianity, then, was the part that it played in the embodiment of Reason. The key to Marx's break with Hegel, and hence to his philosophy of praxis, is, so to speak, a sociologising of epistemology. In what at the time was a very influential work among the Young Hegelians, Ludwig Feuerbach had argued that Christianity was, in fact, a slave religion, a vehicle for protest and a reaction to oppression. Its doctrines and forms in the earliest years were shaped by the social conditions of its members, not by the requirements of some abstraction such as Universal Reason. If we want to understand Christianity, then, we should look for the clear parallels between its organisation, forms and doctrines and the social, political and material conditions of its adherents. Commonplace though that might be today, we should not underestimate its impact 150 years ago. Instead of a body of ideas being shaped by and expressing non-material, spiritual determinants, Feuerbach is arguing that Christianity, any body of ideas, is a human artefact. Rather than treating Christianity as an 'instance', an 'objectification' of *Geist* as it struggles to overcome its alienation and comprehend itself, Feuerbach insists that it and all religions are human attempts to locate and cope with their social conditions by alienating them and mystifing them. An other-worldly freedom is achieved in place of this worldly oppression. Marx takes this idea and pushes it to its conclusion. Instead of an ontology of active Reason and acted upon humanity, Marx inverts the subject-predicate relation. Men make history; they are the active force. They are the subjects of history not its objects. The opposition between the reality of Mind and Matter, is replaced with an ontology in which Matter is all that is real. If religion is the alienation of social conditions so, by extension, must philosophy be. If it does not present the material determination of ideas, it too will be mystification. For Marx, therefore, it cannot be enough, as it was for Feuerbach, to simply expose and criticise religions, philosophies and other bodies of ideas. The social conditions which give rise to such ideas must be transformed. Knowledge cannot merely be contemplative; it must be active. A body of ideas must either contribute towards the transformation of the material conditions which create alienation or be alienating itself. The goal of human history is the creation of the material conditions which would overcome the alienation of consciousness. Society would then understand the nature of its material basis.

The roots of the theory of alienation which forms the kernel of the philosophy of praxis are a set of responses which Marx makes to the central philosophical questions of his time. Hegel had tried to overcome the dualities of mind/body, reason/nature, matter/spirit by universalising them and proposing the dialectic of embodiment as a logical synthesis. The source of human spirituality was its expression of *Geist*. Marx locates the origin of human consciousness in human life, not outside of it. Mankind's essence is the relation it stands in towards the natural world. That relationship is transformational. By creativity, the expenditure of themselves, mankind masters the natural world. Rather than the dialectic of embodiment, it is that of labour which allows the synthesis of the dualities. Through labour power, mankind externalises creativity and acts upon the world to transform it. The expression of this creativity is not individualistic but social. It is carried out in society. Mankind's essence, what was termed his 'species being', is collective, as is consciousness. This is the crucial idea. If forms of human consciousness such as religions, political doctrines and philosophies are collective mystifications and alienations, this is not because something *external* to mankind is struggling to express itself and only manages to do so in distorted ways, but because the *internal* relationships of production and creativity — the labour process, in a word — are debilitating and alienating. They create the distorted or false collective consciousness. As with the central tenets of Hegel's system, we are not being offered an empirical finding here; a proposition to be 'tested' against the facts. This is a metaphysical theory about the character of human relationships and their expression. In place of expressive idealism we have expressive materialism.

The important question to be asked is how such alienating conditions could come about. There are two ideas to keep in mind. One is the need for collective productive relations to overcome the constraint of material wants and needs. We obtain release from these constraints through labour, a collective process. The other is the Hegelian idea that freedom is self-expression within an ethical community. When productive relations are such that labour is channelled away from the expression of creativity and instead 'objectified' as a commodity to be sold for wages, there is a loss of control over creativity and self-expression, and hence a loss of freedom. Alienation is expressed in the changed relationship to production. For Marx, the crucial point in this process occurs with the extension of the division of labour and its requirement for specialisation, and the 'privatisation' of the means of production. The means of production cease to be collective and become private property. The process of extension and privatisation is theorised, legitimated and mystified in ideologies such as the religions, political theories and philosophies that dominate human consciousness. Each of these ideologies has the shape and flavour associated with the particular stage in the development of the process of alienation at which it is found. It follows, on this argument, that the central Hegelian tenets such as the role of Reason in history, the necessary separation of the state and civil society, the unification of human and cosmic subjectivity are all expressions of a form of alienated consciousness. It is ironic that this is exactly the same line of argument that Hegel used against the Utilitarians. As with Hegel, Marx is not arguing that these are deliberate fabrications but simply collective false consciousness, the expression of the attempt of particular sets of interests to locate, understand and legitimate their place in history.

Immediately we are face to face with the problem of how to bring this spiral of false consciousness to an end. The answer is well known. It is the abolition of private property through collectivisation of creativity. But how do we know this will work? Why isn't this idea just another piece of alienated consciousness? Notice how the form of this question is precisely the same as that used to define the problem of 'objective knowledge' in the Introduction to this section. It is here that the philosophy of praxis bootstraps itself. The break between Marx and prior philosophy is in the conception of knowledge and its purpose. Knowledge is not gained in contemplation, but in action towards particular ends. The alienated consciousness of Christianity or Hegelian philosophy are not passive but practical knowledge; they serve practical ends, namely the mystification of alienated labour. Philosophy is the activity of society trying to understand its own relations. This will only cease to be alienating and mystifying when mankind realises as a collectivity that it is the subject of history. Such an expression of collective consciousness could only be articulated in a set of ideas, a philosophy, which served not *particular* interests but the interests *of all*. This philosophy would have to be expressed in the ideas of a class which stood outside the system of relations of private property which produced alienated consciousness. The proletariat is just such a class. This declassé class must be the bearers of society's ultimate self-understanding. The bourgeois can gain freedom for themselves by demanding the rights of private property. The proletarians hold no such property. They have only their rights as human beings. In freeing themselves, they will free all. Once the proletariat realises its world historical role, it will cease to be a class in itself and will become a class for itself, and thus a class for all. Having achieved such an understanding of history and their place in it, proletarians will overthrow private property and so liberate mankind.

As with Hegel, this will take the form of the freedom of self-expression, but this time in the community of non-alienated labour. The historical role of the proletariat is not an empirical, historical discovery that Marx culled from his study of history, but the logical entailment of his arguments in the philosophy of praxis and the theory of alienation that it includes. He spent the rest of his life trying to show just how the historical truth of the entailment was to be demonstrated.

Historical Materialism

The philosophy of praxis is anthropocentric. Man is placed at the centre of history. It also replaces a contemplative attitude towards knowledge with an active one. The philosophy which is required is one which will further the goal of history by enabling the proletariat to achieve self-understanding. Such a philosophy can only do so by identifying the revolutionary role of the proletariat in history. This philosophy is the cornerstone of Marxism, and is known as Historical Materialism. In all essential features, it is a philosophy of history formulated in direct opposition to Hegel and is based upon the philosophy of praxis. It comprises three major components: an account of the nature of social life; an account of human consciousness; and a theory of history. All three are predicated on the theory of class which we have presented in a fragmentary form above and which was never fully worked out in Marx's writings.

Social life

In explaining his view of social life, Marx drew on an image which has since become somewhat of a liability, namely the distinction between the base and the superstructure of social relations. In general terms, the image is used as follows. The essence of humanity is the productive creativity of labour. This has a collective character because humans are collective creatures; their species being is collective. The expenditure of labour requires the conjunction of *productive forces*, namely raw materials, technology, knowledge and labour. When we produce things we enter into productive relations with one another. Central to all modern (i.e. non-primitive) production processes is the privatisation of the means of production. Because of this privatisation and the specialisation it is associated with, the alienation of labour has occurred. It follows that the crucial relationship is that of ownership or non-ownership of the means of production, that is, the social relationship we stand in towards production itself. It is this relationship which forms the basis of all our social life. Because the relationship is bivalent — there are owners and non-owners — it has created two great classes. But the relationship is not one-dimensional. Owners are no more free than non-owners. They have the illusion or the appearance of being free, but in reality are dependent on the non-owners. Because the owner needs the non-owner, he is constrained by that need. The dual aspect of dependency is the dialectic of production. As technology, motivated by the forces which led to the alienation of labour, proceeds, so the productive relations that are presently in being become outmoded and have to be replaced. This transformation of the means of production and relations of production is the essence of historical development and can be marked off into stages or epochs corresponding to the dominance of particular forms of production.

The foundations or base of social relationships are the particular forces and relations of production which constitute a *mode of production*. In the theory of praxis, Marx argues that each mode of production gives rise to its own forms of alienated consciousness enshrined in ideologies such as types of law, philosophical theories, familial organisation, state institutions, forms of education and so forth, all of which articulate, legitimate and mystify the alienated nature of the productive relationship. Because ownership and non-ownership is definitive of the productive relation and separates the two classes, the social structures which fit particular forms of ownership are class-determined. What this means is that, for instance, parliamentary democracy as a theory of the organisation of the state is a legitimation of certain orders of productive relations. Parliamentary democracy places a premium upon individual rights and is a form of radical utilitarianism which, in turn, is a consequence, or 'epiphenomenon', of the homogenising and atomising of social life brought about by the extension of the division of labour. Utilitarianism's theory of the state, namely parliamentary democracy, legitimates the breaking down of all class and other communal bonds thereby isolating the individual. It matches, is symmetrical or homologous with, the individuated character of production.

This sociology of social formations is not a mechanical recipe. The connection between relations of production and other social structures is not a reflex, wholly determined and wholly one-sided. Precisely how it ought to be viewed is one of the central issues of debate in modern Marxism. In any event, it is quite clear that it could not be just one way, that developments in the base come prior to changes in the superstructure. As we shall see, Marx's own analysis of the contradictions within capitalism show that the account is not as simplistic as that. Religious, political philosophical and scientific *ideas* can all have economic effects, but they can do so only when the conditions for their realisation are present. To change Marx's image but to capture his thought, we can say that they will only bear fruit when they are sown in fertile ground. Here is, yet again, another Hegelian resonance. The cunning of Reason is cast in materialist terms. Individual politicians, scientists, priests and philosophers are not the dupes of the owning class which dominates society. Despite what is often thought, Marxism is not an *ad hominem* critique. The dominant ideas, the prevailing ideologies must be seen as homologous with the needs of productive relations. Just as, for Hegel, successive philosophies and political forms expressed how Reason overcame alienation in the world, so for Marx successive ideologies express the necessary stages in labour's struggle to overcome its alienation. This struggle will culminate not in Hegel's ideology of Idealism but in the truth of Historical Materialism.

Hegel's philosophy of history was built upon a proto-evolutionary scheme organised around the regaining of universal freedom. In the rational state, all would be free; such freedom would embody the realisation of Spirit. Marx materialises this. The stages in world history are redefined as so many modes of production characterised by their particular relations of production. The scheme is set out in the famous quintet of primitive communist, slave, feudal, capitalist and communist modes of production. In each case the forms that social structures take is determined by the dominant mode of production, which in turn is characterised by the form which ownership relations take. Since all modes of production consist in the use of technology to apply human labour power, it is this combination which provides the dynamic force to history, not the overcoming of the limitations set upon Reason. According to Historical Materialism, it is the constraints set by and the supercession of forms of the alienation of labour, the tension between the dominant mode of production and that which will replace it, which drives history on. We do not have the space to spell out in all its detail the interpretation of history which this philosophy allows. It is part of what Marx came to call Political Economy. It would require the dissection of the complex inter-relationships between the many different elements within a mode of production and the ideological superstructures to which they give rise. This would involve showing first how contemporary understandings of the processes of production and social life were forms of false consciousness and resulted in the mystification of the forces at work. Nevertheless, we ought to sketch out some of the ways in which the philosophy of Historical Materialism has been implemented as the grounding for interpretations of history. To do this we will look at the most contentious case, the diagnosis of the ills and impending demise of capitalism.

The Contradictions of Capitalism

What gives capitalism its peculiar character is not that there are owners and non-owners of the means of production, nor that workers are forced to sell their labour-power for wages, but that prime among the forces of production is capital. This is a direct consequence of the increase in the scale of production. Classical utilitarian economics recognised four factors of production: land, labour, organisation and capital. To each of these factors was derived an appropriate return, rent, wages, profit and interest. As a theory formulated at a particular historical time (notice the sociologising epistemology again), Marx says that this theory is partly right and crucially wrong. It gives the factors an equivalence which in reality they do not have. Capital dominates. In utilitarian economics value is defined as utility which, in turn, is measured by price — the willingness to pay. Thus the metric of use value (utility) is exchange value (price). The value of any article is the price it can command in the market, be that good a piece of furniture, food, or labour. But, asks Marx, where does all the value that is being distributed among the factors of production come from? What creates the value that inheres in goods? Following Ricardo, Marx locates the origin of value creation in labour itself. It is only when goods have been *produced*, when raw material has been transformed by labour, that they have value. If the expenditure of labour creates value then any return which is not made directly to labour must be an expropriation of value created by labour. It is important to notice the 'normative' character of this argument. If value is being distributed among the other factors of production, it can only be at labour's expense. Hence labour is exploited. This exploitation is made possible by the alienation of labour, and in particular by the treatment of labour as a commodity, wage labour. Value is created by the expenditure of labour over time. During his working time, the labourer creates the value which is returned to labour as well as to the other factors. The minimum level of value required to reproduce labour, that is to keep the labourer working, is created in what Marx called the 'socially necessary labour time'. For reasons we will not touch on now, Marx sees in capitalism a tendency for wages to be forced down to the level of value associated with socially necessary labour time. The rest of the value created by labour is, therefore, *surplus value* available for redistribution among the other factors including the owners of the production processes who, as capitalists, merely hold shares and do not create any value at all. What Marx is describing, of course, is how the economic system works in the aggregate, not how each and every firm in the capitalist mode of production operates. Capital receives surplus value without contributing any creativity to the productive process. Since the expression of creativity is the foundation of human morality, this form of production, which expropriates value to those who do not create it, is both immoral and dehumanising. Individual capitalists, such as Engels, may hold and advocate libertarian and even socialist views. That does not matter. It is the institution of capital which, like the biblical Moloch, is devouring its victim, labour.

The key question, of course, quite apart from its morality, is why the development of capitalism should be self-contradictory. Why should capitalism's presuppositions lead to its eventual downfall? To show this, Marx invokes the second of his central ideas, the alienation of labour. The alienation of labour has been facilitated by the extension of the division of labour. Under capitalism this has led to the replacement of labour by machines. The expulsion of labour from the productive process must mean, in the long run, a narrower and narrower base of value generation. The obvious consequence, Marx thought, was that in any set of circumstances where the return to labour was above the minimum necessary, the rate of profit must fall. In the short run this can only be countered by extensions in the division of labour, mechanisation and the forcing down of wages. As the rate of profit falls, those least able to compete fall by the wayside. At the same time, more and more labourers join the 'reserve army' of the unemployed. Society becomes polarised. While all this is going on, production is concentrated in fewer and fewer hands and located in larger and larger complexes. Labour is *socialised* in huge factories and towns. At the same time, labour is *homogenised*. All bonds other than that of class are broken down. In response to this there arise social and political ideas which are met with repression or 'token incorporation'. Political, philosophical, religious doctrines circulate which offer explanations for the plight of all by making existing conditions appear immutable and inevitable. Though promulgated in the name of all, these doctrines actually legitimate the rule of a few.

As the crises grow and the contradictions become more exacerbated, workers become more and more alienated, both from their species being and from the system of production. Increasingly repressive measures are required to hold society together; capitalism staggers on from crisis to crisis until, becoming aware of its world historical role, the proletariat seizes power. As the universal class, it takes over society in the name of all.

Before we look at how this historical vision has been extended, developed and reshaped in modern Marxism, let us just summarise the major features and underline what we think are the most important things to bear in mind. The first of these is, as we said, that on the whole this framework was fully laid out by 1850 and was the product of a confrontation with Hegel's philosophy. It was not the outcome of empirical studies. These came later. It is also clearly a non-deterministic view. There will be leads and lags between the various stages and elements or 'uneven development', which will create tensions of their own. What it provides is a *reading of history*, a way of organising historical facts, trends and events, of picking out what is significant and disregarding what is not. In offering a class theory of history, Marx claims that it is class relations and their origins that motivate history and social change. Where Hegel invited us to see Greek philosophy, medieval Christianity and modern science as the manifestation of Reason, Marx tells us they are the epiphenomena of class relationships. Where Hegel sees the separation of the state and political processes from civil society, or economic and social life, as necessary following the collapse of the polis, Marx insists they form a unity. The state is always a class state; the history of all societies is the history of class struggle.

The philosophy of praxis was predicated upon the *practicality* of knowledge. Knowledge always served interests. Since the end of capitalism could only be brought about by the proletariat realising its role, then the most pressing task was the application of the philosophical anthropology and the theory of history to capitalism. This would require the specification of the inner workings of capitalism as an economic process. The promulgation of this theoretical work was a necessary preliminary to the raising of the consciousness of the working masses so that they can fulfil the goals set by the philosophy. Having arrived at this vision of what was required and how it was to be brought about before he was thirty, Marx spent the rest of his life in theoretical studies of capitalism and its forms of alienation, and in political struggles to organise the working class.

Modern Marxism

In our account of Marx, we have drawn on three elements: the philosophical anthropology, the theory of history, and the analysis of capitalism. These elements are to be found in what might be thought of as the essential texts of Marxism, the early manuscripts, *The Preface to the Critique of Political Economy* and *Capital* itself. The philosophical movements we shall dwell on now — each in its own way — construe the importance of these texts differently. Critical Theory, certainly as Marcuse exemplifies it, is a theory of liberation and alienation and so picks out the Hegelian thematic of the early manuscripts. Cohen is much more concerned with what sort of status the theory should have. To determine this, he brings debates from within the philosophy of the social sciences and applies them to Marx's 'scientific' theory of history, and hence is occupied with the *Preface*. Althusser wants an analysis of the structures of capitalism to set beside the structures of the natural and physical world given by the biological and physical sciences. He focuses his attention on *Capital*. Both Althusser and Cohen want to combat the Hegelian interpretation of Marxism by replacing the philosophical framework derived from Hegel with something else. Because Marcuse stresses the continuity between Marx and Hegel we will begin with him. We will then look at the counter-arguments.

The Critical Theory of Herbert Marcuse

To his contemporaries as well as himself, Hegel's system of philosophy marked the culmination in speculative metaphysics. We have seen that it generated one reaction, a revolution from within by Marx and the Young Hegelians. However, there was another line of opposition not concerned with Hegel directly or solely but with all such philosophising. In many ways, this second reaction marked a return to the empiricism of Hume. It wanted to move beyond the dichotomies of appearance and reality, potentiality and actuality, subjectivity and objectivity by means of a technical concern with logic, and particularly the logic of the natural sciences. Part of this philosophical programme involved professionalising philosophy and the definition of philosophical problems in distinct and technical ways. Critical Theory as it was propounded by Horkheimer, Adorno and others is a rejection of this professionalising, 'positivist', — as they called it — tendency. In their eyes, positivism was a modern form of alienated consciousness. Its philosophy involved the 'eternisation' and acceptance of present social and political conditions, a turning away from the central problems of human creativity and self-fulfilment as the expression of man's essence and a failure to engage with the limitations placed upon human potentiality in modern life. The professionalisation of philosophy was an accommodation to social institutions and thus an acceptance of the illusion of freedom and the confusion of freedom of thought with liberated consciousness. To Critical Theory, positivism was an ideology. It mystified the real nature of social life by wrapping it up in a myth of the 'objectivity' of scientific method and the certainty of what, earlier, we called 'passive' reasoning. Above all it involved a denial of the proper tasks of philosophy.

Critical Theory's critique of positivism works through the argument in the following way. To begin with, it argued that positivisim had not transcended the old antinomies of body and mind, fact and value, subject and object, appearance and reality but merely reintroduced them in a novel form. It stipulates the existence of a pre-given order of 'facts' about which it is possible to obtain 'objective knowledge' simply by using the appropriate methods for organising experience. These methods are those associated with science. The key to science's 'objectivity' is the use of the tools of mathematics and logic. The aim of philosophy, according to this positivism, is to show how social and political sciences can codify 'social laws'. In which case understanding social reality, the formulation of these laws, is obtainable by academic contemplation alone. To the Critical Theorist, this marks no more and no less than a return to the Enlightenment doctrine of the primacy of absolute reason which Hegel had demolished and is a complete rejection of Marx's philosophy of praxis which was, in its turn, the transcendence of Hegel. By accepting the epistemology of objective knowledge and extending the possibility of scientific knowledge of social life through disengagement, positivism tears social facts out of their 'real' context and so sanitises them. This 'real context' is the present state of the class struggle. Because social facts are, then, treated as equivalent to natural facts, they are given an immutable character which renders them immune to criticism. The potential for transformation of social life is thereby denied. The character of social life as essentially a human product expressing social relations of exploitation is therefore lost. In the social sciences, the most insidious consequence of this positivism has been the acceptance of the 'myth' of value freedom. By accepting that the scholar can separate himself from his surrounding social context and achieve objective knowledge by use of reason alone, positivism denies the revolutionary and liberating role of knowledge. The intellectual is committed to saying how things are but not to showing what they might become.

According to the philosophy of praxis there can be no neutral knowledge. Knowledge is always in the service of interests. Positivism had to be combatted on every front. In our discussion of Habermas (Chapter 3) we show how he has tried to reconstitute social theory. Adorno and others attempted to form a new theory of aesthetics which did not rely upon the generalising of 'bourgeois' standards of taste and morality. Marcuse takes up political freedom and in particular the positivist definition of such freedom in terms of the rights of the individual within a parliamentary democracy. Such a definition makes it appear inevitable that individuals will have to be constrained and their potentiality limited because of the 'realities' of social life, such as the scale of modern societies and the need for 'efficient' decision-making. In this way positivism contributes to the alienation of consciousness in the modern, atomised society. Marcuse begins with the theory of praxis and the belief that philosophy must be a theory of liberated consciousness. Just as Marx took on Hegel and showed how that philosophical system was rooted in its social conditions, so Critical Theory must show how positivism has permeated into our ways of thinking. In so doing it will demonstrate the possibilities of creativity as the expression of the essence of human nature. Marcuse chooses to exemplify the effects of positivism in two areas: in *Eros and Civilisation* he looks at the use that has been made of Freud's theories of personality development, while in *One Dimensional Man*, he takes up the role of the mass media in modern society as agents of repressive tolerance and repressive desublimation.

Marcuse's treatment of Freud has two distinctive features. First, like Marx's account of Hegel, there is a determination to show how, when properly reframed, its revolutionary potential can be extracted. To do this, the Freudian project has to be taken out of the medical and para-medical context in which it has been located. Such scientism has neutralised its potential. Second, what is central to Marcuse's Freud is the theory of consciousness. He strips this out of the 'scientific' theory that Freud provided for it. The theory of 'neurone flow' and the hydraulic model it is premissed upon is so much unnecessary baggage. In place of this, Marcuse puts the opposition between the pleasure principle and the reality principle. The pleasure principle involves the immediate gratification of instinct and the freedom of expression. The reality principle requires deferred gratification, restraint, toil and productiveness. The process of personality development in the modern world, and the evolution of modern consciousness, is the process by which the reality principle comes to dominate the pleasure principle. The most significant parts of this process involve the exercise of control over the instincts for destruction and death and the channelling of those for creativity and reproduction. In this way, Freud saw in the development of the individual personality the recapitulation of the development of civilised society. The 'savage' child is tamed, controlled, civilised. This is achieved through the internalisation of social norms and a respect for institutionalised social relationships primarily through the acquisition of guilt and conscience with the superego. The stages this passes through are those of the famous 'Oedipus complex' which result in the *repression* of natural instincts. The superego controls by sublimating, that is channelling into accepted forms, the two natural drives of sexual love (*eros*) and death (*thanatos*). Civilisation represents the triumph of eros over thanatos but only at the cost of devitalising it. Sexual love becomes reproduction, a means of begetting children, but in a form which matches the reality principle. The primacy of the reality principle is expressed in utilitarian ethics which are themselves a form of positivism. The essence of creativity and its potential are, thereby, repressed and contained. In this instance, positivism leads in Freud's theory to a denial of man's essential character as a necessary condition for social life.

Against this interpretation and use of Freud's central ideas, Marcuse sketches an alternative vision. Here, personality would not be repressed and its potential crushed. The picture drawn is very similar to that offered by Marx in his discussion of freedom in the early manuscripts. However, this 'natural man' is not a savage animal because the liberation of instinct and norms does not mean their complete absence, but their transformation. Their essence would be realised. When Marcuse talks of freedom, he is not championing sexual promiscuity and a lack of license. Far from it, his new moral community, the new *Sittlichkeit*, will be altogether a highly moral one, where instincts are expressed in pure forms and not the distorted and repressed ones popularised in modern society.

The central element in Marcuse's interpretation of Freud, then, is that the theory has become an ideology of fear and dominance. The power of the instincts of eros and thanatos have become feared and controlled. In particular, sex has become an instrument for selfish gratification. In becoming a commodity, a means to an end, sexuality has reproduced, and is typical of, the modern consciousness. Eros is repressed and debased. Freedom — in this instance sexual freedom — has become a shibboleth defined in distorted and illusory terms. We have created more and more novel forms of expressing sexual freedom but they are all in fact ways by which our potentiality for creativity is controlled and denied. The myth of sexual freedom is a decivilising ideology and the expression of an alienated consciousness. Freud had stumbled on the germ of this, but had missed the significance of his own discovery. Instead, he had immured it in an unnecessary positivist 'scientism'.

Marcuse's distaste for the forms of modern society is most clearly brought out in his book, *One Dimensional Man*. In this he argues that forms of production, consumption, leisure, culture have been debased in the aggressive, acquisitive, wasteful philistinism of the modern consumer society. The reality principle has become a universal consciousness which stifles the possibility of alternatives. Criticism is impossible because it is hedged around with qualification, neutralised, and allocated to its appropriate place. The dynamism of our instincts, their potential, has been diverted into frivolity. The masses are fed a diet of sex and violence in sublimated, stylised and hence repressive forms through the mass media. Equally, in the spheres of culture and knowledge no real alternatives are tolerated to the reality principle. There are just varieties of the same thing. Hence, this 'tolerance' is repressive. The homogenisation of production, consumption, culture and knowledge is carried out in the name of economy, competition, rationality and truth, but is, in fact, the reflection of the ideology of positivism and the needs of the bourgeois class for more and more commodity production. Modern industrial life, its administration and production, is obsessed with fitting means to ends, with obtaining value for money. It gives no credence at all to the possibilities of human transformation and the consideration of alternative social forms. They are dismissed in the name of realism and pragmatism. Repressive desublimation is the refusal to confront the alienation of modern consciousness, to see that it could be transformed and that the essence of human nature could be actualised. Modern consciousness fragments criticism into localised issues such as welfare rights, pay and conditions, obscenity and pornography, the intellectual 'fads' and fashionable philosophies. This fragmentation of criticism, and philosophy's endorsement of it in its professional specialisation, is a reneging on the essential revolutionary task, just as wage negotiation is an acceptance of and legitimising of the institutionalisation of class conflict. It is allocated a controllable and defined space.

This argument leads to only one conclusion. Modern consciousness has become so permeated with the rationale of the reality principle that it is no longer possible to expect a revolution from within society. The proletariat will not, cannot, achieve revolutionary consciousness. Instead, the revolutionary consciousness is carried by those who stand outside of modern society, those who reject our technical rationalism or have not been fully socialised into it. These are the young, the marginal, the deviant, the 'irrational'. In their styles of life, in their ideas, are to be found the seeds of the revolutionary consciousness which will transcend the reality principle.

Marcuse's version of Critical Theory looks for a new *Sittlichkeit* and embraces, therefore, the vision of human potential which was expressed in Marx's early writings. Because of this, it has been accused of distorting Marxism by turning it into a form of Idealism. Such Idealism is itself distorted and ideological. It has also been accused of violating Marx's central tenet, in that Marcuse sees the replacement of the working class as the revolutionary force by those who have no class unity. Such objections really boil down to the emphasis that is placed upon the importance of alienated consciousness in Marxism. The consequence of Critical Theory is to turn Marxism back into a social philosophy; there are others who are determined to keep it a science.

Althusser's Structural Marxism

Althusser's vision of Marxist philosophy is based upon a certain view of the organisation of social relationships which gained popularity among French academics in the 1960s and 1970s. This theory of social relationships is structuralism (cf. Chapter 5) and was closely associated with the anthropologist Levi Strauss and later the psychiatrist Lacan. At the time, it was felt that structuralism offered the opportunity of founding a non-positivist science of human relations. Althusser uses a structuralist reading of Historical Materialism to combat what he sees as the over Hegelianised and Idealist interpretation of Marx that was dominant in French philosophy. This interpretation was most popularised by Sartre and the Existentialists (cf. Chapter 4). Althusser wants Marxism to be a science and not a social philosophy. The arena in which this struggle over the definition of Marxism took place was the French Communist Party. Althusser's 'interventions' from philosophy were all forays into practical politics.

In the main, the arguments were all over the attitude that was to be taken towards the Soviet Union. Could there be a distinct variety of European Communism which owed no allegiance to the USSR and which sought to express revolutionary consciousness in capitalist societies? One of the crucial events in the emergence of this separatist movement was the speech made in 1956 in which Kruschev admitted the crimes which had been committed under the Stalin regime and explained them away in terms of the 'cult of personality'. The problem of Stalinism was theorised in two ways within Marxism. On the one hand there was an explanation which centred on Stalin's own personality, his megalomania, and so personalised the 'deviation'. On the other, there were explanations which located the origins of Stalinism in the violations of 'socialist legality' which Stalin was able to institutionalise because of the distortions which Lenin had introduced in his reshaping of revolutionary theory for the Russian case. This reshaping involved the bureaucratising of the Party, the thesis of democratic-centralism and Party rule, and so on. The upshot of the second line of thinking is to distance classical Marxism from Leninism and its consequences. If this is possible, then Euro-communism can claim the Marxist heritage *without* a commitment to support the USSR. The predominant thinking among French Marxists, led by Sartre, was that this latter interpretation of Stalin was the correct one.

Althusser rejects both options. He claims that neither is in tune with the essence of Marxism. Both fail to set Stalinism within the framework of class struggle. The characteristics of Stalinism, the use of terror, are the direct result of contradictions inherent within Russian society after the revolution — contradictions which Stalin tried to deal with by invoking bourgeois methods of repression. In so doing, Stalin stressed the total priority of economic organisation and so showed how much his thinking was dominated by residuary bourgeois modes of thought. In stressing economic factors, Stalin disregarded the class struggle, and so deviated in the direction of what Althusser calls 'humanism'. This tension between 'humanism' and 'economism' created the phenomenon of Stalinism. In many ways, in trying to isolate and explain Stalinism as he does, Althusser's philosophy is very conservative. The soviet model should be given pride of place because the Soviet Union had now recognised, even if it had incorrectly diagnosed, the problem of Stalinism. The explanation which Althusser offers is based upon his own structuralist understanding of Marxism. This reading offers a way between 'economism' and 'humanism' to understand the scientific character of Marxism.

At the heart of Althusser's interpretation of Marxism is the notion of a 'symptomatic reading'. This is one of the many ideas which he takes from Freudian psycho-analysis where it used to describe the diagnostic procedure of examining a patient's actions and utterances as symptoms expressing an underlying pathological condition. Althusser gives a 'symptomatic reading' to Marx in that he addresses Marx's writings as expressions, symptoms, of an underlying *problématique*. This latter idea is a difficult notion but is generally thought of as an overarching frame of reference, a set of theories, methods and concepts. It was used by the philosopher of science, Gaston Bachelard, to describe moments in the history of science. In a symptomatic reading, every text gains its essential meaning by being located in the author's problématique, even though that framework may not be explicitly referred to, nor even developed as yet. Texts are never to be taken in isolation as discrete individuals; each is examined for the contribution which it makes to the final, fully worked out problématique. In Althusser's view, there is no doubt that Marx's problématique is the institution of a science of history theorised in Historical Materialism and displayed in full in *Capital*. All the preceding texts should be analysed from this point of view. This reading implies that we can understand a text not just by focusing on what it contains but by noticing what is absent from it. Such absences are made discernable by a 'retroactive' reading, from the fully developed problématique in *Capital*. Althusser argues that if we do this, we will see a radical discontinuity between the early and the late texts. There is a break from Hegelian influenced philosophy to scientific Marxism. Althusser compares, Marxism with what he calls Thales' 'invention' of mathematics in ancient Greece and Newton's 'reconstruction' of physics in the late seventeenth century. In all three cases, he argues, pre-scientific thinking, or ideology, concentrated upon external appearances only and so gave only the illusion of understanding. In rejecting this mode of thinking, these scientific 'coupures' or 'breakthroughs' penetrated to the essences of mathematical, physical and social phenomena. All three are described in an extended topographical metaphor which grips Althusser's discussion. They opened up new continents. With the sciences to hand, real exploration could begin. The terrain which the science of Historical Materialism explores is the description of the structure of relationships which characterise modes of production, especially that of late capitalism. Modes of production are complex structures which can only be comprehended by penetrating to their essence, the inherent contradictions which they articulate. As with all other structuralisms, and in contradistinction to, for instance, Critical Theory, the reality of social processes is to be found in the relationships between levels within and elements of the 'social formation', not at the level of acting human beings. Individuals do not constitute the correct unit for study of a properly constituted science of history. Each instance in the contradictions gains meaning not from what gives rise to it directly but from the part it plays within the totality. Althusser's theory, then, is a structural interpretation of Marx and a structural vision of social formations. The two are intertwined.

Involved in this interpretation is one novel insight. The traditional role allocated to philosophy is that of adjudicator on science. Through its reflections on logic, methodology and epistemology, philosophy provides a way of comprehending science. Philosophy might even, if the positivists had their way, become the science of science. Historical Materialism, a science, now enables us to comprehend philosophy. Philosophy can never hope for incorporation into science because it will always remain a form of structurally determined ideology. Philosophy, or pre-science, must end before science can begin. The distinction between ideology and science is as fundamental to Althusser as that between truth and error was to the Enlightenment. Incorporating philosophy into science only compromises and distorts it. Althusser holds that the 'coupure' occurs in Marx's writings when he rejects the dualisms of subject and object, man and nature, fact and value, and so on, enshrined in Hegelian Idealism in favour of the monism of materialism. Any attempt to build these philosophical categories back into Historical Materialism, would have the same effect that it would if alchemy and astrology were built back into Newtonian physics or numerology into mathematics. Truth would be compounded with error.

In the short period from 1845 to 1848, Marx broke free of Hegelianism. By dissolving Hegelian dialectics from within, he put an end to philosophy and developed the science of history. That there *has to be* such a 'coupure' is a consequence of the reading which Althusser adopts. If Marx ends in science but does not start there, a break-out is necessary. Without the break, Althusser could not sustain the claim that Marxism was in fact a science and hence would have no basis to argue that the 'truths' of Marxism can be segregated from deviations such as the economism and humanism of Stalin.

Just what does the 'epistemological break' consist in? There are three elements. First there is the transformation of concepts like 'work', 'production', 'exchange' and 'value' which Marx achieves. Prior to 1848 these were set in a philosophical framework and so were ideological in form. By 1850, they had been relocated and transformed. Part of this transformation is the jettisoning of the idealist categories of consciousness, alienation, mankind and species being, and the introduction of scientific terms such as base, superstructure, class and mode of production. Exemplary in this transformation is the 'concretisation' of revolution from an idealist deduction to an empirical fact. This was achieved by its connection to the 'real' processes of class struggle. Second, there is what we earlier called the sociologising of epistemology. Philosophy is seen as the expression of the scientifically identified class struggle. Philosophy is the class struggle fought out in the field of theory. Once this is seen, the attack on philosophy becomes total. There can be no room for argument or reservations. Philosophy *must* contribute positively to the class struggle, it must express the ideology of the working class, or it must be overthrown. The third element — one which has already been outlined — is the prominence given to class struggle. This is a 'real', 'concrete' scientific fact not a speculative metaphysical notion. With it, Marxism ceases to be a philosophy of man and nature, concerned with humanism and the human condition and becomes the science of the class struggle in history. Against any attempts to turn Marxism into a 'bourgeois' philosophy, Althusser insists on the inviolability of the concepts and methods of *Capital*. There can be no compromise, no short cut and no retrenchment. They constitute a complete and integrated science. Lenin's contribution was to politicise the class struggle through the Party. He did not affect the science at all. The hard and fast line which Althusser drew struck many as too doctrinaire and unrealistic. Under pressure from many of his colleagues, he gradually retreated from his strong position and criticised his early extreme 'theoreticist' errors for being too influenced by rationalist dogmatism, by which he means the pursuit of a systematic theory for its own sake, and structuralist metaphors.

In Althusser's symptomatic reading, the science of Historical Materialism consists in a system of related concepts. The most important of these is the mode of production. This designates the twin ideas of base and superstructure, but not in a way that places total and absolute pre-eminence upon the base. The interpretation which does that is economism. A mode of production, while comprising the base and superstructure, has to be considered as a totality wherein the base holds sway 'only in the last instance'. When viewed as a whole, relationships within the mode of production are reciprocal. As we said earlier, it is the whole which is the object of attention. Within any particular social formation — that is a mode of production at some specific historical point and displaying particular social condition — are sets of forces of contradiction and 'overdetermination' which can only in the last instance be explained by the base. In late capitalism these forces have 'condensed' in the state and the economy, giving these 'regions' a pre-eminence. In other social formations, such as that of feudalism, other elements predominated. The contradictions are not merely reflexes of the forces and relations of production within the base but are 'overdetermined', in that they are the expression of many different layers and types of contradiction within the historical circumstances. To use Althusser's terminology, they are 'articulated' as particular 'instances' of the contradictions at a 'conjuncture' of specific historical conditions. In Freudian psychoanalysis, overdetermination means the attribution of causal force to a number of different elements which combine to produce an individual set of symptoms such as a paranoid delusion or a neurotic obsession. The multiple pathological elements 'condense' into one set of symptoms and hence 'overdetermine' it.

The regions which make up a mode of production are all inter-penetrating and overlay each other. The unity of forces and relations of production is just one of these regions. Others are the state ideological and repressive apparatuses. The combination of these regions is not a 'compound' in which each retains its completely separate identity, nor is it an amalgam in which they are fused. Rather the structure of relationships is one of 'relative autonomy', and while the nature of social relations is determined in the last instance by the forces and relations of production, each individual region can express that character in an idiosyncratic way, often in guises very far removed from those which might have been expected. The concept of 'relative autonomy' allows for enough slack to provide for the reciprocity of determination, with causal efficacy lying in the base only in the last instance. We have used that term many times without explaining it. That is because it is far from clear exactly what it does mean. One way of thinking of it might be to say that in Historical Materialism the last principle that one should be prepared to dispense with is the determination by the base of the superstructure.

The theory, of course, only has any point if it can be applied to real historical conditions so that the class struggle can be furthered. In the modern case the application has to be to late capitalism. Here the structure of dominance is represented by the economy and the state. Drawing upon what he claims is an insight into the classical texts, Althusser distinguishes two elements in the state, the state repressive and the state ideological apparatuses. In his analysis of ideological state apparatuses, Althusser collects up the conventional list of social structures, the family, education, religion, culture and so on. The function of the ideological apparatus is to ensure 'voluntary compliance' to the needs of productive relations and, therefore, conformity to the interests of the dominant class. Such voluntary compliance contrasts with the forced compliance achieved by the repressive apparatus of the state system of courts, police, the army and so on. The philosophical point that is being made is brought out in his account of the nature of modern law and education which, by emphasising the free individual and the primacy of the individual's reason, conscience and subjectivity, create the circumstances in which particular people — instances of free subjectivity — can be dominated by the ruling class in that they 'voluntarily' reproduce 'repressive' productive relations. Because such apparatuses are all relatively autonomous and multiple, they are never at precisely the same stage of development. This, in turn, creates relations of strain and contradiction between them. Teasing out the entanglements of these contradictions as 'condensates' of those which hold in the forces and relations of production is the topic of the science of history.

G.A. Cohen's Technological Determinism

Althusser's reading of Marx dominated Marxist philosophy for some considerable time. Certainly it stimulated a re-examination of the roots of modern Marxism in the classical texts. And, as is to be expected, it has provoked many critical responses. Some have simply tried to restate the old positions. Others have sought to carve out new ways of defining and defending Marxism that do not lead towards the dogmatism of Althusser. One of these is the attempt by G.A. Cohen to bring some of the debates presently being carried on within the social sciences to bear upon Marxism. He does so because in his view all previous attempts to expound and clarify Historical Materialism — and that included Althusser's — have not given it the strongest possible defence. That defence would be to show that it conformed at all important points with one of the forms of explanatory theory to be found in the natural sciences. Once we see that, then Marxism's arguments, at least as far as Cohen is concerned, will be irresistible.

To achieve this Cohen adopts a consistent line. Marxism is a version, a defensible version, of technological determinism. Its explanations are functional in nature. These two themes come together in the assertion of the primacy of economic forces all the way though the theory. This is a deliberate downgrading of any of the Hegelian 'residuals' and hence the importance attached to conscious-ness, alienation and so forth, as well as a rejection of determination only 'in the last instance', which he says is opaque unless it means the unilinear and primary determination of economic forces. The link which holds between base and superstructure is one of functionality; the form of social life is a functional consequence of economic arrangements. In his recent writings, Cohen seems to be rethinking his position somewhat. He still holds that Historical Materialism is best seen as a functional theory, but he is less sure that it can be said to be a case of simple technological determinism. He has begun to smuggle consciousness back in.

The central theses of Historical Materialsm, as Cohen outlines it, are quite straightforward. There is a 'real' distinction between the economic base and the ideological superstructure. Priority always rests with the base. Against much of conventional wisdom, Cohen holds that the superstructure refers only to a limited range of things, the state and law particularly, and perhaps religion. The theory is not an all purpose sociology. Giving primacy to the base does not mean that non-economic forces can have no economic consequences. However, they can do so only within very defined conditions. Settling for any particular case just what those conditions are is the job of what Cohen calls 'secondary elaboration'. We will return to this in a moment. Cohen then proceeds to segregate the forces and the relations of production in a hard and fast way. The former have a causal effect upon the superstructure only when mediated through the relations of production. The forces of production are the substratum on which the relations of production, the base, are built.

Cohen systematises the theory by presenting it in a top-down manner. In any set of historical circumstances:

(a) The nature and form of the ideological superstructure is determined by the economic substructure, the base.

(b) The nature and form of the economic substructure is determined by the need of the forces of production, principally labour, to develop.

According to Cohen the items contained in (a) and (b) can be connected if the propositions are cast in functional form. In Chapter 10 on the philosophy of science we show how these are usually arrived at. Cohen sets (a) and (b) out in something like the following form:

(a′) The economic substructure requires stability in social conditions. This can be achieved by the propagation of particular ideas and doctrines in these particular historical circumstances. So, these ideas and doctrines are propagated.

(b′) The needs for the development of labour at any historical time are met by the form that the mode of production takes. This induces certain types of relations of production.

Both (a′) and (b′) can be made to conform to what Cohen calls the 'consequence law':

If it is the case that if a type of event E were to occur at t_1 then it would bring about a type of event F at t_2, then an event of type E occurs at t_3.

t_1 and t_3 could be the same, but t_1 must precede t_2.

The causal connection between the base and the superstructure is like that which holds between the wheels and the chassis of a car. The wheels hold the chassis off the ground and are held up by being bolted to it.

It is clear that the point of reference here has to be the total system of conditions. The functional explanation holds for just those conditions necessary to F. Second, in this case at least, the explanation is a generalised one. One the whole conditions fulfil needs. This does not mean that all relationships are directly beneficial. In this way, strain and conflict can be introduced. It is the relative mismatch of conditions and needs that creates such conflict. Third, and most importantly, Cohen's explanatory strategy of secondary elaboration involves the spelling out of how the super-structure fits the economic system.

To accomplish his aim of showing that functionalism is the best defence one can give of Marxism, Cohen has got to fend off claims that functionalism is a proper form of scientific explanation. We will consider these arguments in the chapter on the philosophy of science. Let us grant Cohen that part of his argument in order to see what difference if will make. Let us also grant him the other contentious element, namely that it is acceptable to cast Marxism in this way. What we are left with is the pay-off, the secondary elaborations; the demonstration of the applicability of the consequence law using the concepts of historical materialism.

Drawing upon examples from biology, economics and anthropology, Cohen identifies four elaborative strategies which he calls the purposive, the Darwinian, the Lamarkian and the self-deceptive. The last is the one which best suits Marxism. If a set of actions, say banning the sale of firearms to the general public, were to be to be instituted because of the beneficial consequences felt likely to flow from it, then this course of action is *purposive*. On the other hand, if such benefits were apparent only to an outside observer, then the action would be *Darwinian* in character. However, once the advantages had been recognised, the course of action might be generalised and so be *Lamarkian*. For example, in developing our computer technology we may not have realised that through the growing use of a limited number of programming languages, linguistic barriers — and hence cultural ones too — are being broken down. If this were to be the case, and it was brought to our notice, then that consequence might become yet another reason for increasing awareness of and knowledge about information technology. In the case of *self-deceptive strategy*, actions are intended to achieve one end but have other entirely unanticipated consequences as well. The example which Cohen uses is that of the famous Hopi rain dance and the creation of social cohesion. In each case we have functional explanations, with self-deception being the type employed in Historical Materialism. The extended example Cohen chooses to show this is the account of the Factory Acts given in *Capital*. Cohen claims that here the state was working against the short run interests of capital since the Acts shortened the working day and so reduced profits. But they were also in the long run interests of capital since they contributed to the preservation of existing economic arrangements in the face of tension and possible upheaval. The explanatory strategy sets the questions for Historical Materialism to answer. Just why did the Acts have the long term consequences they did and what were the mechanisms which connected changes in the legal system with the preservation of relations of production in the economic base?

Cohen's account of the scientific nature of Historical Materialism is entirely different to that of Althusser. In some ways, it seems to underplay Marxism's revolutionary character by treating it as just another social science theory. To his critics, Cohen seems to have embroiled Marxism in just the positivist philosophy it is opposed to. He has tried to secure Marxism as a theory by tying it to a variant of empiricism, and so he has stripped it of its moral and revolutionary edge. In the arguments that Cohen's work has produced, we can see the whole array of philosophical positions we have picked out in this discussion. He has been condemned for neglecting social and political engagement with the repressed and alienated condition of the modern world on the one hand, and for ignoring the unique scientific character of Historical Materialism on the other. In this debate are brought out all of the themes which Marx took from Hegel and Enlightenment philosophy and which he turned to his own use. In arguments over scientism, subjectivism, idealism and theoreticism, positivism and determinism, modern Marxism shows itself as concerned with the problems Marx confronted as he was himself 150 years ago.

Recommended Reading

Peter Singer's *Marx* (Oxford University Press, 1980) is a clear and brief introduction to the major themes. David McLellan's *Karl Marx* (Paladin 1976) provides a comprehensive intellectual biography. The Foreign Languages Press, Pekin, publishes a relatively cheap version of all of Marx's opus. Those of direct relevance are *The Economic and Philosophical Manuscripts*, *The Introduction to a Critique of Political Economy* and *The German Ideology*. A reasonable selection of these is to be found in *Karl Marx: the early writings* (Penguin, 1975). A complete review of Marxism from its inception to modern times is L. Kolakowski's three-volume *Main Currents of Marxism* (Oxford University Press, 1981). For an alternative viewpoint, there is Perry Anderson's *Considerations on Western Marxism* (New Left Books, 1976).

Hegel is difficult, and so are most of the book about him. The best guide is Charles Taylor's *Hegel* (Cambridge University Press, 1975) and his shortened and reshaped version of that work, *Hegel and Modern Society* (Cambridge University Press, 1979). A survey of the young Hegelians can be found in S. Hook, *From Hegel to Marx* (University of Michigan Press, 1962). Max Horkheimer gives a good introduction to the interests of the Frankfurt School in his *Critical Theory* (Seabury, 1972) as do many of the essays in Paul Connerton (ed.) *Critical Sociology* (Penguin, 1976). Apart from *One Dimensional Man* (Sphere, 1968) and *Eros and Civilisation* (Beacon, 1974), Marcuse's thought is best displayed in *Negations* (Beacon Press, 1968).

Althusser's main works are *Reading Capital* (New Left Books, 1977), *For Marx*, (Verso, 1979) and *Lenin and Philosophy* (New Left Books, 1971). The latter contains the famous essay 'Ideology and State Ideological Apparatuses'. Alex Colincoss has provided a reasonable introduction to the range of Althusser's thought in his *Althusser's Marxism* (Pluto Press, 1976), while T. O'Hagan's 'Althusser: How to be a Marxist in Philosophy' in G.H. Parkinson (ed.), *Marx and Marxisms* (Cambridge University Press, 1982) is a good guide to the philosophical aspects of his thought. The most fertile application of Althusser's thought can be found in the work of Nicos Poulantzas, especially in *Political Power and Social Classes* (New Left Books, 1975). Althusser's philosophy has been widely criticised. The least technical and hence the most accessible is Alvin Gouldner's 'The Two Marxisms' in his *For Sociology* (Penguin, 1973). G.A. Cohen's *Karl Marx's Theory of History* (Clarendon, 1978) gives his whole argument in one place. Three differently slanted appraisals of it are: M. Mandelbaum, 'G.A. Cohen's Defence of Functional Explanation', *Philosophy of the Social Sciences*, vol. 12, (1982), pp. 285-7; Peter Halfpenny 'A Refutation of Historical Materialism?', *Social Science Information*, vol. 22, no. 1, (1983), pp. 61-87; and Jon Elster 'Cohen on Marx's Theory of History', *Political Studies* vol. xxviii, no. 1, pp. 121-8., which is followed by a reply from Cohen.

3 HERMENEUTICS

Originally, Hermeneutics was concerned with the interpretation of texts whose meaning is confused, incomplete, fragmentary or unclear. Although as a philosophy it has broadened its interests, it still retains much of its early philological character. During the nineteenth century, the discipline of linguistics began to emerge as an independent branch of knowledge separate from philosophy, literature and the humanities. To begin with, its aims were largely historical, tracing the connections between the Indo-European languages, especially Sanskrit, Greek and Latin among others. This interest was also encouraged by the prominence at the time, especially in Germany, of studies of classical literature and philosophy as well as biblical and Talmudic scholarship.

The material which these scholars had to deal with presented two kinds of problem. First, because of their age, the texts were often incomplete and fragmentary. In addition, the texts, or the portions of them that had survived, were often the work of more than one author. To complicate matters even more, they were also sometimes translations of even earlier texts which had not survived. Unwrapping and recovering the 'original meaning' of the text became a delicate process. Second, such texts were also historical documents in their own right. They reflected societies and cultures which were very different to those of the scholars who sought to understand them. Any attempt to penetrate to the meaning of the text and get some kind of 'objective' understanding of it would have to overcome the linguistic problems of translation and language change, the revisions and reconstructions by successions of authors, as well as grappling with the fact that the texts were part of ways of life no longer directly accessible to us except through other texts and similar 'archaeological' remains.

The complexity of these problems is easily appreciated if we look at a case such as that of the Nag Hammadi manuscripts. These were discovered in 1945 by two Egyptian farmers. Altogether thirteen papyrus books were found, a few of which were destroyed soon after discovery. Those remaining, after disappearing for a few years, eventually found their way to the Coptic Museum in Cairo. It was subsequently revealed that the books contained 52 texts from the early days of the Christian era, including a collection of previously unknown gospels. The texts proved to be translations of Greek materials written 150 years or so earlier. The texts presented a very different picture of the Christian church to that usually given. They showed it to be deeply divided doctrinally and organisationally. They also reported very different facts about Jesus' life to the traditional account. So, making semantic, archaeological and historical sense of these texts involved not only linguistic matters, important though these were, but also required them to be related to the wider social context in which they were originally produced. Who wrote them? For what readership? Why were they concealed? Could their meaning be taken at face value, or were other issues at stake? These are just some of the questions that had to be answered. For our purposes all it is important to notice is that making sense of the materials requires a union of philology and history. It was this that provided Hermeneutics with its central question. How could we gain an understanding of the past through its texts and other remains?

As we mentioned at the beginning, it was largely in nineteenth-century Germany that this fusion of interests took place, in the context of a long running and often bitter debate over the nature and methods of history, historiography and the human sciences. We saw in the Introduction to this Section that one of the features of Enlightenment thought was an attempt to extend the natural science model of knowledge to the study of human life, society and history. The claim made by Kantian philosophy that it had provided a means of avoiding scepticism and empiricism to provide an independent view of the order of the universe lent weight to this tendency. Natural science did provide 'objective knowledge' of Nature. Its models and methods would provide the way, if suitably modified, to gain 'objective knowledge' of history and the nature of social life. At the beginning of Chapter 2 we described one line of resistance to this, that of Hegelian philosophy, and suggested that it was part of a general rejection of this whole attitude. There we called this rejection 'Romanticism.' What the Romantics objected to was that the use of the natural science model of knowledge, with its 'empiricist' and 'positivist' overtones, left no room for the idea that history and social life were *human creations*, and that the essence of all social forms was that they expressed human creativity. In their eyes, the study of human history had to be based on the fact that humans are free, intentional and purposive *creators* whose lives are bounded by a reality which has meaning for them. They act towards the world and each other on the basis of these meanings. The duality of subjectivity and objectivity was indissoluble. What this meant for historiography was that the pattern of history did not reduce simply to the succession of events which were connected only by time. Because the essence of man was his subjectivity, his spirituality as they saw it, and because history was the expression of that subjectivity, then history was of prime philosophical importance. Social institutions, law, literature, forms of government, values, family life, art, all reflected the characteristic spirituality of particular cultures. The historian's task was to penetrate beneath the surface appearances to the deeper reality, the guiding mentality and its place in mankind's spiritual progress.

Given the emphasis upon subjectivity, it seemed clear that historical inquiries could not merely take over and adapt the methods of the natural sciences. What was required was a wholly different but equally well grounded kind of method as that of the natural sciences. This method had to be appropriate to the distinctive nature of history's topic matter. Understanding the actions, events and artifacts that are the expression of human spirituality and creativity requires grasping the place, the significance that they have *within* human life. This task is very different to the observation of an *external* reality felt to be typical of science. The general line that was adopted to provide such a method was to treat human action and its artifacts as analogous to texts. Deciphering the meaning of history was similar to deciphering the meaning of a long lost text. In this way, Hermeneutics came to refer not just to the study of historical texts and the problems of translation, comprehension and contextualising associated with them, but to a broader endeavour: that of discovering or uncovering the meanings of all human artifacts and actions. The way that these meanings were grasped was through a process of interpretation through which the action, event, artifact or text was located as the expression of a deeper, underlying, unifying spirituality.

Hermeneutics was, then, determined to show that the generalising of the natural science model of knowledge to all spheres of knowledge was unacceptable. To do this it had to show that alternative methods — those which it advocated — were as systematic and controlled as those of the natural sciences and, furthermore, uniquely suited to the study of the nature of human life. To achieve this it had to demonstrate two things: first, it had to show that there was a field of objects, a proper body of items for study, about which one could say that their *essential* quality was that they were meaningful and expressed spirituality and that it was this that gave them their coherence and sense. Hermeneutics sought to achieve this aspiration by defining all human action and artifacts as text-analogues. Second, it had to be possible to demonstrate that the distinction between meaning and its expression was not illusory or fallacious. This distinction lay at the heart of the suggestion that the same meaning, the same underlying reality, could take very different forms or expressions. Without it, it would make little sense to say that Hermeneutics was the interpretation of underlying meaning. In addition to these two, invoking the idea that human social life and artifacts can be seen as text-analogues invites us to see such phenomena as having meanings for particular subjects — that is interpreters, be they individuals, groups or the Universal Subject, mankind in general. Meaning does not exist independently of subjects who use it, attribute and respond to it. Nor does it exist separate from other meanings. It is caught up with them and interconnected to them. The phrases that recur again and again are 'a web of meaning' and 'a field of meaning'. As we shall see, it was this idea that gave so much importance in the early days of Hermeneutics to imaginative reconstruction and empathy in elucidating meaning and its life context.

It is clear, then, that the efforts of hermeneutic philosophy to create a systematic discipline were a reaction to and hence dominated by the paragon status accorded the natural sciences. There seemed to be two alternatives. Either interpretive understanding had to be able to match, point for point, the standard adopted by the natural sciences, or it had to be shown that such standards were wholly inappropriate to the understanding of human history and social life. The first course would take the comparison seriously; the second course would reject any attempt at comparison. By and large, hermeneutic philosophy chose the latter. It resisted the comparison. The problems faced by the disciplines engaged in interpretive understanding were wholly distinct from those of the natural sciences, and hence their methods would be wholly different too.

What was being rejected was the appropriateness of a particular image of science as philosophy saw it in the nineteenth century. This image was one of a body of cumulating, objective knowledge obtained by the use of particular techniques and methods governed by agreed rules of procedure. Although scientists might disagree about particular findings, it was held they did not disagree on how one determined what was to count as a finding. The interpretation of meaning could not be predicated upon such communally agreed rules which would operate impersonally to determine which interpretation of a text or text-analogue was the correct one. The empirical method adopted by science was held to guarantee the certainty of its knowledge. Scientific knowledge was objective knowledge. This was because the validation of such knowledge was independent of particular individuals, but based upon formal manipulations and replicability. Interpretive understanding could not use these methods nor make these claims. If the sciences were 'objective' then by comparison the interpretive disciplines must be regarded as 'subjective'. The Enlightenment categories were reintroduced and reworked to justify the contrast. This subjectivity was no more apparent than when choices had to be made over differing interpretations. A successful interpretation is one which brings out the sense, the rationale, the meaning which on the surface appears confused and fragmentary. But how do we know that any interpretation is the correct one? Not only can we not validate interpretations, but any attempt to find a way to choose between competitors simply raises the problem of interpretation to the next level, and thus interpretations proliferate. This arises because the weight that we give interpretations depends upon *our* understandings. We accept an interpretation when we can use it to see just how fully what was puzzling to the interpreter is clarified by the interpretation. If we cannot see what was puzzling nor how it is resolved, all the interpreter can do is to call up more and more interpretations to show what is at issue. Establishing a particular interpretation means grounding it in other interpretations. There is no way out of the interpretive circle through a reference to an independent non-interpretive 'reality'. If we accept the rules of science, all of which are based upon the supposition that reality is outside any scheme of interpretation, then we can say that its results follow independently of what individual scientists might hope, fear or wish. Even when historians have settled upon an agreed interpretation, there is no guarantee of correctness, truth or universality. The interpretation which the historians accept now is *their* interpretation, to be understood through the social and historical circumstances of *their* times. As we will see when we talk about the philosophy of science in Section Three, the rather comfortable view of the 'objective' and 'non-interpretive' nature of science is today very much in retreat, or at least being rethought. The generalising strategy, in fact, is going the other way. To philosophers such as Feyerabend, the way to understand science is to see it as an historically contexted phenomenon.

In the period of which we are speaking, though, the distinction between the 'objectivity' of science and the 'subjectivity' of history was a fixed and rigid one for the most part. Hermeneutic philosophy accepted that meaning and interpretation were historically located and so denied that comparison with the natural sciences was appropriate. The consensus of interpretations that might be on view at any time could only be seen as the common participation of historians in a historically and culturally defined frame of understanding. But, given the importance that was attached to the subjective essence of human life, this was not taken as a disadvantage. Indeed, that the interpretive sciences would be subjective followed from the essential character of their object of study. It was here that its distinctive contribution was to be found. From the first, hermeneutic philosophy tried to show which methods would be appropriate for the interpretive sciences.

Schleiermacher and Dilthey: the Constitution of Hermeneutic Sciences

It was Schleiermacher who more than any one else was responsible for drawing Hermeneutics away from its home in philology and applying it to the problem of historical knowledge. This problem he took to be the question of how we are to grasp the sense of the past from the standpoint of the present. Since all history was to be seen as the expression of human meaning, then we could not treat history and historical events and artifacts as if they were 'objective' and merely causally determined. To understand the past, the historian had to identify with it. What Schleiermacher developed was a method for achieving that identification.

The historian's task, according to Schleiermacher, is to place himself in the position of the person, the subject, who created the original meaning, the text, artifact or whatever. In doing this, the historian will submerge himself in the totality of life that gave them meaning. This 'psychological interpretation' is a coming to share the background against which interpretation takes place. It is because we do not have this background that we find texts, events, movements and artifacts puzzling. We cannot contextualise them. The special method that was required to contextualise the puzzling element within the totality from which it had been extracted, involved two kinds of interpretation; the grammatical and the psychological. The grammatical stresses the need to situate a text by reference to the language shared by the author and the original public. The second tries to show how the thoughts and meaning expressed, emerged in the course of the author's life. This is achieved by attempting to grasp what the author was struggling to convey. This literally means that the interpreter has to identify with the author or social actor. The interpreter has to submerge his own identity in that of the author. If this were possible, the act of interpretation would allow a gradual movement out toward the understanding of the totality. The meaning of the part is determined from its place in the whole, and that of the whole from the way that it contextualises the parts. The movement back and forth, from parts to whole, is one way of characterising what is often described as the 'hermeneutic circle'. By complementing grammatical interpretation with psychological identification, Schleiermacher introduced Hermeneutics into the study of human activities other than linguistic communication through texts and so indicated something of the possibilities and limitations of interpretive understanding.

It was Dilthey who built upon Schleiermacher's beginnings and argued not just that Hermeneutics offered one way of grasping the character of human life but that it was essential for any understanding of human life. Hermeneutics was to be the key human science. In other words, Dilthey takes the argument over method right into his opponents' camp and challenges the paradigmatic status of scientific knowledge. Since the essence of human nature is the creation of meaning, the world which they have created — that is, their social institutions and practices — 'objectifies' their subjectivity and can only be understood by other subjective beings, other people. Our knowledge of human life can only be gained through a hermeneutical interpretive procedure based upon the possibility of 'imaginatively recreating' the experience of others. It is this imaginative recreation that Dilthey takes over from Schleiermacher. We know the nature of other subjective natures by analogy with our own. We can come to understand the cultural and social complexes of meaning of other historical eras by immersing ourselves in the interpretive study of the 'objectifications' of meaning complexes, the actual historical artifacts, texts and so on. Dilthey recognised that all such interpretations must take account of both the point of view of the creator of the artifact as well as the interpreter. We cannot achieve a proper understanding of figures such as Plato or Luther by treating them entirely as figures of their own times, entirely alien to us, nor by assuming them to be contemporaries of ours. Interpretive understanding is not an attempt to recover what it was like to be Plato or Luther and what they were doing, but to understand them in relation to our concerns. Accordingly, because interpretation involves our experiences as well as those of others, imaginatively reconstructed, such knowledge can never be independent of a point of view. As we saw in the Introduction to this Section, Kant argued that it was possible to obtain, and therefore science could be based upon, an independent view of reality from within our experience. For the human sciences, at least, Dilthey denies this. Interpretive understanding is essential to grasping the meaning of human life. At the same time, it remains inescapably historical and culturally delimited because *our* experiences are integral to the process.

Dilthey's argument, then, is that it is a misunderstanding of the nature of the cultural sciences to try to compare them directly with the natural ones. His justification for this stance is a reintroduction of the strict distinction between subjectivity and objectivity as topics of investigation. Human life is the expression of subjectivity and cannot be treated simply as the consequence of causally determined objects. The goal of the human sciences ought to be understanding and not causal explanation. Such understanding recaptures the meaning of social objects and actions. The methods of the natural sciences do not allow them to achieve such understanding. It follows that the cultural sciences are not inferior but simply different.

One of the consequences of holding to this view was that Dilthey was able to make a virtue out of what his opponents held to be a drawback of the methods of the cultural sciences. The relativity of interpretation was not just something that historians and others would have to accept. It was a condition of interpretive understanding and gave it its distinctive value. What the cultural scientists provides is a way for *us* to understand *their* way of life. It is clear, though, that to some this would look like a commitment to a form of knowledge that would be prey to the sceptic's argument that there could be no certain knowledge, no certain morality or truth. Dilthey blocked this by appealing to an idea which he derived from Schleiermacher and which has recently been given extra force in the work of Habermas (cf. below). This is the notion of 'a community of life unities'. Although the aim of interpretation is to understand objects and events as manifestations of the lives of individuals, none of us are *just* individuals. We share in a collective life and so are 'collective individuals' so to speak. Against the tendency in 'positivist' social science to treat individuals as aggregated into collectivities, Hermeneutics rejects the rigidity of the distinction between the collectivity and the individual. In this way, Dilthey could say that we all share in the 'life community' and through it may be able to disentangle our essential community from the historical and cultural specifics of particular societies. This provides the possibility of a firm foundation for the hermeneutic method. As subjective beings sharing in a collective life, we can understand what other similar beings have created. We are all united in our creativity, for that is our essence. Penetrating to this essence, though, is no straightforward or easy matter.

What Schleiermacher and Dilthey began was a long running 'struggle over method' in the cultural and human sciences, particularly in Germany. The rejection of the natural science model required them to formulate their alternative. Since then attempts have been made to bridge the disjunction by showing that interpretive understanding could be combined with causal explanation — in the case of Weber's sociology and Habermas' social philosophy — or how the circle of relative interpretations could be broken by linking such knowledge to its 'real underpinnings' as in the case of Mannheim's sociology of knowledge. Both of these themes are essentially continuations and modifications of Schleiermacher and Dilthey's methodological interest in Hermeneutics. Recently, though, Gadamer has tried to rekindle the original philosophical concern of Hermeneutics in the nature of existence by treating interpretive understanding as the fundamental feature of what he calls 'being-in-the-world'.

Gadamer and the Authority of Tradition

Gadamer advocates a return to the problem of understanding in general. This, he says, has been supplanted by the overriding interest in the hermeneutic constitution of the social sciences. In turning away from such methodological matters, Gadamer wants to illuminate the human context in which understanding occurs, for understanding and interpretation are, as has been repeatedly said, the essential features of human nature. Gadamer is going back, then, to the ontological and metaphysical questions that the Romantic movement raised in its rejection of Enlightenment thought. In dealing with Gadamer, it might be as well to distinguish between 'Hermeneutics' as a philosophical method and 'hermeneutics' as a feature of human existence. Clearly Gadamer's interest is primarily in the latter. In his view, Hermeneutics is concerned with 'breeches of subjectivity', that is those situations where we encounter meanings that we cannot grasp or which require considerable effort to understand. Hermeneutic understanding, both as a philosophical method and in ordinary life, has to bridge the gap between the familiar and taken-for-granted world we are all immersed in and the strange and unfamiliar meanings that we find resist easy assimilation and understanding. Clearly, then, interpretation not only encompasses that which we strive to understand but also that which we already do understand. This is an important observation which, in Gadamer's view, was not noticed by Dilthey and Schleiermacher.

Gadamer's argument is, in essence, that Dilthey and Schleiermacher had not freed themselves from the idea of knowledge being obtained by 'pure reason' which, as we saw, had dominated the Enlightenment. The 'pure reasoner' was the scholar who had detached himself from his social and cultural context by the adoption of methodologically secured sets of rules of enquiry. Dilthey and Schleiermacher seemed not to have rejected this view because they held that the historical and cultural distance between the historian, say, and the society being studied, was an impediment to the acquisition of valid knowledge and had to be overcome by the hermeneutic method. In this sense, our social and cultural location in history is an accidental and potentially distorting feature of understanding. Gadamer rejects this. Our 'historicity', as he terms it, is an ontological condition of understanding. It is because of our historical and cultural location that we can engage in interpretive understanding. It is our present understandings, our conceptions of life, that open up the past to us so that we can have knowledge of it. These conceptions are the grounds of the judgements that we make about other societies on the basis of our understandings. In talking about such prejudgements or 'prejudices', Gadamer reinvokes the Kantian theme of the necessity of knowledge being obtained through a cognitive framework, although there is the clear difference that in Gadamer's view this framework is what we as historically and culturally located beings know and understand about the world and not the Kantian innate structures of the mind. Prejudices, then, enable us to experience and understand other societies through their texts, artifacts and so on. Our historical position can never be entirely held at a distance and left out of account. It is the 'given' which shapes our experience. But our historical position is itself shaped by the past, so the past has a considerable power over our under-standing. The past provides the tradition, which defines the ground on which the interpreter stands. In discussing the role of the past in the present, Gadamer follows many of the ideas which are associated with Heidegger and which we dealt with in Chapter 4.

What we have here is an attempt to expand interpretive understanding beyond the range of historiography and the social sciences to the concern with the essence of human life in history. In Gadamer's view, and it echoes that of Heidegger, most of European philosophy since the Enlightenment has been 'subjectivist' in that it has concentrated on the features of pure reasoning and the rules that the pure reasoner would follow — that is, the development of Logic and logical languages. Such philosophy is alienating because it ignores our location in history as human beings *and* interpreters. Gadamer's own conception of interpretive understanding is not that of reconstructing the past in the present but of mediating the past for the present.

The work of mediation involves attention to the continuity of heritage and tradition. The past already influences the present by shaping the interpreter's horizons and understandings. The prejudices and interests that we bring to understanding are located in history. This should also be forward as well as backward looking. Our interpretations will make a contribution to all those that follow. There is a continual mediation of past and present in which our interpretation marks just a moment. Into this continuity, Gadamer introduces the idea of a plurality of possible meanings. The past is an active force providing an inexhaustible supply of possibilities and not passive, inert, merely an object of contemplation. Texts, events and so on come to acquire different meanings as they become part of new hermeneutical situations; as the interpreter's horizons change with the understandings which he acquires so he reconsiders and reviews the texts, etc., and what they mean *for him*. This movement back and forth Gadamer talks of as a dialogue which begins with the interpreter genuinely opening himself to a text and allowing it to speak no matter how challenging its viewpoint. This opening up throws the interpreter's prejudices into relief by raising them for critical appraisal. This 'collision of horizons', the shock of contact between our own and some entirely alien viewpoint, reveals our own deep-seated assumptions and our historicity. Genuine understanding requires imagination in situations like this; the ability to see what is questionable and what is questioned, to be carried along by it and immersed in its flow. In this rendering, the hermeneutic circle of interpretation becomes a process of hypothesis and revision as understanding develops. As we come to grasp a part we conjecture a sense of the whole. This conjecture is then revised as our knowledge progresses. The 'unity of sense' toward which interpretation strives is the integration of all of the parts in a meaningful whole.

All Hermeneutics is tradition bound, and therefore historical. These traditions are integral to understanding and cannot be set to one side. Gadamer makes the connection to the central problems of philosophy, as he sees them at least, by arguing that Hermeneutics is not just a method or an ideal; it is the original form of 'being-in-the-world'. Since it is fundamental to our existence, our being-in-the-world, it is the universal principle of human thought. His argument here has several closely related steps. First there is the rejection that hermeneutics can be the recapitulation of some actor or agent's intended meaning. To define it thus would be to suppose that there was just one, fixed meaning to be attained. This would make unintelligible the host of differing interpretations that are to be found in history and which make up the tradition we bring to interpretation. These interpretations cannot be treated as *mis*understandings as Gadamer felt Schleiermacher did but as varying understandings. This variety gives us an 'excess of meaning' in the tradition which we bring to bear in our understanding well beyond that of any particular author or agent's intentions. What a text means is a growing, changing, live matter not a mummified intention. The ways in which such developments are shown, found, and presented, how meaning 'discloses' itself as he puts it, is its being. In this way, Gadamer circumvents objections premissed upon a requirement that knowledge be objective. There can be no standards of objectivity independent of the intersubjective fusion of horizons reached by partners in the dialogue of interpretation. This fusion is brought about through the interpreter's willingness to review his prejudices in the light of those brought by the author of the text in question.

Underpinning the possibility of a fusion of horizons is our possession of language. Our concepts and meanings are expressed in our language. Without language we could not understand for we would have no way of expressing our concepts. The crucial metaphysical question, of course, concerns the relation of our concepts given in language to the world. Gadamer argues that our possession of language is not merely an accidental feature of our existence, akin to the fact that we have two legs, breathe air and have stereoscopic vision. We possess the world through language because we experience the world mediated through our concepts. Language is a precondition of any truth and understanding. It follows since we cannot experience the world independently of our concepts that language sets limits upon the world for us. This, remember, was exactly the same conclusion Kant drew from his deduction of the a priori categories, namely there are limits to what we can know and understand. The limits that Gadamer is pointing to are not those imposed by innate structures of the mind, but the sediments of history laid down in tradition and expressed in our language and concepts.

By its very nature language is communal. This offers the possibility of escape from the relativist treadmill. Knowing a language means knowing how to make oneself understood in it; language has, as Gadamer puts it, 'disclosive power'. What is spoken of in language, what is captured in our concepts, is the common world in which we live; as we noted above, our language constitutes the world in which we live. Language is, therefore, the universal medium of understanding. Just as prejudices are not bars to our understanding but its starting point, so to know a language is to be open to participation with others in dialogue that can transform and broaden the horizons from which we begin. Language discloses realities and assimilates them within itself. Since there can be no experience of the world outside of that given in a language, the question of the relativity of language does not arise. There is nowhere else to view the world from, nowhere that is fixed and independent of language. Just as we cannot escape from language, so we cannot escape from prejudice, although interpretation allows us to transcend particular prejudices. What Gadamer is reminding us of here is the essential creativity of language and interpretation. Meanings that are disclosed through the dialogue of interpretation pose further questions and puzzles for us. The spiral of understanding and interpretation is a creative process which constantly fuses and enlarges the horizons provided by the interpreter and the interpreted. The linguistic nature of interpretation is the way that tradition is able to communicate with us. At each point in the spiral, tradition, interpretation and horizons are encountered and transcended at a more universal level. There can be no end to this transcendence.

Gadamer takes Hermeneutics back to philosophy and thereby rejects the need for a special hermeneutic method to overcome historical and cultural relativism. His is an even more radical interpretation of hermeneutics than that of Dilthey and Schleiermacher. Tradition and language form the context for interpretation; there can be no understanding outside of language and history, and so there is nothing for our understanding of a text or artifact to be relative to. In

the Introduction to this Section we said that time and space constituted the axes of experience for Kant; history and language constitute
the axes of understanding and hence of experience for Gadamer. We
cannot escape from history and tradition. In our interpretations we
contribute to history and the sedimentation of tradition.

Habermas and Depth Hermeneutics

In Chapter 2, in our discussion of Hegel and Marx, we indicated that
one of the central features of Marx's philosophical anthropology was
the idea of 'alienated consciousness'. In outlining Marcuse's
interpretation of this theme, we suggested that Critical Theory
attacked contemporary philosophy for failing to recognise and
confront the possibility of alienated consciousness. This is precisely
the charge which Habermas lays against Gadamer. In stressing the
community of language and tradition, its consensus, Gadamer fails to
point out that language can be deceiving and distorting as well as
disclosing. The traditions which we take over from the past can be
ideological in form, masking the oppression and exploitation that
determines our being-in-the-world. Hermeneutics as a philosophy
cannot ignore this possibility; it must confront it and so become
critical of the conditions which give rise to alienated consciousness.
    What Habermas is bringing to Hermeneutics is the theory of
praxis, and with it a rejection of abstracted reason. All knowledge is
gained in the pursuit of cognitive interests; these can be 'hermeneutic',
'technical' or 'emancipatory'. The familiar dichotomy between nature
and reason reappears here in that the natural sciences, what are
termed 'the empirical-analytic sciences', seek a technical mastery
over nature. The 'hermeneutic disciplines' seek to further understanding of intersubjective, rational beings by interpretation of the
purposes, motives and intentions of actors as these are displayed in
action. The third cognitive interest is concerned with the securing of
freedom from constraint; especially that imposed by the distorted
communication of ideology. In this way, Habermas hopes to give
Hermeneutics a critical edge by introducing into it the concerns of
Hegelian Marxism. It is aimed at a critique of ideology which would
uncover the power relationships embodied in the communicative
process and tradition. What Gadamer had failed to take cognisance of
was Marx's discovery that forms of communication and tradition both
shape and are shaped by the material conditions of life. His

philosophy, therefore, succumbs to the 'idealism of linguisticality', whereas for Habermas the framework for understanding social action is that provided by language, labour and domination. In elevating the hermeneutic process to constitute the character of our being-in-the-world, Gadamer ignored the economic and political factors which 'limit' our horizons. In making the connections in this way, Habermas has to recall the distinction between subjectivity and objectivity of knowledge. He has to do this in order to say that Gadamer's Hermeneutics does not go deep enough. It does not penetrate beneath the historically contexted traditions to the real determinations of our knowledge and understanding, those socio-historical processes which restrict the ways that our needs and wants are defined and the means we have for satisfying them. Although human history does express our subjectivity, it is still constrained by the objective character of domination, repression and ideology. Emancipation from domination, repression and ideology can only occur when the spiral of interpretive understanding that Gadamer described is linked to a critical evaluation of the constraints on knowledge and all cognitive processes; when hermeneutics is revitalised by praxis. Such a revitalisation will be a 'depth hermeneutics'.

The recalling of the distinction between 'subjective' and 'objective' meanings presents Habermas with a problem. Gadamer had dismissed the duality by arguing that all interpretations were formed from within a community of life interests. There was no way outside to an independent point from which to take an 'objective' view. If Habermas wishes to argue that the expressions of our subjectivity are determined by forces which we can know 'objectively' — and he must say this if he wants to make a distinction between ideological and non-ideological knowledge, between distorted and non-distorted communication — then he has got to show how this 'objective' viewpoint is arrived at. He cannot fall back upon an invocation of the rules and procedures of the natural sciences because they are predicated upon the universality of objectivity. Hermeneutics is predicated upon subjectivity. Habermas looks for a synthesis. He seeks a unified framework within which the natural and the hermeneutic sciences can be accommodated. The exemplar of a critical theory which displays this synthesis, for Habermas, is Freudian psychoanalysis.

The general strategy that Habermas adopts is to show how Freudian theory extends and complements that of Marx, to give a fuller account of the nature of distorted communication than is to be found in the theory of ideology alone. Habermas sets the argument up in the following way. In his view, Freud saw strong similarities between the development of the individual and that of the species, particularly since the survival of both involves the repression of needs and wants. This repression results in patterns of distorted communication. In the individual, these appear as neurotic symptoms; in societies, as ideologies. Marx's account of alienation, emphasising as it does production and labour, is unsatisfactory even though it does reveal the power of ideologies to conceal the facts of domination and oppression. What Freud showed was that unsuspected patterns of distorted communication can be seen even in the speech patterns of ordinary life. By focusing on the development of socially repressed needs and wants, Freud saw that the power of social norms resides in their ability, albeit unconscious, to provide substitute or 'displaced' gratifications. These repressed socially unacceptable motives and channelled them into acceptable forms of expression. This repression, in the Freudian theory, comes about through fear and domination and is expressed in the demands for conformity expressed in the superego. Habermas suggests that such demands could account for the 'false consciousness' of groups within a class society. If this is so, then emancipation from the constraints which dominate and shape human life can only be achieved through an interpretation of both the development of the personality and human society; an interpretation which would allow us to identify those points at which development became arrested and so produced distorted communication. In this way, the therapy of self-understanding and analysis which is integral to Freud's method becomes the task of critical hermeneutics; guided self-reflection will enable us to overcome distorted communication.

Habermas is attracted to psychoanalysis not because it has all the trappings of a bona fide science — which it is not — but because it is essentially hermeneutic in character. It involves the systematic and methodical interpretation of behaviour, speech, dreams and so on. At the same time, it admits causal processes into its accounts of neurosis and other pathologies. By bringing out, from the pattern of behaviour, the latent significance of that part of the patient's life history which had been repressed, it penetrates beneath the surface to the 'underlying' forces generating the surface meanings. Psychoanalysis is a unity of hermeneutic method and science. By reconstructing his own childhood traumas, the patient is able to give these repressed areas of his life a new significance. Depth hermeneutics will apply the same 'therapy' to communication and behaviour in social life. Here the level of conscious intentionality — what we think we want and strive for — will be linked to our unconscious, repressed needs and wants. The meaning of what we do and say, our surface interpretations, can only be fully understood by causally relating them to the unacknowledged and unrecognised determining factors of power and domination. In this way, depth hermeneutics will raise for analysis the very character of language itself, the distorted forms which we use to communicate. In so doing it will go beyond the limits of language and experience and show what brings about our language and experience. Rather than the 'ordered view from within' language and experience sought by Kant, Habermas seeks to break through to that which determines our experience.

Part of therapy in psychoanalysis is the stage at which the patient comes to accept the analytic interpretation of the neurotic or other symptomatic behaviour. The patient can understand his behaviour when he comes to see how it is to be explained by the causal factors which produced it. Once the explanation is accepted, the patient's distorted understanding of his actions (what he thought he was doing) and the self-conscious realisation of his condition are mediated. Therapy can only succeed when self-understanding and explanation unite. Such acceptance is not simply an agreement, a consensus in interpretation. It is the patient's own reconstruction of his life history. The neurosis is overcome only when the patient cures himself.

Psychoanalysis, then, is the prototype of depth hermeneutics. Through the self-reflection it requires, the patient can overcome distorted communication. Habermas now brings that proposal to historical materialism. If it were to be reconstituted as a depth hermeneutics it would become a realisable critique of ideology. The combination of hermeneutics and the theory of praxis would create the possibility of social emancipation in the same way that the patient in psychoanalysis ultimately cures himself. Such a depth hermeneutics would be a new social philosophy of liberation. Guided by this social philosophy, the human and social sciences would have a diagnostic and therapeutic role.

Following the hermeneutic method, this philosophy begins with an object, say a social process, whose meaning is in doubt. As in traditional hermeneutics, dialogue is employed to disclose the interpretive possibilities. To move beyond these and remove the distortions in communication, explanations involving causality must be developed. Once we have a theory of societal evolution which accounts for the emergence of class societies to hand, it should be possible to reveal the fundamental distortions which, at present, limit our self-understanding. Such a theory could be 'tested' through the reconstruction of the case in question to see the extent to which distorted communication is disclosed. The final verification for the whole process depends, as it does in psychoanalysis, upon its practical success. Does it reveal the barriers to self-understanding and aid in their demolition? In capitalism, social existence consists in class domination, a fact which is distorted in ideologies of one sort or another. These ideologies encourage the subjugated mass to subordinate their interests to those of a social order whose injustice remains hidden and repressed. Capitalism hides its contradictions behind a veil of pseudo-scientific explanations and emotive appeals to the common good, the nation, the needs of economic growth, and such like. The assent by the subjugated to their subjugation amounts to a passive but repressed acceptance of a 'false reality'. Awareness of this false consensus should lead to the questioning of this tradition of assumptions which has been inherited from our history and so, like the patient's self-understanding, be the crucial step to overcoming them.

The critical edge to depth hermeneutics is provided by the theory of distorted communication. However, this itself is premissed upon the possibility of non-distorted communication, a possibility which is sketched out in the theory of communicative competence. Historical materialism has indicated the overall nature and origins of ideology. Depth hermeneutics will show how it is to be comprehended and overcome. But to hold a distinction between true and false consciousness, Habermas has to show that non-distorting communication is possible and, furthermore, how we could recognise it. Habermas does not appeal to a simplistic notion of 'truth' to help him out here since he realises that the possibility that any procedures for ascertaining such truth would be open to the allegation of distortion remains. Instead, he takes the route of appealing to the notion of a rational community in which interests are fully acknowledged and all positions open to critical inspection. In this idealised, rational speech community, false consciousness could be detected and brought to light *because we know the preconditions which give rise to it*. Our sensitivity to these preconditions would alert us to the possibility of distorted communication; that our arguments might be ideological.

The point of Habermas' critical hermeneutics is to argue to the possibility of the idealised speech community and so contribute to the transformation of the conditions of human life. Whereas traditional Hermeneutics was concerned with the achievement of a unity of interpretation — be that as a methodological problem for the social and historical sciences, as with Dilthey or Schleiermacher, or as the ontological prerequisite for human existence or being-in-the-world as in Gadamer — Habermas wishes to transcend the illusory unity imposed by ideology through tradition and language and so liberate mankind from the forces of domination and oppression that require these ideologies. Such liberation will be achieved with the attainment of the rational, free society built upon critical self-understanding. In so doing, Habermas has sought not simply to move beyond Gadamer's philosophy and Dilthey and Schleiermacher's methodology but to synthesise the duality, the distinction, between the scientific and the hermeneutic disciplines. The synthesis in depth hermeneutics will be a social philosophy that marries the philosophical anthropology of Marx with the hermeneutic method.

Recommended Reading

Dilthey's works are voluminous. H.A. Hodges, *Wilhelm Dilthey, An Introduction* (Routledge, 1944) contains some fifty pages of translations. Similarly H.P. Richman, *Meaning in History* (Allen and Unwin, 1961) provides a full discussion of Dilthey's philosophy of history along with selected passages. Z. Bauman, *Hermeneutics and Social Science* (Hutchinson, 1978) offers an extensive and accessible discussion of the hermeneutic strain in the social sciences. J. Bleicher, *Contemporary Hermeneutics* (Routledge, 1980) contains selections from a discussion, sometimes difficult, of more contemporary hermeneutic thinkers. The fullest statement of Gadamer's views, though it is long, is his *Truth and Method* (Sheed and Ward, 1975). Habermas' critique of Gadamer's views, 'A review of Gadamer's *Truth and Method*', is to be found in F.R. Dallmyr and T.A. McCarthy (eds.), *Understanding and Social Inquiry*, (Notre Dame Press, 1977). Habermas' own corpus is, like Dilthey's, enormous and growing, though his *Knowledge and Human Interests* (Heinemann 1971) is, perhaps, the best treatment of his response to hermeneutics. D. Held's *Introduction to Critical Theory* (Hutchinson, 1980) and T.A. McCarthy, *The Critical Theory of Jurgen Habermas* (Hutchinson, 1978) are both excellent, and readable, detailed expositions and commentaries on Habermas' thought and its development. A more than usefully clear essay setting out the logic of Hermeneutics and its implications for social analysis, using examples from political science, is C. Taylor's excellent essay, 'Interpretation and the Sciences of man', in R. Beehler and A.R. Drengson (eds.), *The Philosophy of Society* (Methuen, 1978), pp. 156-200.

4 PHENOMENOLOGY

Two questions preoccupied nearly all Enlightenment philosophers. They were: 'What is the basis of our knowledge of the world?' and 'What is that knowledge, knowledge of?'. In the Introduction to this Section, we saw that several different answers had been offered. The arguments over them continue even today. However, the progress of science had considerable impact upon philosophy. By the end of the nineteenth century, science's success had seemed to vindicate the empiricist epistemology on which it was based and the logico-deductive method it had adopted to order its investigations and theories. For many, the success of science had solved the problem of epistemology, namely the way to objective knowledge. In so doing, it had also answered the questions of ontology.

One of the consequences of the success of science was a persistent attempt to export its methods to the social sciences. The many and various arguments put forward to justify this move could be collected together under the banner of 'positivism'. Such a transformation of the human and social sciences would place their inquiries on a firm and 'objective' footing. The discipline that was most amenable to this suggestion and which took positivism to its heart, so to speak, was psychology. Psychology in the positivist vein offered the objective study of subjectivity. It showed how human consciousness and knowledge acquisition — the premisses of epistemology — could be the objects of scientifically rigorous study. Ultimately, some felt that this would lead to the dissolution of philosophy as traditionally conceived to be replaced by science. This argument proved very attractive to a number of philosophers and philosophically inclined scientists who urged that the methods and logic of science constituted not just the paragon of knowledge but also the only proper topic of philosophical inquiry. Philosophy was parasitic on science; it had no problems of its own.

From its inception, Phenomenology resisted this 'scientism' and the fawning upon science which so often accompanied it. Phenomenology did not reject the achievements of science nor deny its power. What it did question was the claim that scientific knowledge had somehow wrenched itself free of subjectivity. The argument was deceptively simple. All knowledge begins in consciousness, in subjectivity, even science. The 'impersonal', 'objective' rules of scientific procedures and argument are just as rooted in consciousness as any other form of knowledge. To suppose that a set of stipulations which, if agreed to, organise consciousness in determinate and fixed ways could overcome subjectivity and the philosophical problems posed by it is misconceived. Science sets these problems aside; it has no interest in them. Scientism in philosophy, because it accepts that they can be ignored, reneges on philosophy and is no more than idolatry. If we seek answers to the philosophical questions about knowledge, then it is to subjectivity, human consciousness that we will have to return. We will have to find a method that allows us to bring consciousness into view for philosophical scrutiny. To accomplish this, Phenomenology went back to the modern origins of Rationalist thought, namely the Cartesian Method of Doubt. Descartes' project, the demonstration of how the world is constituted in consciousness as a world for us to have knowlege of, is the correct one. However, it is fatally flawed. It was these flaws that had to be corrected if we want to supplant 'scientism' and resurrect philosophy.

The return to the Method of Doubt was initiated by Husserl. Descartes' fatal error was to suppose that the distinction between the *res cogitans* (the thinking being) and the *res extensa* (its embodiment) was foundational; that beyond this distinction no further steps could be taken. The relationship between the thinking subject, mind, and the non-thinking object, matter, has been central to epistemology and ontology ever since. What do we have to say the mind knows a priori for it to be able to have knowledge of matter a posteriori? As we saw in our Introduction, this was the question that Kant felt had to be answered if sceptical empiricism was to be kept at bay. Husserl takes it up again. Using the Method of Doubt in a wholly new way, the presupposition of mind and matter, in Descartes' ontology can itself be suspended, and thus the world-in-consciousness brought into view.

Husserl begins by proposing that all forms of knowledge have their roots in consciousness. Consciousness is always intentional; it is consciousness of things, be they ordinary objects in the world, mathematical proofs, or scientific discoveries. All of these enter our consciousness as *phenomena* for us. To see how we constitute them *as* phenomena, how they come to be objects for consciousness, we have to suspend the presupposition of their reality. In so doing we will go back beyond the dualism of objects and consciousness, mind and matter, to see how we constitute the objective character of objects in consciousness. By reflecting upon experience, we will have transcended it. This was what both Descartes and Kant were after. What they did not achieve was what Husserl thought he had achieved, namely the constitution of 'pure consciousness', what he termed the Transcendental Ego, as the departure point for knowledge of the world. To see why he thought he had achieved this, we will need to look a little more closely at Husserl's philosophic method.

Husserl insists that philosophy involves a distinctive cast of mind. He contrasts it with what he terms 'the natural attitude'. The natural attitude has two essential features. First it presumes that there is a world of objects existing independently of us which we can know. Second, the possibility of our having knowledge of this world is indubitable. Thus the reality of the world and of our knowledge of it is never questioned. This natural attitude was not confined simply to ordinary commonsense. It could be seen in science, mathematics, including, significantly, mathematical logic. (Why Husserl should have thought this significant can be seen in the Introduction to Section Two). The sciences and mathematics differ from commonsense in that they take up a theoretical attitude towards the objects presupposed in the natural attitude. Commonsense adopts a practical attitude, or even a moral and aesthetic one. Practicality, usefulness, morality and aesthetic considerations are excluded from the theoretical attitude. The philosophical attitude is predicated upon the questioning of all presumptions; there are no presuppositions that cannot be questioned and suspended. By extending the premiss of doubt to all presuppositions, philosophy can transcend the natural attitude and so bring the premisses of science, commonsense and so forth into view. Scientism fails to take this step; it is locked into the natural attitude. It simply is not rigorous philosophy as Husserl defined it; it fails to penetrate to the foundations of scientific knowledge, let alone knowledge in general. The first task that Phenomenology set itself was the description of the constitution of consciousness. Only when such a description is available could we seek to show how the theoretical attitude of science is both predicated in and a transformation of consciousness.

The step from the natural attitude to the philosophical attitude, Husserl called the 'phenomenological reduction' or epoché. As we have seen, it involves 'bracketing' our presuppositions about the objects of consciousness. In this way, the philosopher distances himself from commonly held theories about the phenomenon in question. The shift in attention that this involves is very difficult to describe in the abstract. It does not mean that the reality of the world disappears from view, but that it is viewed in a wholly new way. For example, there is a television playing in the next room and someone is cooking in the kitchen beyond. I can hear the sounds through the open door. The phenomenological reduction asks how we come to take the sounds as the indubitable evidence that the television is on and someone is in the kitchen. If you were to ask me how I know, I could only say that I can hear the sounds. To keep the example at a manageable level, we can say that it involves asking how the reality of real objects like televisions and people cooking dinner is constituted in consciousness. Bracketing the world means returning to consciousness of the world. We cannot now take the bracketing any further. We cannot in consciousness bracket consciousness. This consciousness, purified of assumptions, beliefs and knowledge which *I* might have about the world, is a Transcendental Consciousness, the consciousness not of a particular thinking being (Ego), but of the Transcendental Ego. The exact nature of this concept has, of course been the subject of much debate. Many attempts, none of them really successful, have been made to clarify it.

The process of abstraction from my particular conscious experience to the transcendental consciousness is long and extremely painstaking. It involves the description of the various horizons of my consciousness, the relationships between elements in my consciousness, as well as their individual character. The examination of consciousness is not delimited by the field of perception in the here and now; I identify a sound as 'the mixer' because I have heard it before. It is 'the same' sound. I can imagine 'courses of action' in which mixers are used and so can say what is happening. Here we have further objects for phenomenological reduction. What makes a perception the same? How are courses of action conjured up in the imagination? The description of each of these and many, many more is the unified field of phenomenology. It is its proper field of study. Its task is to show how each of these constitutive components is synthesised within the unity of consciousness. In stark contrast to the empiricists, Husserl offers us the image of the active mind organising and constituting the world as real and not as an inert *tabula rasa* waiting to be stamped with 'impressions' of the world.

The point of the Rationalist Method of Doubt, even in Descartes' hands, was to be able to formulate an ontology, a list of what, stripped of all appearances, there must be. Husserl follows the same path. He argued that the phenomenon given in pure consciousness is the essence of the object experienced empirically in the natural attitude. The 'essence' or 'eidos' of a phenomenon is that which is present in pure consciousness, and hence that which makes the object knowable, experienceable by consciousness. The method for isolating or intuiting essences is the 'eidetic reduction' whereby the object's location in consciousness is set aside and its unchanging, universal characteristics revealed. The ontology of essences that is arrived at in this way is the grounding on which science and all other knowledge had to be based. It gives us the indisputable categories of how things must be for us to be able to constitute them in consciousness and so have experience of them. The method that Husserl recommends for the achievement of this 'eidetic reduction' is that of 'free variation'. 'Free variation' enables us to strip an object of any given empirical reference — what it is and what it does, how we usually constitute it in our consciousness — so that its possibilities can be explored. The object being examined is, in a literal sense, a fiction, an imaginary object. We can, for example, imagine what Captain Oates' state of mind might have been after he walked out into the snow. We do not have any 'facts' to constrain us, only what we take to be essential to Oates' character. Perhaps the model for 'free variation', though, is geometry. We are perfectly free to imagine a geometrical shape, a triangle or a parallelogram mapped onto a curved rather than a plane surface. We are not thinking about that triangular set square or that piece of A4 typing paper, merely the shapes. We can then ask what will happen if the shapes are drawn on a curve. Will the internal angles of the triangle still add up to $180°$? They might, but they don't have to. Will the parallel sides of the parallelogram never meet? Some might, but others might not. In this way we can extract what is immutable in the shapes and what is not; what is the essence of 'triangular' and 'parallelogram' and what is not.

The important feature of the 'eidetic reduction' is that it was Husserl's attempt to steer between the twin alternatives that previous philosophy had tried not always successfully to avoid, empiricism and psychologism. If carried out rigorously enough, the method provided the possibility of a foundational transcendental science illuminating the data constituted as phenomena in each of the derived sciences. For Husserl each of the sciences adopts a particular attitude or way of defining its objects and its modes of study. These are the means by which phenomena are selected and conceptualised. The eidetic reduction would enable the sciences to see 'the ground on which they were standing', the essential character of the phenomena which they studied. Each of the derivative sciences was a science of appearances-under-particular-attitudes, the eidetic reduction would enable the formulation of an 'eidetic science', a first philosophy on which all science must be based.

Earlier in this chapter we suggested that for Husserl, all knowledge begins in the natural attitude of commonsense and by stages of reduction and rigour proceeds from there. Having set out the character of his method and the epistemological and ontological foundations that the method can provide for the rigorous sciences, Husserl turns the philosophical view back onto the empirical world of daily life, the *Lebenswelt*. In so doing, he takes up the possibility of an empirical science. The 'lifeworld' of commonsense is not directly accessible to science because, more often than not, many of its basic features, such as the existence of the external world and the possibility of knowledge of it that we mentioned before, are essential to both. The attitudes that the sciences have adopted, such as formalisation, measurability and so on, are ways of treating with the world given in the natural attitude, ways of rendering it amenable to science, or of making it scientifically tractable. What science has failed to do, because its interests do not require it, and what 'scientitistic' philosophy could not see had to be done, was to show just what the attitudes of the sciences take over and what they leave out from the natural attitude we all adopt in the lifeworld. In turning back to the lifeworld, Husserl wants to remind mathematicians, scientists and philosophers that the phenomena they study are *all* seen from a vantage point that is constitutive of them. It is only when we suspend vantage points in the eidetic reduction that we transcend them.

The basis of meaning, the concepts used and the objects studied, all have their origins in the lifeworld. However, the 'sensory fullness' of objects in our experience of them in the lifeworld is systematically abstracted in the sciences. Galileo when carrying out his famous experiment with the cannon ball and the pebble in Pisa was not interested in the fact that one object could be used to prop open doors, placed in pyramids in palace gardens etc., while the other could be used for children's games, fired from a sling or whatever. They were, for him, objects subject to uniform acceleration but of different masses. The cannon ball and the pebble are masses in motion and no more. The ontology of physics with mass, acceleration, motion, particles etc. etc. is a constitutive one. It selects from the lifeworld those aspects it is going to pay attention to. For Husserl, then, it was an absurdity to suppose that what the sciences reveal could possibly be certain truth about nature when they were premissed on a systematic disregarding of many of the features of nature and natural objects. It should not be surprising that, under the gaze of science, such objects reveal a high degree of mathematical orderliness since as objects for science they are defined in ways that will make them mathematically orderly. The difficulties that relativity theory created in physics and elsewhere were precisely that the premises of earlier mathematical orderliness were being violated, and the fact that they were premisses and not invariant features of the world had been obscured. As we shall see in Section Three, much the same conclusion is now being pursued in modern philosophy of science.

There is a fairly strong conection with the social sciences to be made here because one of the disciplines that Husserl was particularly contemptuous of was psychology. In Husserl's view, psychology claimed to be the science of consciousness but in its most prevalent forms it was committed to a strategy of experimentalism which meant that it could not in its studies do other than caricature consciousness. Human subjectivity and intersubjectivity simply are not amenable to experimentation and 'objective observation' of this sort. Instead of blindly following the natural sciences, psychology ought to derive a methodology which fits its subject matter's essence, namely the immersion of human consciousness in the flow of intersubjectivity in the lifeworld. When behaviourist and non-behaviourist psychologies alike sought to achieve formality, objectivity, replicability and all the rest they so distorted their subject matter as to make their 'findings' irrelevant. The identities which are presumed between, say, social conformity in daily life and social conformity in a Milgram experiment, or human learning and the acquisition of habit by rats are simply the result of a failure to reflect upon what their experimentation produces. Such reflection and clarification can only be brought about through a phenomenological sensitivity.

We have seen that during his life Husserl's philosophical method gradually became transformed into a critique of the natural sciences and, as we have just suggested, psychology. All of these disciplines had failed to reflect seriously and rigorously upon their own foundations in the lifeworld and consciousness. They had failed to see just what they had and what they had not taken from the lifeworld. As Alfred Schutz saw, this was of particular importance for the social sciences and sociology because they claimed to provide the 'scientific study' of the lifeworld. In his view the foundations of the social sciences as Husserl would have defined them were non-existent and the methods if not misconceived were systematically misguided.

Alfred Schutz and the Foundation of the Social Sciences

In Chapter 3 we discussed the influence of Hermeneutics upon the debate over the proper methods to be adopted by the historical and social sciences that took place in Germany throughout the latter part of the nineteenth century. Dilthey and Schleiermacher offered the possibility of an interpretive social science rather than an objectivist one. One figure who was profoundly influenced by this debate was Max Weber. Weber was convinced that it was possible to provide sociological explanations that were adequate both at the level of meaning and at the level of causality. Subjective understanding had to be an essential part of any thoroughgoing sociological explanations. In Schutz's view, while Weber's ambition was wholly admirable, it was not clear that he had provided the framework to make it realisable. Declaring that interpretive social science was not simply a luxury but a necessity did not indicate what its philosophical premises were to be. At first, Schutz felt that the gestalt psychology of Henri Bergson and William James might provide such a framework, but he soon came to see that it could not do so. Instead he turned to Phenomenology and Husserl's analysis of the lifeworld. In so doing he uses Husserl's philosophic method and findings to indicate what sort of ontology and conceptual framework interpretive social science would have to have and how it could be arrived at. In what has become a famous phrase, he treats the concept of subjective understanding as a topic heading for a set of problems which Weber failed to examine in any detail.

Schutz's exploration begins, as Husserl's did, with a rejection of 'positivism' and the naïve use of the 'natural science' model in the social sciences. The argument, following Husserl, is that the lifeworld of ordinary understandings is carried through from the natural attitude into that of the scientific one. It is not bracketed and examined. This, remember, was Husserl's criticism of the natural sciences' view of reality. The social reality which the social sciences take as their topic has its origins in the lifeworld of ordinary social actors. What Weber and other advocates of interpretive social science as well as those of the more familiar 'positivist' view have not done is to examine just how much of the natural attitude of commonsense has been carried over into social science. In order to clarify this and to set interpretive social science on a firm footing, it will be necessary to examine how the character of social reality is constituted and maintained in daily life as the outcome of the actions of intersubjective social actors. The path to be followed then is exactly parallel to that which Husserl recommends for the proper constitution of the physical and mathematical sciences. For them to be fully rigorous they have to elucidate how scientific and mathematic reality is rooted in the lifeworld of commonsense actors.

The heart of Schutz's examination is the 'postulate of subjective interpretation'. By this he means that all accounts have to begin by treating social actors as beings with consciousness whose own activities and the activities of others have meaning. The social reality in which we move and act as interpretive social actors is the outcome of the interpretations we make and the courses of action we initiate. The primal question is how the social scientist is to constitute the intersubjective lifeworld as a phenomenon for study. What 'objects' will it investigate and what concepts will it need? The answer is to be found in the phenomenological analysis of the lifeworld, and the concepts of intersubjectivity, subjective meaning and actor.

The phenomenon studied by the social sciences is social action. Such action is meaningful because of the intrinsic intentionality of consciousness. I do not see behaviour and infer meaningful action; I see meaningful action. I do not see someone moving his hand and infer he is waving, I see that person waving. It is only an occasional feature of our lives that we have to interpret behaviour at the level of consciousness. 'What on earth is he up to?', we ask. The second element in this is that the meanings which are given to actions are shared. Other social actors are interpreters too. The social world is intersubjective; we share schemes of meaning. In this way, not only are we able to make sense of our own and other actions, but others can too, and the sense which they make is similar to ours. The interpretations which we jointly make in daily life are based upon what Schutz calls the 'common stock of knowledge' which we all share. This stock of knowledge is partially idiosyncratic since it is formed out of the particular biographically defined experiences which each one has. But it is also formed out of the knowledge which we inherit simply because we are members of society. We are born into and become members of a continuing endeavour. We do not invent social life *de novo* at each generation. Our involvement in the flow of action and our use of the stock of knowledge is, in the natural attitude, one predominantly directed towards practical ends. We have letters to write, the children to fetch from school, classes to prepare and give. We do not stand back and reflect upon the processes we utilise and the knowlege that we have of the social world. We take them for granted.

Although the structures of knowledge at the call of each one of us are continually changing, none the less they are all structured along the same lines. As Husserl emphasised again and again, we do not experience a stream of sense data, a booming, buzzing confusion, but see and hear and feel discrete objects constituted for us in our consciousness. We see mountains, trees and bicycles, we hear the dog barking and the radio playing. If we go to stay in an acquaintance's home for the first time, while we will not know exactly how his family will behave, we know in general terms what his family life will be like. We assume, though we admit we could always be wrong, that it will be fairly typical. Our knowledge of families, objects, courses of action and everything else is organised into typifications. These typifications are not put together by the exhaustive review of all possible cases; we do not run surveys of families, nor climb every mountain. Rather they are collected together — related might be a better term — by our motivations and relevances, the interests that we have in them. My typifications of mountains and cats are very different from those of a mountain climber or cat breeder. And yet, even a cat breeder need not have a cat breeder's interest in the family pet. Our interests and relevances are fluid and responsive to the courses of action we are engaged in. The most important feature of the typifications that we use in daily life is that they are taken for granted. I know the difference between a dog and a cat, I know that a mountain is not a mole hill. To bring out just how my typifications of dogs, cats, mountains and mole hills are organised requires reflection in the theoretic, analytic stance.

Having elaborated the crucial notion of a typified stock of knowledge, Schutz is able to move out from the constitution of the conscious subjective actor as an object for social science into the systems of relations that such actors engage in. Here he notices several domains. There is, first of all, the world of primary face to face relations with other subjective actors — the world of joint action, the 'we-relation'. This can be marked off from the world of contemporaries. What I know about this student, this shop assistant, this family is different to my knowledge of students in general, shop assistants in general etc. My knowledge of the general type and the general courses of actions they engage in is not necessarily the same as what I know this particular individual will do. The taken for granted character of daily life is underpinned by the fact that in most of our ordinary actions we assume (and we are right to do so in that things generally run their expected course) that members of types will behave in typical ways. The post office clerk does not throw the letter we hand in into the waste bin; the postman delivers it to the address on the envelope and not to the first house he comes to, and so on. Although Schutz never fully worked out the typology of domains, none the less it is clear that he felt that they all, including those of predecessors and successors, shaded into one another.

Alongside and overlapping with the notion of domains of relations, Schutz introduces an idea which has been given a certain notoriety in discussions of his sociology. He talks about there being multiple realities. From all that has been said so far, it ought to be clear that Schutz could not have meant by this that the way the world is 'in itself' is subject to transformation at human whim. Such an idea is unintelligible within the phenomenological framework. What Schutz means by the term is simply that within different finite provinces of meaning — that is to say clearly defined and demarcated forms of social life — the systems of relevances invoked and the stocks of knowledge available enable us to bestow the character of 'factuality' in different ways. The paramount finite province of meaning is, of course, that of daily life. But we also know that when dreaming things which in waking life would be impossible have a reality for us; similarly, to the insane, their paranoias and neuroses are real for them. But the disjunction between daily life and these 'odd' or 'bizarre' occasions is not the whole story. Schutz suggests that the theatre, novels, science and the social sciences are all distinct finite provinces of meaning. In each of them 'reality' is constituted in widely differing ways.

This idea of science and the social sciences as finite provinces of meaning is of great importance in understanding the contribution which Schutzian philosophy might make to the human sciences. Both the natural and the social sciences adopt a theoretical attitude towards their topic matter. They are not primarily concerned with practical consequences except and in so far as these are theoretically given. For example, the social scientist may be oriented to the practical concern of doing social science in a rigorous way. He need not be concerned that his work have some practical point. Although the scientist may engage in research to further his career, gain promotion and so on, these practical concerns are bracketed off when he adopts the attitude of science in doing his science. The system of relevances appropriate to the scientist is determined by the problem in hand and the rules, procedures and traditions of the science in question. These rules, procedures and traditions limit the horizons of the theorist. Most importantly, they make it unnecessary to demand that the object being subjected to scientific scrutiny be treated in just the same way that it might be in ordinary life. As we mentioned in the example of Galileo used a little earlier, it does not matter to the scientist that the cannon ball is black, made from cast iron and can be used as a door stop. It is a mass in motion to him.

For Schutz, the social sciences had failed to grasp this fundamental feature of their method. They seemed to want to suppose some sort of direct identity between social action and social actors as constituted for social science and as they are experienced in daily life. They did not seem to have realised that while it was perfectly proper to wish to satisfy the requirements of testability and verifiability that ought to be invoked in all sciences, it was what was involved in making subjectivity available under the theoretical attitude that necessitated a disjunction between 'ordinary life' and 'social science'; or probably more accurately between social actors as experienced in daily life and social actors as constituted for social science. It was the trans-formation that was required to effect this latter constitution which marked sociology off from social philosophy. The social scientist is *not* concerned with the experiences and meanings of actual individuals. He is concerned with typical actors with typical motives who seek to realise typical goals by means of typical courses of action. These idealisations are puppets, analytic fictions, constituted under the theoretical attitude and subject to variation, manipulation and replacement.

It was on the basis of this observation that Schutz felt that he could make recommendations for the foundations of the social sciences. He proposed a set of postulates which if adopted would put them on a firm footing. The first postulate is that of logical consistency. Like all theoretical scientific disciplines, the social sciences should ensure that its system of constructs conforms to the highest standards of consistency, clarity and logical connectiveness to help secure the objective validity of its theories. The second postulate is that of subjective interpretation, which we mentioned when we introduced Schutz's ideas. Social scientists must seek to attribute to social actors in their theories typical consciousness, typical motivations and typical stocks of knowledge. They must treat action as meaningful for social actors. The third postulate is that of explanatory adequacy. Our explanations of courses of action and social behaviour must be in terms of the models we have utilised. We cannot attribute more to actors than they can meaningfully have in the social world of which they are part and in which they are acting. This does not mean, as many have thought, that we have to content ourselves with only reproducing commonsense explanations and accounts. What it means is that we cannot attribute to our actors-in-the-theory anything other than commonsense theories. And if these commonsense theories are not enough to generate the courses of action we wish then the model is inadequate. We cannot make our theoretical actors do the things we want them to do by attributing to them knowledge, beliefs, desires and motives they do not know about or know that others have.

Schutz's work in the foundations of social science is a direct application of Husserl's phenomenological method. Utilising it, Schutz came to see most contemporary sociology, at least, as woefully unsuited to its subject matter and hence in need of a thorough-going rethink. This was, we might say, a methodological use of Phenomenology. At the same time that he was writing there were others who felt that Husserl's own conclusions were in need of deep philosophical revision and extension. Husserl's conception of consciousness was, to them, far too restrained and restricted. Once it was put in its proper setting the possibilities of Phenomenology, especially for the human sciences, became positively revolutionary.

Heidegger and Existential Phenomenology

Husserl's phenomenological method required the abstraction of consciousness from its empirical embedding in the world. To Heidegger this process necessarily involved the disregarding of some of the essential features of human consciousness; the ontology that it produced was, therefore, inadequate. The essential features of consciousness that Husserl ignored were what Heidegger calls the 'basic modalities of being in the world': our separation from others, our anxiety about the future, our fear of the certainty of death. All philosophical systems on this view, in trying to use Reason to constitute consciousness, do so by some method of abstraction from the world, whereas our existence is one in which we are located in the world. The essential feature of human reality is that it is existence in the world, or perhaps better, it is existing in the world. *Dasein*, as Heidegger calls the basic component of human reality, is 'being-there', being in a concrete situation. It is important to recognise that Heidegger's use of 'being' does not pick out a distinct property of humans or some entity which somehow is associated with us. His is a gerundive use, a verb used as a noun. His use of 'being' is like that of 'doing' in the sentence 'His doing of the deed was doubtful'. Our being in the world is not the structure of consciousness but the premiss for our consciousness. It is the ontological condition of consciousness. Being in the world is how our essence, our being, manifests itself. What Heidegger is attempting to do, then, is to ground the analysis of human consciousness in the here and now flow of time and the reality of the situations in which we find ourselves.

Once Heidegger has taken consciousness back to being in the world, he has to face the possibility that the world as we encounter it — socially, materially and so on — can constrain our mode of being. Where such being in the world is constrained, where we are not free, where we do not understand the nature of our existence, where our expression of hopes and fears masks the essential modalities of anxiety and fear, our being is 'inauthentic'. The task of philosophy — and notice how much this is a re-echoing of a prominent theme in Romanticism — is to lead the individual towards an understanding and hence overcoming of the difficulties and impediments that lead to inauthenticity. This understanding is provided by the analysis of being in the world. At the heart of this analysis is the suggestion that inauthenticity derives from the 'forgetting' of our temporality and hence our 'historicity'. Our being in the world is only understandable by seeing it as a 'being toward death'. It is because we are located in history as mortal beings that our being in the world has the typical character of 'angst' that Heidegger feels it has. Inauthentic being is a denial of this.

The important contribution which Heidegger makes to Phenomenology, then, is to insist on being, and hence consciousness, being treated within a temporal, historical mode. Everything has its existence in history. Even the language that we use to communicate our ideas and concepts is an historically given and shaped phenomenon. We cannot abstract it, nor any other feature of our subjective lives, out of history and out of its location here and now in the situations in which we find ourselves. But not only was consciousness given in the flow of time, it is also an embodied consciousness. Merleau-Ponty insisted that we had to treat consciousness from the point of view of our bodily being. Human consciousness is, first and foremost, consciousness of a material being. Others, such as Aaron Gurwitsch, sought to illuminate the phenomenology of consciousness by bringing to it some of the insights of studies in gestalt psychology and elsewhere. Like Schutz, but in an entirely different way, Gurwitsch wished to insist that the examination of the lifeworld of face to face social interaction was the primary arena for phenomenological analyses. However, to most human and social sciences, the single most important mediating influence between their concerns and those of Husserl and Heidegger must be the work of Jean-Paul Sartre.

Jean-Paul Sartre

Sartre's influence has been felt in two ways. As a novelist and as a literary critic he has been able to bring out in his own work and sensitise us to the ways in which other novelists have struggled to capture the dimensions and predicaments of the modern consciousness. In his philosophical work, which has always been closely related to his purely literary output, he has sought to analyse and locate this predicament. In many ways — although this is to grossly oversimplify — one could say that the central thematic to all of Sartre's work is transience and transformation: how places, objects, persons become something or someone else and so cease to be what they were. This theme, of course, is not Sartre's invention. It is at the heart of Hegel's philosphical system and is crucial for Heidegger as well. What is distinctive is the way in which Sartre approaches this tension, the dialectic between present being and what it will become, between being and not-being. The key to Sartre's understanding of becoming or transformation is the intentionality of consciousness. It is always something which we are conscious of. Our consciousness of objects is the realisation in consciousness of objects and hence of their possibilities. Whenever we 'see' an object — a chair, a desk, a typewriter — we have chosen among the possibilities that were available to us. The chair might have been a makeshift ladder, a door stop, an heirloom. Our consciousness that the object is a chair or a desk is itself the making of these choices. Whenever we behave towards others we do so as the acting out of our choices. Heidegger's being in the world has become Sartre's being in consciousness.

The ontological conclusion that Sartre draws from his analysis of consciousness is that man has no essential being; he simply exists and must construct his being through the choices that he makes. This absence of essence, of being, is a nothingness that must become being. Here temporality enters again since we are all in the process of becoming. The taking of choices and the construction of being in our lives is the exercise of freedom and responsibility. These two, of course, are recurring motifs of his novels, especially the *Roads to Freedom* series. Although the horizons of choice may be limited by events, by objects, by other beings, Matthieu for example, cannot decide that he will be unaffected by the German invasion of France: what he decides to do, whether to collaborate, to be apathetic, or to join the Maquis is a choice he freely takes. He may feel impelled by circumstances and the wishes of others, the fact that the war won't leave him alone, so to speak, but even that is a feeling he chooses to have.

It is in Sartre's work that Phenomenology has taken on its revolutionary guises. His *existentialism* has led him to reappraise the appropriateness of Marxism as a philosophy for modern consciousness. In essence what he has done is to deny the deterministic elements in orthodox Marxism (cf. Chapter 2 for a discussion) and particularly the overly dogmatic interpretation and dismissal of the philosophical anthropology of the 'early Marx' which had become the orthodoxy in many Communist Parties particularly. Sartre wants to emphasise that, while circumstances may be constraining, men do make their own history. They are free to choose to have things differently. But if they do make those choices, then they must accept the responsibilities that go with them.

The connections between Phenomenology and the social sciences seem to have gone forward on many different fronts and to have been mediated by many different influences. All, however, have involved the movement of intentional consciousness to the centre stage. Husserl's philosophic method was used by Schutz to try to indicate the sorts of clarifications and decisions that had to be made in order to found a rigorously grounded interpretive social science. Heidegger reintroduced the traditional metaphysical and ontological questions of philosophy and so reshaped the notion of consciousness as the central feature of any possible social philosophy. As we pointed out in Chapter 3, this was very influential on Habermas and, through him, much of modern social philosophy. Sartre's influence has been not only in creating the possibility of an existential Marxism, important though that was for a time, but in bringing the problems of existential philosophy to a non-specialist audience through his novels. There and in his literary criticism, Sartre shows how the author mediates the particulars of individual biographies, both his own and those of his characters and the constraints set by the format of the novel or play or whatever he is writing, the audience he is trying to reach, the historical circumstances he is writing in and about, and so on and so on. The mediation between consciousness and constraints are to be seen in the choices the author and his characters make in the text.

Recommended Reading

R.M. Zaner's *The Way of Phenomenology* (Pegasus, 1970) is a helpful introduction to phenomenological thinking and T. Luckman (ed.), *Phenomenology and Sociology* (Penguin, 1978) gives a good selection of readings from the major phenomenologists. The most straightforward introduction to Husserl is *Edmund Husserl* by Maurice Natanson (Northwestern University Press, 1973). A sensitive and systematic account of Husserl's place in the European tradition can be found in L. Kolawkowski, *Husserl and the Search for Certitude* (Yale University Press, 1975). The easiest entries to Husserl's own work are probably *The Cartesian Meditations* (Martinus Nijhoff, 1969), *The Paris Lectures* and *The Crisis of European Sciences and Transcendental Phenomenology* (North-western University Press, 1970). A more demanding exposition of Husserl's views is to be found in M. Faber, *The Foundation of Phenomenology* (State University of New York Press, 1943). Schutz is, generally, his own best expositor. His *Collected Papers*, especially Vol. I (Martinus Nijhoff, 1962) are a good place to start. The detail of his analysis of the lifeworld can be found in *The Phenomenology of the Social World* (Northwestern University Press, 1970) and *The Structures of the Lifeworld* (with T. Luckman) (Northwestern University Press, 1973). Two distinctive approaches to the use of phenomenological insights with regard to the social sciences can be found in Maurice Merleau-Ponty's *Phenomenology, Language and Sociology* (Heinemann, 1974) and Maurice Natanson's *Phenomenology, Role and Reason*, Charles Thomas, 1974. His two volume collection *Phenomenology and the Social Sciences* (Northwestern University Press, 1973) considers the contribution which phenomenology might make to a range of social and human sciences.

Heidegger's work is extraordinarily difficult. His seminal work is *Being and Time*, trans. J. Macquermi and E. Robinson (Blackwell, 1967). Also worth attempting is his *On the Way to Language* (Harper and Row, 1971). Sartre's work, apart from his *Roads to Freedom* novels, all available in Penguin, his *Critique of Dialectical Reason* (Verso/New Left Books, 1982) and the shorter statement of his argument, *Search for a Method* (Vintage Books, 1963) are worth looking at. His more completely phenomenological work, the dimension we have emphasised here, is *Being and Nothingness* (Washington Square Press, 1966), a long and difficult work. R. Aronson's, *Jean-Paul Sartre: Philosophy in the World* (Verso/ New Left Books, 1980) is an excellent and recent review of Sartre's work.

5   STRUCTURALISM AND POST-STRUCTURALISM

Several features make Structuralism quite distinct from the other topics which we deal with in this book. To begin with, no one would want to claim that Structuralism offers a philosophical programme of any sort, nor even that, like Phenomenology, it is a philosophical method. To be sure, it is a method, but one *within* the cultural and social sciences. It does not offer an ontology or metaphysics of its own. As we shall see, its epistemology is more or less a version of Kantianism.

The most important figure for Structuralism, Saussure, was not a philosopher nor engaged in building philosophical systems. Many philosophers have found a great deal that was significant in his work, but no one would define him as a philosopher. What structuralists see in Saussure is the delineation of the possibility of the structuralist method. Here we have the third distinctive feature. Structuralism as a general movement within the social and cultural sciences is almost entirely a one-generation phenomenon. The body of authors and researchers, mostly French, who sought to apply Structuralism to a range of cultural and other topics were largely contemporaries. There has been no extension and elaboration of the method comparable to that which occurred in Hermeneutics or even Phenomenology. Indeed, one could say that the work of later scholars such as Derrida and, to a lesser extent, Foucault is post-structuralist in that it reveals the inability of the method to satisfy the ambitions set for it.

Although Structuralism is not a philosophy none the less it does make use of several philosophical or philosophically inspired distinctions. Probably the most important of these is that between appearance and reality. This dichotomy is made use of in a variety of differing guises. It can be seen in the opposition that is made between the surface configuration a phenomenon may have and its underlying, deeper reality; in the dichotomy between the form that a text, communication or social process takes and the content which the form carries; in the contradistinction made between the individual as a discrete item and the collection of relations that any individual stands in; and in the emphasis that is given to seeing the part-within-the-whole. This last distinction brings out the second most important general theme. Alongside appearance and reality, structuralists place unity and diversity. The diversity of surface appearances masks the unity of structural realities.

The use that these distinctions are put to gives Structuralism its peculiar cast. Primarily this can be seen in the determination to pitch analyses at the level of the totality; elements, parts, internal relations are all viewed with reference to the totality. Given this totalising proclivity, Structuralism quite naturally rejects any form of empiricist epistemology. Appearances express the diverse overmantle and should not be taken for reality — a mistaken view which it attributes to empiricism. This rejection of empiricism involves a rejection of the possibility of certain knowledge being obtained by the efforts of isolated reason and individual subjectivity. The individual cannot discover reality in isolation. In this way, Structuralism marks itself off both from empiricism and from Phenomenolgy and Hermeneutics. What has to be provided — and this is what the structuralist method was felt to provide — is objective, universal knowledge which was not grounded in particular, individual, historically given subjectivities.

Of itself, though, Saussure's structuralist method prescribes no content; it is content-free. In a sense this is part of its attractiveness. It is not confined to one realm of social phenomena and could be applied across the range. To provide the content for their studies, French Structuralists turned to the figures who dominated post-war French intellectual life, Marx and Freud. The readings which they gave to Marx and Freud specified the content. In each case what was being looked for was a way of making strong connections between the analyses of social reality to be found in Marx and Freud, the accounts that are given, on the one hand, of the composition of social formations and, on the other, of the structure of the unconscious. For Structuralism there had to be some way of relating these two. The importance of finding a reading which achieved this is most clearly on view in Althusser whose major work is actually entitled *Reading Capital*. But it is of equal importance in Lévi-Strauss, in Lacan, who was more concerned with Freud than Marx, and in Foucault, who in recent years has extended the reading to Nietzsche. It is only with Derrrida that the question of what it is to give a reading of a text is taken up. In pursuing that question, Derrida ends by subverting the whole structuralist project.

In this chapter first we will look at the general structuralist schema as that is provided in Saussure's semiology. We will then look at two prominent applications of Structuralism; Lévi-Strauss' anthropology and Lacan's psychoanalysis while at the same time making passing reference to Althusser whom we have already discussed in Chapter 2. We will complete our survey by reviewing the way that Foucault in the analysis of history and Derrida with regard to texts have pushed Structuralism beyond its limits and the conclusions that are to be drawn from this.

Saussure's Semiology

At the beginning of this century, in so far as linguistics was a separate discipline to philology and the study of particular languages, it was mainly concerned with linguistic history. That is, it tried to itemise and catalogue the important and not so important influences upon an individual language's particular grammar, phonetics and semantics. Saussure tried to reorient linguistics toward the examination of the principles by which language itself worked. To do this he drew a crucial distinction between *langue* and *parole* — language as a system of communication, and speech as the use to which we put that system to achieve the goals we wish. The system which makes up a language is the body of rules or principles which give it its coherence as a communicative medium. The proper task of linguistics, in Saussure's view, was in the examination of language as a system of rules and principles existing and being implemented at any particular historical time, and not the tracing out of the subtle changes that particular systems might undergo through time. The former is a *synchronic* interest in language, the latter is *diachronic*. This distinction is at the heart of all structuralist analyses.

To what did the rules apply? Here we find the second central contribution that he made. The basic unit of language is the sign; language is a system of signs, what he termed a 'semiotic'. Sounds only count as part of language, that is as expressions of something, when they are treatable as signs of or standing for some idea and hence as conveying meaning. The sign is composed of two elements; the signifier, that which is used to make the articulation — for example the sound in language — and the signified, the idea or concept that the sound refers to. It is important to see that the signified is not the actual object or entity that the signifier points to, it is not the dog that we call 'Fido' but the idea of Fido that is signified, because the system of signs is not a reflection of how the world is but how we organise the world in consciousness and language. This is a clear influence of Kantianism. The system that we use is not fixed and externally determined. The signs we use are quite arbitrary, or rather, there is no general principle guiding their selection. It may be that the cuckoo gained its name from its call, but the same could not be said of the wren, the magpie or the bar-tailed godwit. Since there is no essential link between signifier and signified, the connection between them is a conventional one. The signifier and its relation to the signified derives solely from the place that it has in a system of signs. This place is identified by the differences between it and those around it. The meaning of the word 'wren' is not to be found in some natural or even logical connection between the object in the world and the sound. 'Wren' only takes on the meaning it has when we use it to distinguish this small brown bird from sparrows and starlings, great tits and mistle thrushes. The differences that the term picks out vary with each case. Wrens look different to starlings, they sing differently to mistle thrushes and so on and so on. The meaning of 'wren' is given by the contrasts that we can make using it.

The arbitrariness of a semiotic system is the third central idea that Saussure gave to Structuralism. Language is not a fixed body of essentially defined signs. Rather, the units which comprise a language are constituted by the systematic differences that mark them off from one another. The elements of language gain their identity by their use in combination with and in opposition to others. They have no value in themselves; their value and their meaning derives from their relationship within the system as a whole. The key to this relationship must be difference, for without difference there cannot be meaning. If a language was composed of just one word, or a semiotic system of just one sign, then the term would have to apply to everything. It would be impossible to pick out anything and so communication would be unable to begin. At least one other term would be required. The differentiation which gives each sign its identity is the system of rules for a language. Indeed, for Saussure language is first and foremost a formal system of rules for differentiating signs. The synchronic analysis of the system as a whole seeks to relate individual signs to the whole by identifying the system of relations in which they stand — what they are used in conjunction with, what in contrast to, and so on.

Saussure realised that his semiological conception of language could be extended to other phenomena. This would involve, of course, the acceptance of the conventionalised character of such semiotic systems. The table manners that we observe, the combinations of food we serve, the ways we organise kinship ties might look to be natural, but, for Saussure, they must be treated as conventional. Cuisine, manners and blood ties are defined and organised quite differently in different cultures. As we shall see this conventionalised approach to social phenomena is one of the important motivations in Lévi-Strauss' anthropology. If we were to use the Saussurean model to analyse the conventional character of systems of signs other that language, we would have to attend to the way in which meaning is determined within the system. It is on the basis of this that particular sentences, concatenations of signs, can be uttered to achieve the results they do. The activities that make up the institutions of marriage, exchanges of goods and services, religion, even literary work, will all be governed by structurally defining rules and principles. These provide the synchronically given system of relations that individual signs stand in.

The idea of culture as a semiotic system, a system in which meaning can be accomplished, is one which proved very attractive to Lévi-Strauss. It enabled him to see ways in which he could pull together, unify the extremely disparate anthropological data that he had collected during his fieldwork in South America; an analysis which could do for those societies what Marx had achieved for capitalism. It also enabled him to work out a method of analysis which broke with the anthropological tradition which he encountered in French social science.

Lévi-Strauss and the Structuralist Method

As we hinted just now, one of the principal attractions of any form of structuralist anthropology is that it prevents the descent of the discipline into academically legitimated traveller's tales and collections of exotica representing the diversity of human life. The surface differences have to be set aside in the search for the underlying unity of principles. These principles express our common humanity,not in the sense in which we are a community of morally responsible beings, but in the sense that our cultural artifacts and social institutions are ways in which we express meaning in systematic and structured ways. This was Marx's insight. Just as language is a system of meaning in which particular utterances can be made and meanings conveyed, so social institutions are meaning systems in which particular meanings and intentions can be realised. The task of the anthropologist is to elucidate the system of meaning, the whole in which the particulars have a place.

Once he had adopted this point of view, it becomes quite clear why Lévi-Strauss had to reject the general sociological tradition in which he found himself. On the one hand, he could not accept the modelling of social science upon the natural sciences as the science of 'objective social facts' which exist independently of individuals, since the objective existence of social reality is only possible in and through the systems of meaning that individuals create. Nor could he accept the evolutionary psychology that was implicit, and now and again explicit, in such sociology. All societies have semiotic systems based upon similar principles and rules. It is a peculiarly arrogant ethnocentrism that promotes one, that utilised by Western rationalist philosophy, above others. At the same time, he could not acquiesce to what he saw as the rampant subjectivism of Hermeneutics and Phenomenology, giving, as they seemed to, pride of place to the meaning and consciousness of the individual. It was in Freud's psychoanalysis that, like Althusser, Lévi-Strauss found the concepts that would enable him to apply structuralist methods to anthropological data. What Freud had done in his discovery of the unconscious was to show how the surface, apparently irrational symptoms of a patient could be expressions of an underlying logic. Diverse behaviour was unified when seen as the articulation of this logic. For the neurotic and the psychotic, Freud dissolves the distinction between logicality and illogicality, rationality and irrationality. Lévi-Strauss wishes to do the same for anthropology. Instead of treating other cultures as exhibiting an embryonic, premature version of scientific rationality, the 'pre-logical mentality', Lévi-Strauss suggests that their cultural forms are constituted by a different order of logic altogether, that of *bricolage*. The *bricoleur* is a handyman who is able to make anything — buildings, tools, machines — out of whatever happens to be available. Furthermore, while the forms it takes are different, the principles of bricolage are precisely the same as those of Western science. They are built around the differentiation of binary oppositions just as languages are. In using bricolage, the native takes whatever is available in the local social, cultural and natural environment and turns it to the use in hand. Kinship systems, for instance, may vary vastly within a small area. Some may be based on ties we would not recognise as those of blood. But no matter how they are constituted they are local and idiosyncratic expressions of the need to draw boundaries between 'us' and 'them', 'insiders' and 'outsiders', 'males' and 'females', those to whom property can pass and those to whom it cannot, those who are marriable and those who are not, etc. etc. Any kinship system, like any semiotic system, is to be treated as the unconscious expression of these deep-seated principles. Just as Althusser argued that developments in capitalism do not take place in order to achieve the conscious goals of the bourgeoisie all the time, and that, hence, they may literally not know what they are doing, that the goals of such developments have an underlying dynamic that is not reducible to individual motivations, so Lévi-Strauss argues that our forms of religion, our myths, our cuisine and our kinship systems are not reducible to individual consciousness either. These principles are laid down, stratified, in the collective unconsciousness of mankind. They are what we share with the Amazonian Indian. If we become preoccupied with the differences between the content of what we and they think, with the exotic nature of their customs and institutions, we will have given up the universal for the particular. We will have sacrificed objective, universal knowledge for subjectivity.

Lévi-Strauss pursued his structural analyses with a variety of different topics: kinship, totemism and myth. It was in his treatment of the latter that the method was at its clearest, although even here it is almost opaque at times. In outline, his analysis treats myths as variations upon a single theme. The variations are produced by the structured arrangements of the locally defined elements in the myths in question. The message that is carried by the myth is one that it shares with many other myths, and it is this which forms the basic structure of the myth. Let us change the image a little here. Imagine each of the different myths, their narratives, as the notes to be played by the different groups of instruments in an orchestra. When looked at separately, there seems to be no clear sense to them. When they are gathered together in the score we can see how they harmonise together and how each contributes to the development of the melody. They carry the melody as inversion, counterpoint, variations in different keys and so on. The sense which the run of notes has can only be appreciated when it is heard as a part of the whole. The parts have what is called a *synechdochal* relation to the whole. The task of fitting the myths together — if you like of writing the score — is one of revealing their intelligibility, the underlying logic of harmony and melody, similarity and difference that is the logic of the unconscious mind.

What Lévi-Strauss is drawing attention to is the common logical structure which different myths display. As we say, this logic is one of binary opposition. However, the units to be opposed and the form which the opposition takes within any particular myth are distinctive expressions of the culture in which it is found. Take, for example, the story of Solomon's accession to the kingship of the Jews as it is told in the Old Testament. As Edmund Leach points out in his analysis of this story, it is not whether the details of the biblical narrative are accurate that concerns the anthropologist but the simple fact that the Jews believed it to be true. What does the structural form of this firmly held belief tell us about the culture of the Old Testament Jews?

If we get away from the diachronic character of the story and look at its internal organisation, says Leach, we will see that the story culminates in Solomon's legitimate accession to the throne as a resolution of a variety of sexual and political oppositions. We do not have the space to go into all the details here and strongly recommend that those who are interested should consult *Genesis As Myth* to see precisely how the complexity is teased out. In brief, though, the analysis incorporates the following elements. The central themes are sexual excess and political conflict. The former is connected with the strict rules of endogamy (marriage and sexual relations within the group) which the Jews had adopted. Sexual sin is associated with foreign women, since all foreigners are contaminating. Such sin is punished by impotence, or by failure of male children to achieve maturity. This theme would be of direct interest to Jews of the time because they determined legitimate inheritance through the male line. Only if there were no surviving sons could inheritance pass through daughters or females more generally. This rule applied to kingship too. Solomon's genealogy, as it is given in the Old Testament, has to show him to be the legitimate heir of David. This is achieved by demonstrating that unlike the other women with whom David had liaisons, Bathsheba, Solomon's mother, was not a foreigner but only married to one, Uriah the Hittite. The second theme of political opposition is interwoven with this. Legitimate kings are opposed by potential usurpers, the two kingdoms of Israel and Judah — one in the north, one in the south — are in opposition, brother fights brother for the throne, so do father and son. In the end, David's adultery is punished by Absolom's (his legitimate son) rebellion and death. David is impotent and can have no more sons. All these oppositions are mediated through Solomon. He can claim direct descent through a Jewish woman. David came from the north, Bathsheba from the south, so Solomon unites Israel and Judah, north and south. In so doing he ends rebellion and strife. He is the legitimate High King.

In what is a throw away analysis tagged on to the end of the discussion of Solomon, Leach suggests that just the same themes of oppositions in sexual and political relations can be seen in the familiar schoolroom story of the accession of Elizabeth 1. If we construct what might be a twelve year-old's essay plan, the schematic form brings out the oppositions quite clearly.

(1) Henry VIII
   strong male monarch
   married many times
   killed most of his wives
(2) Edward VI
   weak male monarch
   remained unmarried (a virgin) to his death
(3) Mary Queen of Scots
   weak female monarch
   married many times
   killed most of her husbands
(4) Elizabeth 1
   strong female monarch
   remained unmarried (a virgin) to her death
(5) Henry VIII *divorced* his wife (the King of Spain's daughter) because she had been married to his elder *brother*.
(6) Elizabeth I *refused to marry* the King of Spain's son because he had been married to her elder *sister*.

In telling the story in this way, the inversions and transformations of political and sexual categories become obvious. The common logical form that the myth takes is what we share with the Old Testament Jew and the Amazonian Indians. It is an innate feature of human cognition.

The task of analysing a myth is both complex and painstaking. It requires comparison of as many variants as possible and the isolation of their invariant components, the 'mythemes'. These are then traced out as inversions, homologies, transformations of one another. From these it is possible to deduce an idealisation of the myth to which all the variants have a correspondence but of which they are cryptic expressions. The ways in which each myth has encoded the idealisation can be explained by reference to the culture in which they are to be found.

There is, then, more than a little hint of Enlightenment rationalism in the emphasis that Levi Strauss wishes to give to human universals.

However, he locates these in the unconscious rather than in consciousness. In so doing we can see him rejecting both Phenomenology and Hermeneutics. The presupposion of continuity that Levi Strauss felt that Phenomenology made between appearance and reality left no room for science. Science has to penetrate through appearances to reality by decomposing and recomposing them. Freud and Marx had indicated just how this might be achieved in social science, how we can set aside the illusions that appearances often give us. What Lévi-Strauss seeks is the dissolution of the radical discontinuity of the human and natural sciences. Human life is placed back into nature by showing how culture is part of nature itself.

The vast majority of Lévi-Strauss' anthropological studies have taken up the theme of the transition from culture to nature; how human beings mark themselves off from the natural world. Latterly his attention has been focused on how the distinction between culture and nature can be produced as a cultural phenomenon itself. The line of connection is not a simple decomposition of social institutions and practices into vehicles for the expression of biological 'drives'. Rather cultural products are the products of human rationalising which, in its turn, is a function of brains. And brains are biological entities. Here we find Lévi-Strauss calling into play a metaphysical stipulation. The very same laws that govern natural objects like the brain govern human thought. There is a structural homology between the image of reality expressed in our thoughts and ideas and the way the world is. There is a fit between the binary categories of the world and the ways in which we express our thoughts in myths, table manners, cuisine, kinship groupings, and texts. In the various systems of thought expressed in table manners, myths and so on can be found the natural functioning of unconscious thought, that is the very structures of our minds. To show how among all the complexity and diversity of culture are to be found fundamental laws of the unconscious is, for Lévi-Strauss, to put man back into nature.

Jacques Lacan: Language and Psychic Structure

As we have pointed out repeatedly, Freud is an important figure for Structuralism. We have already seen that both Althusser and Lévi-Strauss make use of psychoanalytic concepts. However, it was Jacques Lacan who provided a complete reappraisal of Freud from the structuralist point of view and in so doing attempted to liberate psychoanalysis from a confinement within the profession of what he witheringly calls 'soul management'.

Freud's achievement, for Lacan, was not so much the discovery of the unconscious but the insight that the unconscious possessed a structure which affected what we say and do. We are in the grip of the unconscious. As far as Lacan is concerned, to speak of a structure is to speak of language. The unconscious is structured like a language. It is a mere accidental quirk of history, in Lacan's view, that Freud made little or no use of linguistic science. He was very well aware of the importance of language for analysis as can be seen in the care that he gives to examining slips of the tongue, puns, jokes, and, of course, patients' own presentations of their symptoms, dreams and so on. What Lacan is able to point up here is the clear image that Freud used of such 'behaviours' as forms of communication. The unconscious speaks through our jokes, puns, dreams and the like. What Lacan does is apply the method of structural linguistics to the Freudian account of the unconscious.

In organising the unconscious around a small number of concepts derived from linguistics, Lacan deliberately goes against one interpretation of Freud which sees the unconscious as a stratum of biologically given instincts which are repressed and controlled but which, on occasion, erupt into our conscious lives. Instead of this, Lacan suggests that the unconscious is a syntax, a body of rules for the organisation of patterns of behaviour. Just as, for Saussure, language was a body of rules realised or actualised in speech, so the unconscious is realised or actualised in our behaviour.

In common with Lévi-Strauss, Lacan feels that a syntactical interpretation of Freud allows an approach to be made to some of the universal features of human life. These are to be revealed by the examination of the common syntactic structures. In this way, the real significance of the Oedipus Complex could be shown to be the way it regulates the incest taboo, for example — a feature which many anthropologists would claim is universal in human societies. The Oedipus Complex, although 'discovered' in Western European patients, is found to be of universal significance. Cultural diversity is replaced by unity. Naturally enough, each local culture would have its own specific form of the complex.

The relationship between the unconscious and language is difficult to specify. We could say, for example, that language is a mirror of the unconscious. Certainly there are grounds for such an interpretation in Freud himself. Lacan does not accept such a view. Rather it is language which creates the unconscious. The acquisition of speech involves taking over an existing symbolic order. The acquisition of speech is the primary element in the acquisition of culture, that is in the submission of free ranging instinctive drives to that symbolic order. By acquiring language, we allow our instinctive energies to be canalised and organised. Although we are oblivious to it, this process makes us what we are. To echo a phrase used just now, for Lacan, we are in the grip of language. The unconscious takes on the pattern of language; the distinction between the two is dissolved.

In that language and the unconscious are syntactically organised, both must be regarded as semiotic systems. They are governed by what Lacan calls 'the law of the Signifier'. This is not simply an uncritical application of Saussure's concept here though, but an attempt to use the resources of both psychoanalysis and linguistics to throw light on each other. In particular, Lacan is extremely sceptical about Saussure's attempt to disentangle the complexities of the relations between signifier and signified as a requirement for the examination of 'pure thought', the word-free structures of the mind. For Lacan this was bound to be pointless since language has a constitutive role in thought. Rather than seeking to break the chain between signifier and signified, the linguist and the psychoanalyst should be looking at the relation of signification itself. This is a relationship of structural connection. What in effect this does is to set aside the hermeneutic and interpretive aspects of Freud's theories in favour of the structural. In the analysis of dreams, for instance, Freud had connected the images that appear in dreams, the signifiers, to the latent dream thoughts lying deep in the unconscious, the signified. In making these separations and connections, there is a tendency to place all of the emphasis in the explanatory power of wish fulfilment. What is neglected is the importance of the structural relations between signifiers. Here, Lacan points out that the pattern that Freud has noticed is similar to that used in rhetoric. 'Condensation' is homologous with 'metaphor', while 'displacement' through which the libido attempts to avert censorship is paralleled by 'metonymy', the use of a name or attribute in place of the thing meant. The levels of signifier and signified should not be separated but their linkage in the process of signification brought out. This process is syntactic, and just as with Lévi-Strauss' analysis of myths, dreams have to be treated as cryptic texts whose meaning can only be revealed in analysis.

The introduction of the process of signification into the heart of Freudian psychoanalysis makes a certain rearrangement of priorities and concepts necessary. To begin with, the notion of the unconscious as a relatively stable collection of things, forces or aptitudes regionalised into the Id, the Ego and the Superego has to be dispensed with. The unconscious is a constant process of restructuring. Similarly, he sees the subject as a continuously future oriented arena of tensions and upheavals. Access to this subject-in-process is obtained through the chain of signification. The signifier both constitutes and governs the subject, while the subject mediates between it and other signifiers.

Central to Lacan's reinterpretation of psychoanalysis is his attack upon the notion of the unity of the subject. From early childhood onwards we view ourselves as a fully integrated, coherent identity, a whole, or at least as potentially so. In the round of daily living, we seek to overcome divisions of identity, the non-identicality of self and ego, how we *seem* when we act in the world and how we *are*. But for Lacan such unification is an illusion. The subject is always divided. This 'decentred view' of the subject is a major break with orthodox psychoanalysis, much of which is given over to achieving the reintegration of the personality. Primarily, the division has its origins in the subject's relation to 'the Other', a particularly obscure conception of Lacan's. The Other may be encountered in others as significations of authority and dominance — the symbolic father — which evoke both aggression and subservience. The Other constrains the subject and so makes and remakes it in these encounters. The subject is a vortex of tensions induced by the gap between the desires held and the goals set.

Lacan's psychoanalysis posits the unconscious as a bundle of deep syntactic patterns. As with other structuralists, he is fascinated by language and the extent to which we surrender our uniqueness to it. His work urges us to treat the autonomy of the Ego as a free agent as an illusion. In his view, Freud's discoveries of the nature of this repression were so shocking that they were set on one side. In their place was put a subjectivism that allowed psychoanalysis a therapeutic role in controlling the subject by creating the myth of the integrated personality and whole identity. In so doing, the liberating potential of Freud's structuralism was converted into subjugated subjectivism. In many ways this interpretation of the history of Freud's thought is akin to the general theory of history provided by Michel Foucault, although, as we shall see, in Foucault's case the structuralist method has proved overly constricting.

Michel Foucault: Structuralism and Beyond

Partly because of the style, and in part as a result of a deliberate policy, Foucault is extremely difficult to summarise. Throughout his writings, Foucault's thought twists and turns, struggling to break out of the confines of the concepts available to him and shifting its emphasis, intention and approach. Most importantly, although structuralist ideas do inform his work, recently he has been at pains to distance himself from Structuralism and has attempted to lay down a new historical method. As with all the other structuralists that we have discussed so far, the backdrop to Foucault's thought is a dissatisfaction with both the subjectivism of Phenomenology and Hermeneutics and the empiricism of the naïve application of natural science models in the social and cultural sciences. Like Lévi-Strauss, Althusser and Lacan, Foucault seeks to uncover the structural principles that govern human action. Like them, he makes heavy use of notions drawn from structuralist linguistics. Perhaps the most well known of these is his use of the term 'discourse' to refer to the historically located and individually shaped sets of institutionalised definitions, practices and procedures associated with any body of knowledge. The term 'discourse' was applied by him to psychiatry and to medicine in his analyses, *Madness and Civilisation* and *The Birth of the Clinic*. The patterns of action which articulate definitions of madness and sanity, sickness and health and the appropriate responses to persons so designated are a discourse located in and the product of the distribution of power. Thus, the discourse of medical science was deeply enmeshed in debates concerning political matters such as constitutionalism, sovereignty, the rights of individuals and so on, which were taking place at the time that the profession of medicine was emerging. Foucault's concern was not just with the history of ideas, or with political sociology. What he tries to do is to approach what Hermeneutics called the *Weltanschaung* associated with a particular body of knowledge, belief and action, using the structuralist method as a point of departure. By the beginning of the nineteenth century a new scientific discourse was emerging that articulated new definitions of illness and health. This new classificatory framework separated the disease from the organism by means of theories of infection and the diagnostic method. In examining the emergence of the modern medical discourse, Foucault focuses on the changing connections between what doctors were able to see, what they saw as the significance of their observations, and most importantly how they managed to get these new ideas, this new discourse, accepted.

What the idea of a 'discourse of knowledge' pulls upon is the suggestion that knowledge can be encoded in different ways. But, various though these ways are, the principles on which they are based are universal. So, descriptions of illnesses and their causes given in the Middle Ages may, from our point of view, be wholly strange and nonsensical. That is because we have 'lost' their discourse. The history of medicine might seek to recreate it by something akin to the hermeneutic method, just as a student of Old English might try to understand and then explain just what *Sir Gawaine and the Greene Knight* was about. Foucault's structuralist method, though, does not seek to recreate the meaning of medicine but to treat definitions, diagnostic procedures and therapies as 'meaningless' objects, particular arrangements or encodings of knowledge. By relating medicine with other arrangements and codings, the harmony — as we termed it earlier — of the culture, the schemes of perception, the techniques, values, practices and definitions of reality can be drawn out. The important insight of this, as Foucault sees it, is a cultural relativity. Once we see medieval medicine as a code of knowledge expressing a formalised structure, we will have to see that modern medicine is exactly the same. Both allow truth claims to be made; and both indicate what will count as validation of these claims. Where the break with Hermeneutics is the most significant is in Foucault's resistance to any attempt to leave history at the stage of interpretation or what he calls 'commentary'. Questions of truth or falsity, either within the discourse or by some external measures are of no concern. It is the systematic structure of the discourse, its actualising of the syntactic form which is the object of scrutiny.

While Foucault's method is structuralist in origin and shape, it also departs from Structuralism in a quite significant way. From the beginning, Foucault has been interested, not in atemporal universal features of the human unconscious, but in the historical location and transformation of codes of knowledge. This interest is pervasive in *Madness and Civilisation* and *The Birth of the Clinic* and crystallised in *The Order of Things*. It involves an attempt to place metaphysical theory in history. Putting it rather crudely, we can say that Foucault draws a distinction between an outlook which emphasises language as a tool, an instrument, a medium for grasping reality and one which sees language as itself creative giving form to reality. In the former, the role of consciousness was that of clarification by means of ideas that were certain. During the eighteenth century the issue of representation became itself a problem. The mind was no longer conceived as a mirror for nature. Consciousness became the shaper of reality. Instead of God at the centre of the universe, we have Man. This produces the tension between Man's 'real essence' and his representational capacity that, as we have seen, albeit utilising a different terminology, has been the preoccupation of philosophy since the Enlightenment and which has led to the feuding camps in the cultural and social sciences of today. Since they are only the modern equivalents of the 'codes of knowledge' of previous ages, the sciences of Man will never attain a unity and are bound to disintegrate and be replaced.

The use to which Foucault puts the concept of a discourse eventually leads to a break with Structuralism. A discourse is a set of propositions which gains credence and autonomy by being validated by a community of experts. What is not at issue is whether such propositions are universally true, nor what they might mean either for us or for those that enunciate them. What he looks for are the unities of form displayed by sets of propositions. These unities delineate the 'conceptual space' that sets of statements can occupy. So, unlike other structuralists, Foucault has not dispensed with meaning altogether. But now it is not a question of what forms of knowledge are really saying but their significance in history. Why they, and they alone, appeared where and when they did. The answer of course is to be found in the system of rules underpinning the discourse. Yet again Foucault has to dispense with atemporality. The 'archeological' method he uses is not concerned with abstract laws defining the permutation of formal elements but with the local, changing rules which in a particular era define what is to count as meaningful. A proposition belongs to a discourse as a sentence does to a text. 'Archaeology' can only describe specific formations and their discourses. It cannot reach back to sets of transcendental rules. At the same time, the propositions that are made in the discourse are not reducible to statements made by individuals. They have an autonomous existence. While they can be thus isolated, Foucault denies that the knowledge which we thereby have of them has any epistemological primacy. It is knowledge encoded in our discourse.

In a fairly clear way, then, Foucault has returned to the problem of knowledge as that was conceived in the eighteenth century, although he has formulated it in his own terms. The adoption of a position of total detachment, utilising concepts that are 'discourse free' to obtain theoretical knowledge, is impossible. And, like others before him,

Foucault has turned to a novel method, one which he terms 'genealogy' as a means of gaining an appreciation of the significance of social practices from within.

The traditional historical method, of which Foucault himself was an exemplar, seeks for the unity of essences, the underlying laws and principles. The genealogical method stresses discontinuities not continuity. It avoids searching for deeper meaning, but tries to obtain the degree of 'distantiation' from which the totality becomes visible. The task of the genealogist is to expose and destroy doctrines of unchanging truths, universal morality and progress, and to substitute for them themes of subjection, domination and conflict. All meanings, values, virtues and even psychologies are the working out of 'force'. For the genealogist no individual or collective moves history. The play of forces is confined and determined by the space within which they operate. History is the play of the rituals of power and force as humanity moves from one domination to another. Our understanding of history and of our own knowledge of the world is enmeshed in this power. It cannot be autonomous.

One theme that is carried over from the early studies is the importance that Foucault places upon the body as an aspect of what he calls 'political technology'. At first the interest was in the conceptions that scientists had of the body and the way that their treatment of it was an expression of institutionalised power. Now he sees the body as a locale for knowledge and power to express force. Yet again the analysis is not simply an account of the professionalising of the 'bodily sciences', nor even of the institutional matrix within which this is possible, but in the connections between the biological body and the institutions of force as these emerge both in scientific, non-scientific and commonsense knowledge of bodily processes and functions. The key is the connection between knowledge and power; it is used to itemise the genealogy of the forms which power and knowledge take as they are articulated through discourses. Thus, for example, he traces the modern concern with sexuality and sexual freedom back to rituals of power, the confessional culture of monasticism and a particular technology of the body. The constant discussion of sexual matters transforms sexuality into a discourse about it. Anatomy and talk are the forms of sexuality. As this process proliferated, so control was extended over sexuality. Scientific, 'experimental' sex is a form of management of sexuality.

Foucault argues that, in the nineteenth century in particular, sexuality emerged as a central component in a strategy of power which linked both the individual and the population at large into the network of 'bio-power'. What the discourse of sexuality did was to produce a specific technology, confessions by individual subjects, which brought the body, knowledge, discourse and power into a common 'localisation'. From the beginning, the discourse of sex was an adjunct to a concern for the welfare of the population as something to be administered. Procreation had to be regulated and hence so did sexuality. This was a direct contrast with the previous religious discourse which linked sexual relations with sins of the flesh and hence something to which moral judgements were to be applied. We do not have room even for a summary of Foucault's views on this topic, none the less we can now see how he might arrive at his conclusion. For him, the technology of the confession, especially confession about one's sexuality, is a central component of technologies for the discipline and control of bodies, populations and society itself. Some cultures seek knowledge of sex through erotic arts, but in the West sex has become enmeshed in scientific and pseudo-scientific discourse. Even the most private self-examination is tied to powerful systems of external control. The cultural desires to know the truth about oneself prompts the telling of truth in confession after confession to oneself and others. This places the individual in a network of relations of power. Others through their possession of knowledge, which is the key to interpretation, can extract the truth within these confessions. They are then in a position to impose their interpretation upon the individual.

Foucault's writing of history is not an attempt to understand the past either in its or our terms. He does not look for 'objective' historical causation nor to decipher the meaning of events. What he is after is the intelligibility of human practices. His genealogy says that human beings are nothing but their history. There is nowhere either in thought, experience or the external world in which a total, objective and detached picture can be obtained. None the less, genealogy is not whimsy. Because we have nothing but our history, we must always read history in terms of our present practices. The 'interpretive analytic' of genealogy enables us to realise that we are the products of what we study; we can never stand outside them. Our own cultural practices which are themselves located in history, have no essence, no fixity, no underlying unity. Their coherence is what 'archeology' and 'genealogy' are concerned with. It follows that there are no objective laws to be discovered, no universal theories to guide us. Indeed, the genealogist must mistrust depth, finality and appeals to unity. Things have no essence. Philosophy as the search for ultimate knowledge is finally over. Determinate interpretation, too, is dead since there is no firm ground to interpret from. Underneath all knowledge is interpretation.

The latter works of Foucault represent a radical attack on all forms of knowledge including Structuralism. Knowledge is indistinguishable from power. And yet despite the fact that power is ubiquitous, it remains elusive. It cannot be acquired, nor does it inhere in any one location or relationship. It is immanent in all relations. It manifests itself in a discourse which is always about something else. It has the capacity of 'infinite displacement' and can only be caught 'in flight', so to speak, and analysed indirectly. The place to grasp it most effectively is in sexuality, for this discourse, promoted by the operation of power in modern society and by giving it access to the human body, has control over the group and life itself. The immanence of power in all discourses raises the possibility of regress for Foucault. If all knowledge and discourses are about power then presumably so is his own. Foucault accepts this and advises intellectuals to abandon their pretensions to detachment and universal knowledge. However, even though we can never escape the embrace of power, we can loosen its grip by showing, as Foucault claims his own analyses do, that our present culture has produced both the objectification and subjectification of reality. His analyses are able to do this because it is a reality which he shares. There are, however, no objective laws to be discovered, no pure subjectivity to be attained, no universal theories to guide us; all we have are the cultural practices which make us what we are. To know these we have to know the history which produced the present; its 'archeology' and 'genealogy'.

Although he has been immensely influential as an interpreter of historical process, and despite the fact that he has broken out of the confines of the structuralist method, Foucault remains for many associated with the main stream of structuralist thought. This could not be claimed of Jacques Derrida. Derrida has turned Structuralism back on itself and so revealed its shaky foundations.

Jacques Derrida: Deconstructive Reading

Unlike many of his structuralist precursors, Derrida's aim is not to provide a unifying method, a common approach to all problems, derived from a overall framework. Indeed, he rejects the possibility of ever arriving at such a sythesis. His ambition is not the construction of a system of general concepts but the critique of the Western European mode of thought that yearns for such schemas. His approach is unorthodox, consisting in the main in critiques of texts and their metaphysical presuppositions. This procedure he calls a 'deconstructive reading'. His own writing style is equally unorthodox, making use of literary devices such a puns, jokes and incongruities to produce a conjunction of non-synthesisable meanings with the intention of breaching or undoing the presuppositions of the text — and the reader. As a result, Derrida's writing often evades comprehension. But this is part of the point he wants to get us to see. Clarity is not the only virtue in writing, and at times it may even be a disadvantage since clarity of expression and ease of comprehension encourage the belief that language is under control. Derrida also refuses to be bound by the conventions of normal academic writing. He is determined to challenge our expectations and so highlight what we do when we give a text a reading.

The theme that runs through Derrida's work is what he terms the 'logocentrism' of Western thought. By this he means 'the metaphysics of presence' which he claims underlies all of our thinking. Although it finds expression in different ways, this metaphysics postulates that reality is made up of a set of present states which form the elementary constituents of the natural, social and cultural worlds. Descartes, for example, argued for the existence of the self by claiming that at each instance in consciousness there had to be something, the Ego, which was experiencing the consciousness. Similarly, the modern theories of meaning are, for Derrida, all predicated upon the idea that meaning is present in the mind and expressed in signs, symbols etc. Meaning is articulated in symbolic forms. However, although it is pervasive, the 'metaphysics of presence' cannot escape confronting the paradoxes it creates. Each account of the present requires reference to states which are not present. This is the nub. Nothing is ever simply and essentially 'present'. Individual states present at any instant depend for their identity upon states which are not present. It is differentiation that gives present states their identity. Such is the grip which the metaphysics of presence has upon us that we think only in terms of presence and absence. Something is either one or the other.

It is fairly obvious that this use of differentiation that Derrida has is close to that to be found in Saussure. However, Derrida takes it further and applies it to the structural conception of language. If we think of the meaning of a word as given in the use that the word has for speakers, then we might argue that the structure of the language is derived from and determined by acts of communication. The trouble is we could never get this conventionality off the ground as a coherent vision of language use. Each individual communicative act is determined by the prior existence of language and meaning. But language and meaning cannot be invented as totalities. This is what earlier in this chapter we called the problem of synechdoche; the part–whole relationship. Even if we invent a story in which language starts with the use of a grunt to signify food, we still face the problem of making the first ostension. We have got to have distinguished one grunt as meaningful from others that are not and to have a world which is classified into food and non-food. Furthermore, we have got to have the social institution of naming by pointing or ostensive definition. And how could we have all these things without first possessing a language? Saussure realised that signification depended upon difference. What is present can be brought out only by reference to what is not present, just as the definition of the wren (the example we used earlier) is a means of marking it off from other species of birds. Differences are only available through differentiation and this, in turn, in any particular case is dependent upon prior differences having been made. We can move back and forth between prior events and present ones, prior differentiations and present ones, but we cannot synthesise them.

Although Saussure provides Derrida with the conception which he turns upon the metaphysics of presence, unfortunately Saussure's own work is an exemplary case of its working out. Although the notion of difference is central, Saussure's logocentrism can be seen in the role that he allocates to writing with regard to that of speech. Writing is a derivative of speech, a mere technical representational device. This association is, to Derrida, common to all Western thought, especially about language. He rejects it. Speakers and listeners are in each other's presence. The words issue as the signs of the speaker's thoughts. Writing, on the other hand, is at one stage removed from the thoughts which gave rise to it. Further, it is an uncertain representation of such thoughts and their creator. Indeed a lot of writing is designedly anonymous. Giving speech this privileged status and treating writing as a parasite upon it is an expression of the way in which certain features of language can be repressed. The hierarchy of writing and speech oversimplifies and so distorts the complex relations between them.

To draw out these complexities, Derrida introduces the 'logic of supplementarity'. It is the use of this logic which makes society, culture, art, everything that is human, possible. He identifies this logic in a number of texts but most importantly in Rousseau's account of the relationship between nature and education in *Émile*. Education supplements nature for Rousseau. In which case, nature must be something complete in itself to which education makes an addition. But it must also be incomplete for education to be able to supplement it. This apparent paradox is resolved by suggesting that education is needed to allow someone's true nature to emerge. In this example, the logic of supplementarity allocates priority to nature but also specifies a lack or absence within nature for education to fill. In this way, education although separate from nature, is a necessary condition of its complete realisation. Whenever we find something being treated as marginal to some other quality or entity, we are dealing with the logic of supplementarity. Writing is marginal to speech and identified as a substitute for it, or as something that can supplement it. It thus becomes possible to reveal that the distinguishing criteria of the marginal are the defining properties of that to which it is being related. Thus in rejecting writing because he identifies it with some characteristics of language which he wishes to set aside, Saussure privileges speech over writing thereby invoking the hierarchical metaphysics of presence.

The question which Derrida asks is quite simply 'What is the basis for this metaphysics of presence?' He suggests that it has its origins in the primacy that is given to the act of speaking in all philosophical systems. The act of speaking is defined as the moment that thought and the material world, the inner and the outer, mind and matter empirical and non-empirical are fused. This moment of fusion is taken as the central reference point in our metaphysics. The distinctions which our metaphysical schemes distribute and relate express the elements that are fused. In Derrida's view, if one were to undercut the priority that speech is given, then the whole of our metaphysics would crumble. When I speak, my words seem to be transparent signifiers of my thoughts. As such they are a fusion of mind and matter, nature and reason, the empirical and the transcendental. My words are not external to but are coextensive with my thoughts. Because words seem to give such a direct access to thought, speaking is taken as the model for communication. Writing is treated, as in Saussure, as a deficient and marginal process.

Derrida now makes a quite startling move. He suggests that, in fact, speech is a form of writing. Speech and writing have the same structure and if one wishes to reveal this structure it is necessary, as

Saussure did, to reveal it in writing. This is a principle which Derrida refers to as 'the principle of self-destruction'. In order to characterise what it took to be central, Saussure's text has to employ what it treats as marginal. The 'central' is defined by the 'marginal'. The relational character which units of speech have can only be brought out in writing. Further, a term can only be used to signify if it can be repeated, cited, produced as an example. This characteristic inheres in writing rather than in speech. The hierarchical relation of Saussere should, therefore, be inverted. It is writing which ought to be the model for speech. Both speech and writing are exemplars of 'archi-writing'.

Derrida's 'deconstruction' of the subordinate role of writing invites us to see language as the play of differences, traces and repetitions which have meaning. However, he does not see this as making a 'logocentric-less linguistics' possible. Escaping from logocentrism to found a new semiology is impossible; we cannot rid ourselves of metaphysics, nor stand outside ours to build a new one. 'Deconstructive reading' means working from within to describe how one can use the arguments within a text to call its premises into question and, thereby, using its concepts to question the coherence and consistency of the system. This dual aspect is a form of 'cohabitation'; presuppositions and critique live side by side in the 'deconstructive reading'. Deconstructive readings cannot be the foundation of a new discipline but are 'only' interventions from within any discipline — interventions which put pressure on the limits of the system thereby making their limiting function visible.

Derrida does not confine his deconstruction to Saussure. He turns it upon the writings of the Structuralists. As we have seen, they all begin with the suggestion that social phenomena, the unconscious, history, are structured like language. In this presupposition Derrida sees the metaphysics of presence. As with Saussure, he finds their texts express the principle of self-destruction. Foucault, for example, lays bare the limits of reason and sanity through which particular discourses have defined madness. But what he has not done is to make clear what relationship his discourse has to the categories he uses. As a consequence, Foucault offers us just another attempt to define madness and sanity. His critique of definitions of madness is self-destructive.

The problem of the privileged status of the writer's own discourse is particularly acute for philosophy. Philosophers, from Plato onwards, have drawn a distinction between philosophical and literary discourse.

Since philosophy aims at truth and certainty and literature is fictional, metaphorical, rhetorical, then philosophy is taken to be superior. This, says Derrida, is philosophy's way of neutralising the threat of language by defending the status of its own discourse. Literary discourse is less serious, derivative, marginal to philosophy. Philosophy invokes, then, the law of supplementarity. But, whenever philosophy tries to use language in a purely logical fashion, whenever it tries to write purely logical languages, it fails because it runs up against the reflexivity of language. The reaction is to invent logical languages which are inflexible parodies of the natural languages we use. The self-destructive nature of this reaction is revealed, says Derrida, in the rhetorical character of philosophy. It seeks to convince. As such, it is but a special case of that which was said to be a derivative of it. Both literary and philosophical discourse have a common progenitor in the archi-literature that is the condition for both. In Derrida's deconstruction of philosophy and literature, he finds that each shares the features of the other.

In putting writing at the centre, Derrida indicates that here is a method by which subjectivity and individualism can be overcome. In writing, the text is set free from the writer. It is released to the public who find meaning in it as they read it. These readings are the product of circumstance. The same holds true even for philosophy. There can be no way of fixing readings outside of the metaphysics of presence. We are enmeshed in the net of our own categories. Clearly, such a conclusion subverts any claim which Structuralism might make to the superiority of its methods and the veracity of its knowledge of the universal essences which lie beneath the surface of social life. Structuralism is just another textual form articulating the metaphysics of presence and so is self-destructive. In denying the possibility of stepping outside metaphysics, Derrida has taken us back to where we began this chapter. Structuralism's claim to have developed a method for avoiding scepticism and relativism has been rejected. There is no sense in the idea of an independent view of how things are.

Recommended Reading

There are several good introductions to structuralist thought. Philip Pettit's *The Concept of Structuralism* (University of California Press, 1975) gives prominence to Saussure, Barthes and Lévi-Strauss. S. Clarke, *The Foundations of Structuralism* (Harvester, 1981) is a very good and thorough account of the origins of Lévi-Strauss' ideas. For a discussion of the contribution which structuralism may make to the social sciences see M. Glucksman, *Structuralist Analysis in Contemporary Thought* (Routledge, 1974). E. Kurzweil's *The Age of Structuralism* (Columbia University Press, 1980) contains essays on the most important structuralist thinkers including Lévi-Strauss, Althusser, Lacan, and Foucault. Lévi-Strauss is extremely difficult, especially at first. The essays in his collections of papers, especially *Structural Anthropology vol. I* (Penguin, 1972) provide some help. Dip into these before looking at *The Savage Mind* (Weidenfeld and Nicolson, 1966) and *Totemism* (Penguin, 1974). C.R. Badcock, *Lévi-Strauss*: Structuralism and Sociological Theory (Hutchinson, 1975) is an accessible discussion. J. Sturrock (ed.), *Structuralism and Since* (Oxford University Press, 1979) provides a collection of reviews of the major contributors including Lévi-Strauss, Lacan, Foucault, Derrida and others. H.L. Dreyfus and P. Rabinow, *Foucault: Beyond Structuralism and Hermeneutics* (Harvester, 1983) is the most thorough account of Foucault's work and ideas. Sherry Turkle's *Psycho-analytic Politics* (Andre Deutsch, 1979) if not exactly racy is none the less easier to get along with than Lacan's own prose. Lacan's own writings are extremely difficult, much of them untranslated. However, selections are to be found in his *Écrits: A Selection* (Norton, 1977). Also, his *Four Fundamental Concepts of Psychoanalysis*, trans. A. Sheridan (Penguin, 1979), is worth attempting. Newton Garver's introduction to Derrida's *Speech and Phenomena* (Northwestern University Press, 1973) gives a reasonably clear account of the background to and early development of Derrida's philosophy. Also, Derrida's *Edmund Husserl's Origins of Geometry: An Introduction*, trans. J.P. Leavey (Harvester, 1978), gives a good taste of his approach. The volume also contains an English and French bibliography of Derrida's writings. Again, his work and thought are by no means easy to comprehend at first reading.

PART TWO

6 INTRODUCTION: LOGIC AND LANGUAGE

In this Introduction we will give a brief and fairly non-technical resumé of some of the more important background issues that inform the discussions which follow. Rather more than for the matters discussed in the Introduction to Section One, it is important to realise the philosophical character of the arguments we will touch on because, unlike those we have already dealt with, there has not always been a close relation between the debates carried on in modern philosophy and the interests and relevances of the human and cultural sciences. Because of the gap between them, social scientists are apt not to appreciate exactly what sorts of things are at issue for the philosophers and philosophies we cover in this section. The consequence is, unfortunately, incomprehension, misunderstanding or, even worse, misappropriation. This happens when the social scientist fails to notice that the epistemology, or the ontology, or even the conclusion that he wishes to make use of has been fashioned for particular philosophical arguments. They come with strings on.

Much of the time, these strings are tied to Logic. Formal symbolic Logic is a looming presence in all of the debates that we will survey. However, the exact nature of its presence often goes unnoticed in commentaries given for, and by, social and cultural scientists. Even in those suburbs of philosophy seemingly far remote from Logic and logical concerns, its presence is felt. Husserl's Phenomenology, for example, was partly an attempt to formulate a non-psychologistic grounding for mathematics. Derrida, the most influential of the post-structuralists, has elaborated and extended his notion of the 'reading of a text' in the introduction that he has provided to Husserl's *The Origin of Geometry*. It might appear that only Marxism has remained unmoved by the tide of Logic. But even here, as we saw in Chapter 2, there have been those who have tried to introduce some forms of argument and theoretical aspirations proposed by logicians for the social sciences. At the same time, though, Critical Theory has castigated this relapse into 'positivism'. Yet in doing so, in opposing the 'scientism' and 'anti-humanism' of this 'logicism', it has had to cast its arguments in Logic's terms.

The important point about Logic's looming presence is not that arguments in philosophy are now cast in logical terms, nor even that logical notation is used widely, true though both are, but that like physics in the seventeenth century, because of the great strides that Logic has made in the last 100 years or so, it has become the model for philosophical thinking. Its techniques and procedures have been merged with philosophy's. To put it another way, philosophy has been retooled with Logic's technology. A central point follows from this. If, as we shall see, one of the major concerns of modern philosophy has been the classical problem of the relationship between our concepts embedded in our language and the world, then if Logic can be said to be the study of formalised languages, then it ought to be able to tell us something about what our languages must be like. Or, perhaps more accurately, what they could be like if they were tidied up a little. Logical procedures require the definition of relationships between symbols and the objects to which they refer. And that looks like the same concern that philosophy has with concepts, language and the world. To see exactly what we mean by this, we ought perhaps to start with the general aims that Logic sets itself.

In the ancient world, Logic was part of a young person's education rather like mathematics, English and a foreign language are today. In particular, anyone who wanted to be successful in public life had to master the arts of public presentation and argument. Along with Rhetoric (how to speak in public) Logic was one of these. Logicians specialised in the dissection and formulation of good, that is strong and coherent, arguments. To this end, they set out recipes of various sorts, the syllogisms. Departures from these recipes resulted in fallacies, or false inferences. One such recipe might go like this: we can infer from the propositions 'All birds have wings' and 'Polly is a bird' that 'Polly has wings'. Most of us would accept that this is a reasonable piece of inference, if a somewhat uninspired one. The logician would set the parts of the argument out like this:

1. All birds have wings.	*(Major premiss)*
2. Polly is a bird.	*(Minor premiss)*
Therefore 3. Polly has wings.	*(Conclusion)*

The next significant change occurred in the early part of the nineteenth century. Under the influence of mathematicians, Logic began to become increasingly formalised; that is, it began to use collections of defined symbols. In particular, it became dependent upon what is known in mathematics as set theory. Indeed, it came to be argued that if set theory underpinned the nature of logical thought — and just why that was so we will see in a moment — and if mathematics was a priori certain, that is guaranteed by the nature of our reasoning itself, then set theory was the foundation of mathematics and, by extension, all valid human reasoning. Set theory, therefore, was the ground on which the most successful of the spheres of human knowledge, the mathematical and natural sciences, were built — or so it was hoped. For the logicians, then, set theory showed how mathematics was possible, which was, it will be remembered, one of the problems that Kant and other Enlightenment rationalists had set themselves.

To see the basis of this argument, we will need to look at a little set theory. Consider the following diagram, commonly called a Venn diagram.

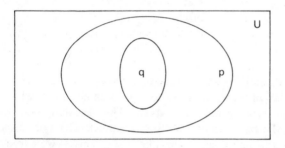

Let us say that the box contains all of the possible states of affairs in a universe (U). Two of these are picked out as p and q. Now let us say that p represents having wings and q being a bird. That is to say, p is the set of states of affairs defined by having wings, and q is that defined by being a bird. We notice straight away that everything which is a bird has wings. But not everything which has wings is a bird. Bats and aeroplanes are not birds. We can say that q is a proper subset of p. We can now present the syllogism about Polly like this:

      1. Everything that is a bird has wings.
      2. This is a bird.
Therefore 3. This has wings.

The syllogism can make use of the notation to simplify matters by writing:

      1. If q then p.
      2. This is q.
Therefore 3. This is p.

However, as well as formalising the expression 'This is a bird' and so on, we can formalise the relations which hold between the sets. The symbols used to define these relations are called 'the logical operators'. Their use enables us to combine p and q in strings of symbols, or logical expressions. When they are used correctly, following the defined rules of use, the sentences they produce are 'well formed'. If the elements that make up the well formed sentence are true, then the sentence will be true *merely in virtue of the formal relationships*. We do not need to look at the world to see if it is true. The most simple of the operators are:

not	—
and	∪
or	∩
if . . . then	⊃
is identical to	≡

The point of all this was that the use of set theory notation seemed to offer a way of representing valid reasoning no matter what topic or subject was being reasoned about. The reasoning was empty of content; the truth was formally guaranteed. The symbols p and q could refer to anything and providing the premises were true then the conclusion would be true. The last step in formalisation was to write out the argument purely in notation. This would give us, in the case of Polly:

$$1. \quad q \supset p$$
$$2. \quad q$$
$$3. \therefore p$$

The relevance of all this to our particular concerns is that the German logician, Gottloeb Frege, tried to use an extended version of set theory to show that arithmetic — and hence mathematics — was completely logically consistent and that it was this logical coherence and consistency which guaranteed its knowledge. In so doing he addressed and created a whole series of problems that constitute the agenda of much of modern, particularly Anglo Saxon philosophy. If we run very quickly through the aims that he had and the difficulties which he and his successors faced, we will be able to see how the central arguments, and the examples even, that recur again and again in the next few chapters, have their origins in Frege and those like him who were working on the foundations of mathematics.

We can start with what we might call Frege's general attitude. Here we meet a first feature that has to be taken into account all the way through the rest of the chapters. Frege thought it was both obvious and indisputable that, if a firm, consistent and logical basis was to be found for mathematics, this would have to be set out in a formalised language using a formal notation. Expressions couched in ordinary language were far too open to ambiguity, local contextual redefinition and just plain sloppiness to do what was required. Ordinary language was not a suitable vehicle for philosophy and would have to be formalised. In two of the chapters which follow, we will see that there are those who are very dubious about this. Ryle argued that the translation in and out of formal notation can make expressions misleading, while Wittgenstein was extremely puzzled by what happened to propositions when they were given logical form. Translation into logical notation seems to require the universal application of the true/false distinction, as well as that of the general/ particular one. Yet some propositions that were perfectly acceptable seemed to defy being cast in these terms. These considerations led to a doubting of the superiority of formal arguments over non-formal ones. Frege, though, would not have accepted such reservations.

Greek syllogistic logic had considered expressions to be made up of subjects and predicates. In the sentence 'Polly is a bird', 'Polly' is the subject of the sentence and 'is a bird' is a predicate that can be used of Polly. Predicates like 'has wings' and 'is a bird' are states of affairs that hold with regard to Polly. One of Frege's innovations is to find a means whereby 'Polly is a bird' is not broken down into subject and predicate but 'analysed' into the sentences or expressions which it presupposes. The sentence 'Polly is a bird' can then be treated as the conjunction of these presuppositions. The method is the elaboration of set theory that we mentioned earlier. In general terms it works something along these lines. The sentence 'Polly is a bird' is the conjunction of two presuppositions.

1. There is something that is Polly.
2. The something that is Polly is a bird.

The initial sentence could be further analysed into:

1. There is something.
2. This something is Polly.

The modern technical notation of these sentences would be:

1. There is something. $\exists(x)$.
2. The something is Polly. $(x)(Polly)$.
3. The something which is $\exists(x)/(x)(Polly)\cup(x)(bird)$.
   Polly is a bird.

The two innovations to be used here are the *unbound variable* (x) standing for 'something' and the *existential quantifier* ($\exists$) standing for 'there is'. Another way of putting 'there is something' it to say 'there is some one thing' which is to quantify the expression. Once we have the idea of quantification then it is an easy step to say that $q > p$ really says 'for all q they are p'. Frege introduces a symbol, today it is usually ($\forall$), to stand for the expression 'for all'. The expression 'all birds have wings can now be rendered as:

$$\forall(x)/(x)(birds)\cup(x)(wings)$$

What actually allows Frege to make this advance is the distinction which he makes between a concept and its 'instantiation' in an object. The concept 'being a bird' is instantiated in Polly. The concept is what is expressed by the predicate. It was here that Frege saw the connection to mathematics. The expression $x + 1$ contains two elements, the variable (x) and a function (+ 1). For $x+1$ to mean anything, the expression has to be given an argument; that is, x has to be given a value. It was for this reason that Frege, Russell and the early Wittgenstein all held that the expressions of pure mathematics were 'meaningless'. With different arguments, the value of the expression varies. If $x = 2$ then the value of $x + 1$ is 3, if it is 4 then the value is 5, and so on. The equivalent conjunction of argument and function in natural language is that of *proper name and predicate*. The equivalent of the value of the mathematical expression is the truth value of the sentence. The rules for the combination of proper names and predicates are contained in the syntax of the formal language, be it mathematics or any other. The rules for determining values, what the expressions mean, is the *semantics* of that language. What Frege wants to bring out is the logical nature of mathematics' semantics by casting it in the formal terms which he invents. He felt that if he could show that the operations used in arithmetic (remembering that arithmetic was felt to be the basis of all mathematics) were just the same as those used to produce true sentences like those cited about Polly, then he would have shown that arithmetic was logically consistent. To do that he had to show that numerals were names, or number words, and so the 'objects' manipulated by arithmetic were names just like 'Polly'.

His argument goes like this. Take the following two sets: {the authors of the Gospels} and {the points of the compass}. The elements of the two sets stand in a one-to-one correspondence. Each element has a match in the other set.

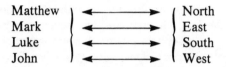

Matthew	North
Mark	East
Luke	South
John	West

Both of these two sets are subsets of at least one other set, the set of those sets having four elements. Other members of this set are the set of sides of quadrilaterals, the set of alchemical elements, the set of kings in a pack of cards. Since the set is distinguishable, then '4' is the name of that set, and the number 4 is the object to which this name refers. If we hold with Frege that any proper name (in the sense that Frege uses the term) names something, then we might feel drawn towards the conclusion that if a name names something then whatever it names must exist. In that case if we say that the sentences 'Unicorns are horned animals' and 'There is a golden mountain' make sense, or have a truth value, then we might also want to say that, in some sense or other, unicorns and golden mountains exist. But, of course, we know that they don't. In that case we have to provide an ontology in which unicorns, centaurs and golden mountains have a different order of existence to cats, paranoid schizophrenics and the Wrekin. This question of whether proper names refer and if they refer whether they refer in quite this way is taken up by Quine and Kripke in Chapter 7 as well as by Ryle in Chapter 9.

The question at issue for Frege is what guarantees the truth value of expressions in arithmetic. The answer is the consistency with which they have been deduced or are deducible from arithmetic's axioms. These deductions involve the use of combinatorial rules for analysed expressions. All and only such well formed sentences in arithmetic will be meaningful. In Russell and Whitehead's *Principia Mathematica* the complexity as well as the scope of the task that Logic had set itself can be appreciated from the fact that it takes nearly 1000 pages to show that $2 + 2 = 4$.

We pointed out earlier that Frege had defined meaning as truth value. Expressions have truth value. The meaning of a word or symbol is the contribution which it makes to the truth value of the expression in which it is found. This is another important idea. It is clearly at odds with the suggestion that the meaning of an expression is the 'idea' in the utterer's mind or something similar. The way that the idea was reworked in the later Wittgenstein and Ordinary Language philosophy to reveal the 'informal logic' of language is discussed in Chapters 8 and 9.

We can, at this point, draw out a connection to the social sciences. For a time, the line which Frege was developing became highly influential in its association with a set of methodological and epistemological doctrines called Logical Positivism. Logical Positivism felt that utilising the logic of the natural sciences was the only way to develop empirical knowledge. To this end it proposed a definition of meaning expressed in the slogan 'The meaning of an expression is its method of verification'. Among other things, Logical Positivism wanted to exclude from any bona fide science any expressions which were meaningless, that is empirically unverifiable. Popper's views on science as they are set out in Chapter 10 are clearly related to this idea. As we repeatedly mentioned in Part One, the influence that Logical Positivism has had in the human sciences has largely been negative. If even those like the Structuralists, the Marxists and the Hermeneuticists who have wanted to reject and counter the model being offered have had to debate with it, largely on its terms. In effect, they have had to debate with one or other interpretation of Frege.

The sentence consisting of a proper name and its predicate, or an argument and its function, is the unit of meaning. Only in well formed sentences do terms have meaning. The meaning which they have, their truth value, can be determined when they assert that something is the case. These ideas had a profound infuence upon Wittgenstein and Alfred Tarski (cf. below). However, we fairly quickly run into snags. To be completely consistent and formal, each definitional axiom will have to be discrete and free-standing. Further, each sentence must be analysable down to such definitions. What do we do when a term has alternative definitions or names and, when joined to predicates, the expressions have varying truth values? For instance, astronomers used to talk about the Evening Star and the Morning Star, Hesperus and Phosphorus, without realising that they were one and the same object — what we call Venus. Sentences about Phosphorus and Hesperus may have had different senses, but they had the same reference. Hence their truth values were the same.

Frege defines sense as the thought that is expressed and reference as the truth value. For Frege, meaning is not sense but reference. This whole issue has erupted recently in discussions of 'mental life' and the 'mind/brain identity thesis' in psychology and the philosophy of mind. One version of the argument holds that descriptions of brain states in terms of orders of neuron firings and descriptions of mental states like being in pain or dreaming, while having different senses, can have the same reference or meaning. Philosophers such as Davidson, Putnam and Kripke have considered this at length.

Frege's attempt to develop a formal semantics and to apply it to arithmetic involved Logic in addressing language in a direct way. He decided that ordinary language was unsuited to his needs and that a formal language would have to be invented. In so doing he gave Logic a topic and philosophy a resource which have been both abiding and the source of much dissension.

Apart from the Logical Positivists, those most directly influenced by Frege were working in England on the foundations of mathematics. Russell and Wittgenstein, particularly, struggled to work through the Fregean programme to its conclusion. The Fregean system was designed to bring out the coherence and consistency of mathematics. Unfortunately, almost as soon as it was completed Russell found that it was irredeemably flawed. He noted that sets could fall into two types, those which contained themselves and those which did not. The set of things which are green is not itself green; but the set of sets is a set. Now, what about the set of all sets that are not members of themselves? Is this a member of itself? The consideration of this question led Russell to formulate a logical antinomy or contradiction which if possible, suggested strongly that set theory could not be the basis of complete, logical consistency. Probably the clearest way to see the point that Russell is making is to put it notationally. Let us call the set of sets that are members of themselves M. The set of sets that are not members of themselves we will call $-M$. The question is, 'Is $-M$ a member of M?'. If it is a member of itself then $-M$ is M. If it is not then $-M$ is not $-M$ (or $--M$), that is M. Either way we have a contradiction. Frege saw immediately that Russell's paradox meant that his system was inadequate. After a period of trying to resolve it within the system, he gave up.

Russell, however, stayed within the Fregean system and tried to get it to do what Frege had originally intended. To do this, two problems had to be resolved. The first and most obvious was the contradiction. The second was to find a way of getting round the apparent necessity of postulating an ontology which included imaginary objects. He thought he might find a way of achieving the latter if he distinguished between those subjects or arguments that were proper names and those which were descriptions. He suggested that the term 'the author of Waverley' in the sentence 'The author of Waverley was Scottish' is a description of Sir Walter Scott and not, as Frege seemed to think, another name for Sir Walter Scott. The theory of descriptions, though,was never satisfactory. It had become clear that Russell had mixed up two sorts of contradiction in his paradox: those produced by an inconsistency within the system's formal syntax, and those produced by ambiguities in ordinary language or the way that ordinary terms are being used. It is with the latter consideration that Ryle's discussion of the paradoxes begins (Chapter 9). They can only be resolved by looking at the technical use that 'meaning', 'truth' and 'name' are being given and how that jibs with our ordinary concepts. A solution to the internal consistencies requires a formal definition of truth in a language other than the language under consideration, which can then be applied to it. It is this which the work of Alfred Tarski tries to supply. It offers the possibility — or so philosophers such as Donald Davidson (cf. Chapter 7) believe — of a rigorous definition of the difference between truth and falsity, meaningfulness and nonsense. In so doing it provides a way of extending the formalisation of semantics from the logical languages to the natural ones.

Tarski sets out from the intuitive notion that any conception of truth must involve a correspondence with how things are. The statement 'The cup is on the table' is true only if the cup is on the table. The state of affairs (p) satisfies the sentence (S). Putting it formally, ' "S" is true if and only if (iff) p'. ' "S" is true iff p' is the definition of truth from which a formal account of meaning can begin. Once the definition is in place then any sentence equivalent to S, such as 'La tasse est sur la table' is also true. Because the cup is on the table, the truth conditions for both sentences are satisfied. Because reference is thus secured both sentences have meaning. While the argument is intuitively acceptable at this level, what Tarski wants is a fully formal definition and a procedure for determining truth values based upon it. We can have this if we hold a distinction between the language which we want the truth criterion for — Tarski calls this 'the object language' — and the language we want the criterion expressed in. If we tried to codify the semantics of the object language from *within*, we soon hit two obstacles. First, any natural language is an infinitely large collection of sentences. We cannot draw the upper limit of an infinitely large collection and so cannot list all the sentences, let alone all the true ones which would be a subset of that set. Second, natural languages are intrinsically reflexive and indexical. Terms such as 'this', 'there', 'me' and 'above' cannot be defined in isolation from the context in which they appear. This being so, they cannot be given a purely formal definition. Tarski concluded, then, that if we wanted a formal criterion of the intuitive kind we suggested, we would have to develop it for a non-natural language which we could codify and define. Tarski proceeded to specify the criterion or convention in a formal language which would have a clearly defined, that is *canonical*, relationship to the object language. Simon Blackburn in *Spreading the Word* has a very neat story to show how this works. Imagine a language which only has one predicate (a) which stands for 'is bald', and two arguments: L for Lenin and M for Marx. Though the language is tiny, consisting of just two sentences 'Marx is bald' and 'Lenin is bald', the principle will work for all languages. The sentences are made to fit the criterion by saying '"Marx is bald" is true iff Marx is bald' or formally '"M is a" is true iff M is a'. The list of true sentences in the formal language maps on to the list of true sentences in the object language with a one-for-one correspondence. The set of true sentences in the formal language satisfies the set in the object language. It is clear enough what is going on in our restricted example. It works because we have a complete semantics, an exhaustive list of sentences and their meanings.

It is when we turn to the natural languages that the trouble begins. Here we do not have such a semantics. Although a sentence could be true, it is also possible that we cannot determine the state of affairs to which it refers. This is where Quine's problem of the inscrutability of reference has its origin (cf. Chapter 7). We would not know what to translate in and out of the object language. This is because although we might know what the truth value of a sentence was, there are infinitely many sentences which could be of the same truth value. To use an example which Quine himself has made famous, it might be that the sentence 'Gavagai' as uttered by the speaker of an alien language when a rabbit hops by, is true, but does it mean 'There is a rabbit' or 'There is an undetached rabbit part' or 'There is dinner' or what? We can get into this position precisely because the definition Tarski gives is a formal or content free one. It can be applied recursively to any sentence in the object language.

What has proved fascinating is the *idea* that Tarski has promulgated. Some have rejected it simply because, *ab initio*, it cannot be applied to the most important case, natural languages, and restricts itself to formal ones. Others though think that Tarski has provided the beginnings of a method for formalising semantics which, if it proves possible to solve the translation and inscrutability of reference problems, ought in principle to be extendable to natural languages. Once we could do that, we would have a fireproof way of determining truth, meaningfulness and so on.

Clearly what is at issue for us is what the relevance of all of this is to the social and cultural scientist. On the face of it, there doesn't seem to be much in the squabbles over paradoxes and logical languages of direct interest to us. It is here that we return to the idea of Logic as a looming presence. Unlike many of the philosophers covered in Part One, many of the authors we deal with now are not much interested in the human and social sciences. Their interest often seems to be in how the sort of data that such sciences produce, the stories that are told, so to speak, can be used as grist for the mill of their arguments. What they say about the social sciences, then, are what they take to be implications of views that they hold about other and, for them, clearly related matters. We could say that the arguments are nearly always over formality, and that every now and again the arena happens to be the philosophy of the human and social sciences. That is, the sort of logic they should have, the epistemological and ontological commitments that such a logic requires. It is just for this reason that we have to be very careful how we approach such philosophy and what we take from it. If we can change the image a little, we could say that while tracking their quarry of logical consistency, clarity and certainty, every now and again these philosophers have blundered into the human sciences. Somewhat perplexed they have looked around to examine what they have found. All too often, what then happens is a hasty and often unfortunate annexation of their remarks on behalf of some proselytising programme *within* the human sciences, or, on the other hand, the outright rejection of what they say because it looks so esoteric. Neither is a particularly sensible response. In the chapters which follow — and it goes for those in the Part One as well — we will try and show that, providing care is exercised and enthusiasm moderated, exposure to philosophy can help students of the human sciences learn a great deal. It can also show them just how much they have to unlearn as well.

Recommended Reading

John Passmore's *A Hundred Years of Philosophy* (Penguin, 1966) remains in the forefront of the introductions to modern philosophy. A general introduction to reasoning and logic can be found in S. Toulmin, R. Reik, and A. Janik, *An Introduction to Reason* (Macmillan, 1979). More technical introductions abound. One such is I. Cope, *An Introduction to Logic* (Collier Macmillan, 1978). Frege's work and the proper interpretation of it has been the centre of much controversy of late. Simon Blackburn's *Spreading the Word* (Clarendon, 1984) provides most of the background against which these arguments are carried on. A collection of the original papers edited by Peter Geach and Max Black and titled *Translations from the Philosophical Writings of Gottloeb Frege* (Blackwell, 1977) contains most of the seminal and important papers, particularly 'Sense and Reference'. Alfred Tarski's 'The Concept of Truth in Formalised Languages' is extremely difficult and technical for anyone without a firm grounding in mathematical logic. An excerpt from it can be found in D. Davidson and G. Harman (eds.) *The Logic of Grammar* (Dickenson, 1975). Mark Platts, *Ways of Meaning* (Routledge, 1975), while less formidable, is still a demanding exposition.

7 MODERN REALISM AND EMPIRICISM

Introduction

Even the most cursory review of the interest which social and cultural scientists have shown in philosophy will reveal it to have been fired, for the most part, by a debate over what we have called 'the natural science model'. Much of the attraction of the philosophies covered in Part One rests in their almost uniform rejection of this model. At root what is objected to is the combination of 'hard line' empiricism and 'naîve' realism which it was felt was being displayed by defenders of the natural science model *within* the social sciences. Whether these defenders actually did espouse such an interpretation of realism and empiricism is, of course, another matter.

In brief, we can say that 'hard line' empiricism requires that all knowledge be gained directly from sensory experience, unmediated by conceptual categories. Certain knowledge is only such if it is not theory laden. Whatever method the human sciences use, the single overriding constraint on them is that they reduce and preferably eradicate the role of subjective interpretation in the acquisition of knowledge. For our knowledge to be independent of our theories we must be able to estimate the fit between the theory and the world, which is only possible if the world actually does have an independent existence and organisation which we can come to know about. The organisation and existence would be captured in the true description or correct theory of it. The combination of realism and empiricism led to the conclusion that what fixes our knowledge of the natural world, and of the social one too, is social and natural reality — how things really are.

The rising tide of anti-naturalism emphasised the interpretive character of all knowledge, but especially that of human science. Knowledge is obtained through the use of conceptual schemes, frameworks of meaning and the like. This view emphasised what came to be called the 'social construction' of social and natural reality, since schemes and frameworks originate in the socio-cultural traditions of society. As we will see in Chapter 10, the implications that these views had for the status of scientific knowledge were felt to be immense.

If we have acquired our theories, categories, methods and standards as a consequence of the socio-historical exigencies of our way of life's development, then other societies will have different theories, categories, methods and standards than our own. There will be different ways of dividing up nature, and nature itself appears to have no role in setting limits to what we can truthfully say. It begins to seem that we can say *anything* about how nature is, depending upon our social circumstances — which on the face of it makes nonsense of the whole idea of scientific inquiry. The world, it seems, has been lost — though Richard Rorty was moved to speak of it as 'well lost' — and someone attached to a naïve realism must surely feel that something has gone very badly wrong, for the independent existence of the external world is the fundamental requirement for talk of truth, knowledge, discovery and so forth. The bogey of relativism seems to have been loosed. To accept this, for any realist, is to give up much more than he cares to surrender. It is not surprising, therefore, that the attention of some social scientists began to turn in the direction of the philosophers that we shall discuss in this chapter who seemed to offer more sophisticated philosophical views that could accommodate conclusions about the social construction of reality and yet could still be compatible with plausibly firm realist convictions.

What the philosophies of Quine, Davidson and Putnam try to achieve is a complete redefinition of empiricism and realism. By and large, they have followed their ideas through only as far as their implications for the status of natural science theories. However, Davidson and Putnam have explored some ways in which their ideas might affect what we can say about the social sciences. The emergence of this form of realism and empiricism has stimulated those like Bhaskar, Papineau and Sayer to champion the reintroduction of 'naturalism' into debates over theory and method in the social sciences. To these writers, the programme that Quine and others have initiated offers the possibility of dissolving once and for all the hard and fast distinctions between natural and social science. In breaking with 'subjectivism' this philosophy shows how all scientific disciplines can attain objectivity.

W.V.O. Quine

Willard van Orman Quine is probably the most influential living philosopher in the Anglo-American tradition. Among younger philosophers in that tradition his work, and that of Davidson and Putnam, is enjoying a considerable popularity and its adoption is seen by many as a healthy reaction against 'ordinary language philosophy' (cf. Chapter 9) which, among an older generation, has much greater sway.

Quine's efforts to extend and 'modernise' that strong philosophical tradition of empiricism have set the terms for contemporary debates, and his work has been mightily influential on both the style and the substance of many contemporary practitioners. Often those who disagree with him are compelled to do so on his terms. We will begin this chapter with an account of Quine's refurbished empiricism and will then look at some issues which relate to his work, mainly through a consideration of some of the things that Donald Davidson, Hilary Putnam and Saul Kripke have to say about the relation of language and reality.

As has been indicated in the introduction to this section, the importance of logic to the philosophy of our century has been immense: the achievements of Gottloeb Frege and Bertrand Russell at the turn of the century and their efforts to make logic *philosophically* important have been decisive. It is the response, for or against, that has set the direction and the preoccupations of the most important philosophers in the Anglo-American tradition. The philosophers considered in this chapter, with the exception of Kripke, are those who respond most positively to the suggestion that logical resources are of great potential value in the resolution of philosophical problems, that the making of logical analyses often is the very stuff of philosophical practice. Any reader of the original sources will find that they are relentlessly technical in character in the sense that they use logical symbolism and notions pervasively. Quine's earliest work was within the field of logic and he has continued to produce work which contributes to, rather than just employs, logic. Davidson, too, is motivated in many of the things he does by the need to develop logic's own powers of analysis.

We shall be doing our best to convey what their philosophy is about without recourse to the symbolism and technicalities of logic, though some very minimal mention of these will be unavoidable. We shall, therefore, be underplaying something that is not just important but is rather essential to the nature of the approach we are trying to describe. This is, however, unavoidable.

If Quine's work falls within the empiricist tradition, then it falls most directly in one branch of that, the 'analytic' one, that which aims to proceed through the development of formal logical analysis in order to achieve a grasp of the logical structure of language, the world or both. His empiricism is not uncritical, very far from it; he is himself deeply critical of some of its key assumptions and sets out to dispense with what some would undoubtedly regard as its indispensable presuppositions. He seeks to create a cautious, canny empiricism, one with a modest mien, aware of and ready to acknowledge its own limitations but undisturbed by many of these since they are shared with *any* attempt to know the world.

No First Philosophy, No Final Science

Quine's most basic move is to abandon the idea that there could be a philosophy which is fundamental to science, which is more basic than it or which is more certain than it. By doing this he gives up the goals which many of his philosophical predecessors, at least since the time of Descartes, have sought and whose pursuit was central to their ideas about the nature of philosophy. Quine thinks that *we* can have nothing more certain than our contemporary science, though to say that is far from saying that our contemporary science is certain. It is not.

Quine is sceptical in a very modest and limited way. There is always room for doubt, even in science, but that does not give rise to any sort of blanket doubt about science as a whole. It means rather that we must take a tentative attitude toward the findings of science in recognition that some of these findings will be shown to be false even if we cannot now identify which.

However, we have no choice but to accept these findings for they are the best grasp that we can *now* have on the nature of things and we shall have to rely on them in living our lives. Undoubtedly they will be improved but we live in the present, not the future, and must now get on with what is available. As he puts it in a deliberately ambiguous statement: 'I philosophize from the vantage point of our own provincial conceptual scheme and scientific epoch, true: but I know no better' *Ontological Relativity*, (p. 25).

Quine's primary concern is with problems of ontology — that is, the investigation of 'what there is'. He does not think that it is possible for the philosopher to make an independent inquiry into the kinds of things that there are in order to then use philosophical findings to judge whether science rightly identifies these things. Rather, philosophy depends on the findings of science for these are the best information we have of what kinds of things there are. It is from science that philosophy must take its lead. Quine is, in fact, quite prepared to hand some philosophical subjects over to natural science enquiry: epistemology for one.

This is not, though, to be seen as a matter of giving science pre-eminence over philosophy, in Quine's eyes, for science and philosophy are not to be distinguished in this way. They are, rather, to be looked upon as continuous with each other, joint participants in the venture of finding out how the world is made up, distinguished only by the relative generality of their respective questions, those of philosophy being the more general ones. Science proposes that there are such things as 'particles', 'waves', 'pulsars', 'radiations' among others. What variety of things can we say the world is made of, what variety of 'entities' have been identified by the scientific enterprise? The latter are the kind of questions that philosophy asks.

Let us note at this point that Quine's conception of philosophical method is that it is continuous with that of science, particularly in respect of parsimony. When we ask a question about 'what there is' we *can* if we wish have a universe made up of a vast and teeming ontology. On the other hand we can, if we want, have a much more austere one which portrays a universe made up of very few different kinds of things indeed.

Science has always pursued, where possible, as economical a conceptual scheme as it can get — or so says Quine. It seeks to make extensive and thorough use of Ockham's razor — that is, the principle that we should postulate as few entities as are necessary and no more. Quine wants to follow science's example here and to make the search for economy a prominent and dominating feature of his own approach. What we seek is the most sparing account of 'what there is', the one which requires the least variety of entities that we need.

Quine is influenced by a variety of philosophical traditions, both in ideas that he takes from them and in corrective reaction against what he sees to be their deficiencies. He has been influenced by Pragmatism, which is, to put it coarsely, the view that ideas are created to facilitate our practical transactions with the world around us and that their value, even their truth, is to be tested by their utility for us, by their effectiveness in helping us manage our relations with the world that surrounds us. Quine is certainly influenced, in his pursuit of economy, by the pragmatist standard, and whether something needs to be postulated will depend in part on the answer to the question of how useful it is to us. The desire for economy is very strong in all of Quine's thought but it does not operate unchecked. It must be played off against other considerations. Other things being equal, though, the ontology which requires fewer entities is always to be preferred. We will find, therefore, that Quine's ontology contains things which he only very reluctantly admits, entities he would rather dispense with but which cannot, without great inconvenience, be disposed of.

Another respect in which philosophy's method differs from that of science is that it does not involve us in direct investigation of the world. Science gets to work trying to discover things, but philosophy investigates language. It does not investigate language rather than the world. Quine firmly rejects any suggestion that its findings are findings about language and insists that what he is doing involves the investigation of the nature of the world through the investigation of language. Its method is that which he calls 'semantic ascent'. Inquiries are moved 'up' a level and instead of examining things directly we examine, instead, how we talk about things. We do this on the principle that there is much to be learned about things through the investigation of how we talk about them. It is a matter, therefore, of philosophy having a different method from science rather than a different subject matter. The aim of investigations in both, after all, is to discover what there is. But neither can claim to discover what there is in a theory-independent way. Quine accepts that we only determine what there is according-to-one-theory-or-another and different theories can assume or require different kinds of things.

Quine *is* a relativist, although this does nothing to undermine his confidence in our science. As has been suggested above, he acknowledges that there is no single right answer to the question 'what is there?' because how satisfactory one answer is going to be depends on what kinds of things we can manage without and what kinds of things we cannot dispense with. For example, the concern with the foundations of mathematics raises the question 'do numbers exist'? From a philosophical point of view, looking for as restricted an ontology as we can get, we might well want to 'dispose' of numbers because they give us all sorts of problems; allowing that they do exist might mean we shall have to allow another sort of 'entity' into our scheme — say, 'abstract objects'. However, mathematics is a central and invaluable part of our scientific knowledge, so crucial that it holds the entire thing together and therefore we shall be very loath to do anything that would require us to give up maths because pretty much everything else would go along with it. Mathematics seems to require that numbers exist and though this may be philosophically inconvenient to us, we shall have to go along with mathematics on this point. As a general question, then, 'what is there?' can only receive the answer 'whatever our theories posit' and since there are different theories we can expect that they will posit different things.

The word 'posit' is aptly chosen because we are talking about the kinds of things our theories postulate rather than those they discover. From a point of view *external* to both, there is no difference between our scientific theories with their atoms, forces etc. and the religious theories of ancient Greece with their gods. The latter are no more or less real than the former. However, we do not look at theories from outside; we look at things *through* theories within the background of one theory or another. We operate from some 'home' theory and the first and most telling difference between science and the Homeric pantheon is that science is our 'home theory'. The simple fact is, therefore, that we do believe in atoms, forces etc and *not* in the gods of Olympus. Our scientific theory posits the former and does not need the latter. There is, therefore, no reason why relativism should weaken our attachment to scientific theory since although we can see that there could be alternative theories and ontologies, we judge their adequacy from the point of view of *our* home theory, science. The question Quine is after, then, is what kind of entities must our theories posit? This involves investigating both what kinds they do posit and what kinds they have to have.

There can be no single answer to the question of the kinds of things that are posited, for what one theory may posit another may not. For example our commonsense theories about what there is centred upon and dominated by 'bodies' and the idea that we might 'do without' bodies might seem utterly bizarre and impossible. But this is just what science does (or so says Quine). Science does not need bodies for, from its point of view, these are just congeries of atoms and atoms are just concentrations of energy.

Quine is not criticising our commonsense here, for it is governed by the concerns of practical life and by the needs involved in carrying on social traffic amongst people. But it does not have a definite, coherent ontology; 'bodies' (i.e. people, tables, chairs, teapots etc.) are prominent in it but after that it is rather vague about the kinds of things there are. But commonsense has not undertaken the task to which philosophy and science have appointed themselves, namely that of constructing a coherent, systematic picture of the world and what is in it. It is with the latter that Quine concerns himself in order to see what sort of ontology a systematic and comprehensive picture of the world has to have. This amounts to a programme for the elimination of surplus entities that ordinary language might suggest to us. In turn, this amounts to changing our ways of talking.

What does all this talk about eliminating surplus entities mean? Saying, as we did in the closing of the previous paragraph, that it involves modifying our ways of talking may indicate what is involved but will hardly clarify why that method is effective nor even what it involves.

The programme of eliminating surplus entities involves the attempt to see if we can, by use of logical symbolism to formulate and reformulate things we say, 'write out' certain kinds of expressions and say what we want to without them. If we can organise the logical symbolism appropriately then we may be able to do without, for example, words which appear to refer to things but whose appearances are misleading. If so, we need make no provision for such things in our ontology. One of the tasks of philosophy-and-logic is, in Quine's proposal, to formulate a 'canonical notation' into which statements can be translated as a way of differentiating those expressions which do genuinely refer to things from those which only appear to do so.

At a very simple level, the kind of thing Quine has in mind can be illustrated by his reaction to other philosophers' concern with 'meanings'. They are puzzled as to what kind of thing meanings are. Quine just wants to object that meanings are not any kind of thing at all. When we speak of 'meanings' it may sound as if we are talking about some kind of thing but we are not. Appearances here are misleading. It is as if, says Quine, when we said we did something for someone else's sake that we were proposing that there were kinds of things called 'sakes'. A sake is not any sort of thing, and a meaning is no more a sort of thing than a sake is.

While the notion of 'meaning' has given philosophers trouble enough, there are other similar problems which have created similar convolutions in philosophical thought. One puzzle we mentioned in the Introduction was what to make of things which do not exist, like 'golden mountains' and 'unicorns'. If words stand for things, then when we say 'the golden mountain does not exist' we seem to be saying that there is something, the golden mountain. In the same breath we are also saying that there is no such thing. There is something of a paradox here, or a problem with our theory of meaning.

The trouble is with the word 'exists'. But we can say what we want to say without using the word 'exists' at all and without creating the appearance of a paradox. We can substitute 'the existential quantifier' for 'exists'. The existential quantifier is the more-or-less equivalent of 'there is' and we can say, therefore, 'There is nothing which is both a mountain and made of gold' (in symbolism, like this: $\neg(\exists x)/(x)$ (mountain) $\cup$ (x) (exists). We have said 'the golden mountain does not exist' but without involving ourselves in apparent commitment to the belief that it does. This kind of systematic exploration and recontruction of things we say through the use of logical symbolism should, we might think, enable us to avoid many of the ontological difficulties that other philosophers have faced. It is just such a hope that motivates Quine's proposal for a canonical notation.

Our language is full of expressions which, on first sight, look like the names of kinds of things. Since we know that this superficial appearance can be deceiving we shall need to decide which terms genuinely do refer to entities and which do not. We shall also want to know whether terms which look as though they refer to distinctive kinds of entities can really be translated without loss into statements about other kinds of entities. For example, if we say something like 'those curtains are red', how many kinds of things are we referring to? Are we referring to two distinct things, the curtains on the one hand and their colour on the other? Or do we refer only to one kind of thing, namely red-coloured curtains? In other words, do we need to admit 'colours' into our ontology as a distinct kind of thing? On Quine's economy principle, we should prefer the latter rather than the former, since it requires us only to recognise one kind of thing instead of two. It is this kind of investigation into the role of words in the language which is the programme for the elimination of surplus entities and it can, hopefully, be seen through our illustrations why it should be thought that learning about the structure of the language is the same as learning about the structure of reality. The employment of logical procedures and the canonical notation would settle questions about 'what there is'. The *general* answer that Quine gives to the question 'what is there?' is this: 'to be is to be the value of a variable', which means that the test for whether something exists or not is whether it can be included in a true formula to the effect that 'there is something such that it has these characteristics.' It can, that is, occupy the position of the variable (i.e. the x) in logical formulae like this: $(\exists x)/(x)(\phi)$.

It is important to remember, though, that Quine's inquiries are taking place against the background of an 'ontological relativity' with its conviction that we cannot say, in any general way, just what sorts of things there are, for what things can occupy the position of 'variable' will differ from one theory to another. The best that we can ever do is to determine the ontology of a given theory, if indeed we can do as much as this.

We have already said that Quine's relativism does not shake his confidence in our science, in which he has a firm but limited confidence. Our science and philosophy cannot give us any final statement of how things are but they do give us the best answers we have to date. While we can continue to improve upon what we now have, we are not going to be able to obtain the kind of certainty that, in the past, philosophers have sought. These convictions result from Quine's views about the relation of theory to its subject matter.

The Web of Sentences

Quine says we can have no firmer knowledge than science gives us. The knowledge that science gives us is contingent, revisable. As we noted earlier, though we cannot say which ones they are, we can be pretty sure that *some* of the things that science now tells us will have to be abandoned. We can face this prospect with equanimity and without need for panic at the thought that science *as a whole* might suddenly let us down. Science is immensely useful to us and we can rely on it in all sorts of ways.

Insistence on this, that there can be no knowledge superior to that of current science at any given time, means that knowledge is essentially revisable. We cannot, in Quine's view, say which parts of our current science will be revised, nor which will not. In this connection Quine departs radically from a great many of his philosophical predecessors, especially those who sought to identify some statements which were 'immune to revision' and which we could be completely confident must be true. The task of epistemology, as traditionally conceived, is futile. The quest for guarantees of certainty cannot succeed and instead we must reconceive the task of epistemology as a part of psychology rather than philosophy. It is an inquiry into how we do come to know the world to the extent we do rather than into whether and how we can acquire certainties. Epistemology is to be naturalised, transformed into empirical inquiry. Our knowledge is to be investigated just the same way as any other scientific topic.

Quine has ideas about the kind of psychology that will be involved. His own position is a materialist one. There are in nature only the physical phenomena which the natural sciences describe. There are no mental phenomena as such. As far as he is concerned, materialism means a behavioural psychology, the study of the actions and reactions of human beings, not the operations of mental entities.

Central to the psychological approach to epistemology will be the investigation of the acquisition of language considered as a system of behavioural tendencies to react to certain sorts of stimuli in certain ways. The essential problem is to understand how, from the very minimal input of stimulation that the human organism receives from the physical environment, it is possible for us to construct our rich and complex theories of that world. As far as physics is concerned, there is a number of ways in which the surface of the organism is bombarded by physical stimulations — the irradiation of the eyes with light photons, the intrusion of gases into the nasal passages, the vibration of sound waves within the ears, the abrasion of nerve endings by congeries of atoms. The only evidence that we can have for our theories about the external world must come to us through the senses. Quine is enough of an empiricist to insist on this. Whatever kind of knowledge it can yield us cannot, however, be any more certain than the findings of science.

Quine's rejection of the traditional philosophical quest for certainty is not unreasoned. He has arguments for thinking that we cannot do better than science. He gives some of them in his attack on what he sees as two key 'dogmas' of empiricism. He denies that certainty can be sought from either of the sources to which philosophers have often looked, namely that which we can know independently of all experience, the *a priori*, and that of which we can be certain because it comes directly from experience, the *a posteriori*.

As we saw in Chapter 1, these two terms are often associated with different types of truth. *Analytic* truths are, crudely speaking, those which are incapable of being false. They differ from *synthetic* ones whose truth is dependent on contingent facts and which are, therefore, capable of being false. The latter are the kinds of truths that science deals in and are not certain beyond all possibility of doubt. However sound some synthetic truth may seem we may have overlooked or been ignorant of some crucial consideration. Analytic truths do not depend on contingent matters, they are true come what may and they cannot be affected by any factual revisions, discoveries or recalculations. Thus, a synthetic truth would be of the sort that tells us that the earth is 93 million miles from the sun — we can easily imagine things happening to show this was false. But an analytic truth, for example a mathematical proposition such as '2+2=4', does not depend on facts in this way and we cannot imagine what could possibly happen to show that 2+2 in fact equalled 3 or 33, not 4.

Characteristic of analytic truths, if not definitive of them, are those which are regarded as 'true by virtue of meaning'. Thus, 'occulists are eye doctors' is true just because in our language 'occulist' means 'eye doctor'. This truth is dependent on nothing other than the relation of meaning obtaining between two sets of words, 'occulist' and 'eye doctor' in our language. Quine does not agree that there is a distinction between 'questions of fact' and 'questions of meaning', nor is he prepared to accept that the distinction between analytic and synthetic truths can be sustained.

The trouble is, Quine thinks, that philosophers have thought that the truth of sentences is something to be settled for each sentence separately and singly. No matter how natural and transparent this may seem, Quine follows Pierre Duhem in thinking that sentences are parts of wholes, of language and theories, and that questions about the truth and meaning of any one cannot be answered without regard for their relation to the system in which they are implicated. Quine is, without qualm, an holist. Where Frege thought that the unit of meaning was the sentence, Quine holds that it is the language.

He makes an analogy with a web. The spider's web is anchored at some points by the attachment of filaments to supporting objects, but the great part of the web is not directly attached to those supports — instead, the filaments are attached to one another. A web is structured in that it has a centre and a periphery. But it is a unit. Something which affects one part of the web will affect, in greater or lesser degree, the other parts associated with it. If a fly lands on the web then its weight will distort the part on which it lands in a more accentuated way than more remote regions. None the less its impact will create perturbations throughout the web; it is these which alert the spider and it will induce distortions in the configuration of the whole web and not just the locality in which it is entangled. The web of sentences which make up our theories of the world are structured very like this, or so Quine insists.

At some points the sentences which we will take as true are pretty directly related to our experience as in, say, 'there's a red patch in front of my eyes'. Others are more remote, as in 'two plus two equals four', which doesn't depend directly on one's own experience at all. Still, our beliefs are linked together, as part of an articulated structure. The relationship which they have to our experiences must be affected as much by their interdependence as by the direct linkage to experience. Just like the spider's web, much of their organisation is produced as a result of their interrelation with one another, not just the experiences which may 'anchor' them. If our beliefs are structured in this systemic way, then the alteration of one of them must, surely, affect all the others. It means a change in the configuration of the whole web and must, therefore, affect the character of other beliefs, perhaps ones which are, within the web, very remote from it.

Some beliefs we can give up relatively easily and with minimal effect on the system as a whole. If someone says 'that stick in the water is bent' and then takes it out of the water and finds it is not bent, then giving up the belief about the stick will not have much effect on our system. Little needs to be changed, and indeed the mistake itself can be explained in terms of other parts of our belief systems — the refracting effects of water on light, the consequent creation of an illusion etc. However, if someone proposes that we should abandon '2+2=4', presumably all our arithmetic would have to be altered too in compensating ways. Such a drastic re-adjustment of arithmetic would have far reaching consequences in mathematics and far beyond, into all those areas of life where we have incorporated mathematics into other activities. It would require much more of us to alter this latter kind of belief — if, of course, we could alter it at all.

Quine thinks there is nothing to prevent us making such alterations, though the inconvenience of trying is enough to prevent us making the attempt unless it is forced on us. There is a difference between analytic and synthetic statements, or what are taken as such, but it is a difference relative to their places in our system of sentences. It is a difference of degree, not a difference in kind. There is no distinction between statements which can be revised and statements which it is impossible to revise, though there is one between those we are quite willing to revise and those that we are more than unwilling to alter. There is a difference in the intensity of our commitment to different statements. The fact is we are loath to alter some because we are so committed to them, not that we are committed to them because they are in principle unalterable.

The argument against the analytic–synthetic distinction maintains that there are no statements which are immune from revision. There are some to which we are more strongly committed, but the difference is one of degree only. The analytic–synthetic distinction is also assumed to segregate statements which are true in virtue of meaning from those which are true in virtue of fact. For example, the contrast would be between a statement such as 'occulists are eye-doctors', which is true because 'occulist' means 'eye-doctor', and 'occulists are, on average, 40 years of age', the truth of which depends on how old, on average, occulists actually are. However, Quine attacks the analytic–synthetic distinction in this respect as well. Questions of fact and meaning are thoroughly entwined. One cannot distinguish statements which are true purely in virtue of meaning from those true purely in virtue of fact. Suppose that we believe that the statement 'all swans are white' is true in virtue of meaning. The word 'swan' means 'a white bird of the genus *cygnus*'. An intrepid explorer discovers some birds that are like swans in all important respects except they are black. We could decide that the facts show our belief that all swans are white is false. There are black swans. Or, we could decide to continue defining swans as white birds and so conclude there are no black swans. We could simply say, whatever they are, these black birds are not swans. The discovery of the birds does not, of itself, force either solution upon us.

The point about a web-like structure is that there are many different ways in which its configuration can be altered to cope with a particular impact upon it. The same goes for the system of sentences which make up our theories. If something happens which 'goes against' our theory we can alter our existent beliefs in different ways to respond and adapt to it.

The important point, then, is that the facts, our experience of the world, do not impose any single theory on us, nor do they impose any particular response on us in adjusting our theories to meet any incongruous fact. We can deal with any such in very different ways. In consequence there is a limit to the certainty of our knowledge which is set because our theory is underdetermined by the evidence of experience.

It was the hope of some empiricists that the evidence of our senses would provide certain knowledge, since there could be no doubt about those things which resulted from the unmediated contact of our sensory organs with the external world. The point of Quine's holism is that it undermines this source of security too, for the sentences which report even our most direct sensory experiences of the physical environment are also part of the system and can be adjusted to provide a suitable response to difficulties in other parts of the system. The fact that we have seen something before our very eyes might seem like the sort of thing that we could not doubt, or call into question but we are, of course, willing to withdraw claims to have seen things before us, to let the judgement of our senses be overridden by the requirements of the theory. Even seeing a Uri Geller bend spoons, we may still prefer to maintain that there is some trick because what we appear to be seeing goes against the laws of physics as we know them. We are determined to stick by the latter rather than believe the so-called 'evidence of our senses'.

Quine is thoroughgoingly empiricist in insisting that we have only the evidence of our senses as evidence for our theories. However, he insists those theories must go beyond that evidence and cannot be delimited by it. His point is about the nature of the relationship between theories and the sensory evidence. Theories are 'under-determined' by the evidence, that is there will always be more than one logically equivalent theory with respect to any given body of evidence we have. The simple reason for this is, as shown above, logical or evidential grounds. This is not a matter of there being insufficient evidence available at any one point in time to decide between them. This is a situation which arises however much evidence we have. The simple reason for this is, as we have shown above, that we can accommodate the same facts in very different ways by more or less elaborate alterations of the configuration of the theory.

Of course, the fact that logically and evidentially two theories might be the same does not mean we should be wholly unable to choose one over the other. One might be vastly more complex and inconvenient than another or there might be other pragmatic considerations which would make one preferable to the other. Undoubtedly inertia can figure here. We will remain attached to a theory because we already hold it, and would not just abandon it on a whim in favour of some other more or less equivalent one. We should stress, it is not that *any* theory will fit a given body of data but neither is it the case that *only one* will.

Indeterminacy and Inscrutability

We do not, of course, compare theories with each other from 'without'. We are always operating from within one theory or another. Before we can compare some other theory with our own we have to understand that other theory, we have to translate it into the terms of our theory. It is this which sets up some crucial constraints on the extent to which we can allow another theory to differ radically from our own. The question of translation into and out of incompatible theories and languages now arises. The business of translation, like that of the more general work of theorising of which it is a part, at least on Quine's account of the matter, is open to alternative solutions between which, on evidential and logical grounds, there will be no basis for choice. The limits on the very different solutions which might be given to these problems will depend as much on the nature of the language we are translating into as much as that of the language we are translating from.

We must remember Quine's concern is to say what ontology a theory has. The question to be asked is if we can really tell how someone's ontology differs from our own. There are some significant obstacles in the way of this.

Consider a situation of 'radical translation', the kind in which someone seeks to translate for the first time a language with which he has no familiarity whatsoever. The sort of situation, in fact, that would be encountered by the Martian who discovered the Earth and sought to speak to one of its inhabitants. There would be an irreducible element of uncertainty — so Quine argues — in the attempt to establish that this was the right translation and that the ontology of the language (say English) had been correctly identified.

It is tempting to think that in translating we are trying to identify the meanings of words, to find words in the 'home' language which mean the same as those in the 'alien' language. This idea is misleading, though, for language is a system and we are seeking not to match the meaning of words but to align two entire systems. Attempts to fix how this bit of the whole is to be translated must involve assumptions about how this bit fits into the system as a whole. We are back in the situation that we were with respect to the establishment of the truth of sentences. We can achieve very different solutions for a particular sentence depending on how we compensate for it in the rest of the system. Therefore, we can always give very different translations of the same sentence, so different that on one translation it will be true, on another false, depending on how we construe the system of which it is a part.

It might seem, though, that if we get into a direct face to face situation with a native speaker and interrogate him sufficiently skilfully and systematically that we shall be able to determine, at least, what *he* means by the words he uses. Even here, however, Quine is not optimistic. There is the inscrutability of reference to contend with. Take the famous example of the word 'gavagai' which is part of an imaginary alien language. Suppose a native speaker produces this in response to the linguist's interrogation and in conjunction with the appearance of rabbits. We may feel confident in translating this as 'rabbit' but this will be a confidence arising from the dependence of our own language on the notion of 'body' as an integral and central part. How can we be sure that their ontology is like ours?

We cannot. Beyond a certain point we cannot tell whether they have an ontology like ours. They could have a very different one and it would not make a material difference to our transactions with them and translations from their language. What if, say, they did not have a notion of 'body' at all but thought of everything as fragments of a substance, such that they think of rabbits as part of 'rabbit stuff' and hence mean by 'gavagai' something like 'here's some more rabbit stuff'. Whenever it would be in order for us to say 'there's a rabbit' it would be equally in order for them to say 'there's more rabbit stuff' and so there would be no variation in our respective patterns of linguistic behaviour to betray the fact we are using the words rabbit and gavagai to refer to very different kinds of things indeed. The reference of an alien word is inscrutable. We cannot tell for certain what kinds of things it is applied to. The evidence that we have for translations is the linguistic behaviour of native speakers and that is all the evidence we can possibly have. The noises they make and the reactions they produce are what we try to structure through our translational theory but of course different theories will be compatible with however much of that behaviour we investigate. Hence it is unavoidable that different systems of translation will be possible.

In brief, we can say that Quine holds that translating will involve the translator in some leaps and some guesswork about how things fit together and that his decisions about which ways to proceed will depend on his assumptions about what a plausible translation could be, about what kind of ontologies people can hold. Translators can vary on these matters and there is no right way of deciding, if they do come up with equivalent systems, which is the 'right' one.

Bringing it all back home, Quine notes that the situation of radical translation arises within our 'home' language. The one who must learn a first language — the child — is as much an alien as the imaginary Martian in crucially relevant ways and must learn to 'translate' its way into our language, alien as that is to it. There is, therefore, logical room for doubt that we speakers of a 'common' language do have the same ontology underlying it. The location of such uncertainties does not cause Quine sleeplessness though, because, of course, they are differences which do not make any practical difference to our interrelations. The whole point about these variations, if they exist, is that they are undetectable. It is the pattern of behaviour dispositions that matters and there is no way of telling from such patterns, with absolute certainty, whether someone has the same or a different ontology to ours.

Truth and Meaning

Donald Davidson has conducted two different, though related, sets of inquiries. He has collected the numerous essays which to date, make up the bulk of his philosophical writings, in two collections whose names give guidance as to the areas of inquiry they cover. The first, *Essays on Actions and Events*, indicates a concern for the philosophy of explanation, particularly the nature of causal explanation, and concentrates on two problematic areas, the explanation of events in general, and one troublesome sort of these, namely actions.

We shall say relatively little about this part of Davidson's writings, though we should note that in these studies he attempts to develop and defend a 'materialist' conception of the mind, one called 'anomalous monism', which we will consider below.

The other collection, *Inquiries into Truth and Interpretation*, is the one which is most directly linked into the arguments that have been developed in connection with Quine. We can, indeed, read Davidson's arguments about these matters as exploring what would be involved in creating the kind of 'translation manual' that Quine envisages. What form would a theory of meaning for natural language take? Davidson asks.

He is much influenced by Quine and is no less motivated by the consideration of parsimony than is Quine. In particular, he is every bit as wary of postulating entities called 'meanings'. He thinks that one can get a very great deal of what is wanted from a 'theory of meaning' without mentioning meaning at all and by going instead for a theory of truth. If one can say what it is for a sentence to be true, then one has said a great deal about what it means. As we saw in the Introduction, Frege thought the connection so close that to know what a sentence means *is* to know the conditions under which it is true.

Let us stress that Davidson's inquiry is into sentences, not words. Like many other philosophers after Frege, including Quine, Wittgenstein and Ryle, he thinks that sentences are the primary foci for the study of meaning. The doctrine that a word has meaning only in the context of a sentence may seem counter-intuitive but many important philosophers have found it persuasive, and for good reasons. As far as Davidson's inquiries are concerned, truth is something that can be predicated only of sentences and not of words. An inquiry into truth is an inquiry into the truth conditions of sentences. Davidson thinks that the resources required for construction of the kind of theory that he has in mind are fairly readily available. There is no real obstacle to saying what the nearest practical thing to a theory of meaning might look like. It would look like Alfred Tarski's theory of truth for formal languages.

In talking about 'theories of meaning' and 'theories of truth' we need to be careful to recognise that very different things can be identified by such titles. We might ask for a theory of truth in the sense that we want to know what it is for something to be true and what it is that makes it possible for some things to be true and some things not, what the bases for establishing truth are and so forth. Tarski and Davidson do have a theory of truth, in that sense, a variant of a quite familiar kind, the 'correspondence theory'.

When we sketched Tarski's theory in the Introduction we showed that he thinks that truth requires correspondence in a relation which he calls 'satisfaction' between sequences of symbols and arrange-ments of objects. Davidson also supposes that it is a correspondence between sentences and the world which makes for the truth, though his conception is of a direct correspondence between language and the world and is, therefore, intended to be more economical ontologically speaking than those correspondence theories which suppose that the correspondence is between 'concepts' and the world or between language and 'facts'. There is no need to introduce such 'entities' as concepts and facts into the theory. One can simply say, for example, that it is true that my skin is warm if my skin is warm. There is a direct correspondence between language, what we say, and the world, how things are.

One implication we can point to, by the by, is this: if we do not need to talk of 'concepts', then it can be anticipated that Davidson is going to be extremely impatient with arguments in the social sciences about the problematic relation between conceptual schemes. On his view, this is a red herring. However, at the moment it is the theory of truth that is under consideration.

The thing that Tarski was after, as a theory of truth, was what we can crudely call 'axiomatisation'. The most familiar form of this can be found in Euclid's geometry, where a deductive system was constructed from a series of 'axioms' about the properties of lines and angles, and from which a whole series of theorems about geometrical arrangements, such as the proportions of triangles, circles and the rest could be derived. Tarski sought a theory for formal languages of this kind. He wanted to be able to deduce, from a set of basic axioms, which of the sentences of a given formal language could be true. The objective of such a theory is, then, less to inquire into what makes sentences true — that is, why some are and some are not — and more to find a way of enumerating the true sentences of a language.

Davidson then takes a controversial step. He proposes to use Tarski's approach in the analysis of natural language. In doing this, he goes against Tarski's own claims that his technique cannot be used in the case of natural language. Tarski recognised that natural language does not comprise a coherent system as formal languages do and that the attempt to systematise it around some basic general principles would lead to paradoxes which are of course anathema to logic.

Davidson does not deny Tarski's claim but does not see it as providing an obstacle to making use of the resources of formal analysis to make progress, and perhaps considerable progress, in the analysis of *parts* of a natural language. Davidson's is very much a piece-meal strategy, one of trying to tackle specific problems and to formalise bits of natural language. The fact that we may eventually come up against paradoxes does not mean that we cannot make such progress.

The crucial part of Tarski's theory is 'convention T'. This looks like something absolutely trivial. And in one sense it is. This triviality is not, however, a disadvantage. From the vantage point of someone like Tarski or Davidson the fact that it is virtually self-evident and pretty nearly uncontroversial is a virtue. Take a statement like 'snow is white'. If we ask what are the conditions under which this is true we can say:

'Snow is white' is true if and only if snow is white.

As we say, this looks completely trivial but if one is looking for a way of systematically identifying the truth conditions of a language, then it has the very great advantage of being easily converted into a more general formula. For 'snow is white' on the left hand side, substitute 's' and for 'snow is white' on the right hand side, substitute 'p' and we have:

's' is true if and only if 'p'.

Into that formula one can insert many other possibilities. 'Grass is green' if and only if grass is green, 'atoms are heavy' if and only if atoms are heavy, and so on.

In the eyes of logic, language is a combinatorial business. The meaning and/or truth of the things that we say in it are a product of the combination of parts into wholes. The simple formula can be easily developed into more complex structures. In a simple example, we can give the truth conditions of the sentence 'snow is white and grass is green'. It is true if and only if snow is white and grass is green, and so on and on.

Davidson — in a way that parallels the independent and different inquiries of the linguist, Noam Chomsky — is arguing that the striking thing about human languages is that they enable the interpretation of quite new sentences. Having a combinatorial nature, they produce unprecedented formations which, none the less, native speakers can understand. One minimum requirement of any theory of natural language will have to be, then, that it will provide for 'creativity', for the production and comprehension of quite new combinations of elements. One way to account for this possibility is to include 'recursive' devices in it, things that can be applied over and over again, for this will ensure that we can go on producing combinations endlessly if there is no limit to the number of times we can carry out the same operation. Tarski's formula provides just this sort of device. We can go on and build up the 'string' with 'grass is green, snow is white and ice is cold' is true if and only if etc. A theory of this form, at a very elemental level, can meet one of the requirements that any theory must apparently fulfil.

It might be objected that this kind of theory is not up to dealing with certain sorts of cases. Whilst one can give the truth conditions of 'snow is white' easily enough, it is not so easy to say what they are for, say, 'Hitler could have won the war if he had not invaded Russia'. Such a charge would, however, justify, rather than undermine Davidson's case for working with 'convention T' at least at this stage of things, for it disposes of the complaint of triviality, showing it to be misplaced. In Davidson's view, the same method will work on all cases. For some simple basic ones, the results are obvious and trivial, but for many others they are anything but. He can respond that we are only at the beginning of an effort to exploit Tarski's approach and cannot expect it to tackle tough cases straight away.

We are not just interested in constructing 'T sentences' for our own language, but would want, also, to do this for languages other than our own. This would mean giving truth conditions for that language in our language, as in the case of:

'Schnee ist weiss' if and only if snow is white.

Again problems of meaning can be replaced by problems of truth. Finding out what people in another language mean can be obtained — to most important intents and purposes — by giving the truth conditions of their expressions in our language. A kind of translation is involved here and thus the problem of meaning is closely linked to those of truth and translation.

We know, however, that Quine has raised some serious doubts about the possibility of determinate translation. Davidson is aware of these. If we want to give the truth conditions of a language other than our own, then we have to have established that, for example, people speaking German do use 'Schnee ist weiss' in such a way that it is true if and only if snow is indeed white. The T sentences give a method for making translations, but they do not give us an answer to the question of whether our translations are right. Can we ever be confident of this, or must there always be some fundamental doubt?

Ian Hacking identifies what we might call 'the Goldilocks options' in philosophical 'fairy stories' about translation: too much, too little and just right. He has in mind the case of Quine, who thinks there are too many possible alternative translations for us to single out any right one. This would be a 'too much' view. On the other hand, there is Feyerabend (cf. Chapter 10) who represents the 'too little' conception, since he does not think that we can manage any adequate translation between two different languages. Between those possibilities, there could be the 'just right' position: that we *can* settle on one right translation. Davidson does not think of himself as a 'just righter', but Hacking maintains that, on his own arguments, he ought to be. However, whether Hacking is, in the end, correct, Davidson does not think of himself as holding a 'just right' view because making translations will involve a lot of assumption and guesswork since we are dealing with things which can be 'played off' against each other in varying combinations.

Two things which can be played off in this way are beliefs and actions. Davidson thinks that actions are explained as a product of beliefs and wants (or desires). Suppose we want to show why someone eats something which we regard as absolutely revolting. We can say that they wanted to eat something good and that they believe something different from us — namely that this is delicious. On the other hand, we can say that they wanted to eat something good and that they mistakenly believed that the thing they ate was delicious. In this case, they share our belief that things of the kind they ate are revolting but they made a mistake. Or again, we could attribute to them different wants: perhaps they did believe that this thing was revolting to eat but wanted to see if eating it had harmful effects. They decided to eat it anyway and disregarded its unpleasantness. Which action they are performing depends upon what combination of wants and desires we attribute to them. Speech, being a form of human action, interpretation of the sayings of other humans will involve us in assigning to them wants and beliefs. In addition, if someone says 'snow is white' and we are to translate what they say as being true if and only if snow *is* white then we shall be attributing to them the want to tell us something true, the belief that 'snow' is this kind of stuff, that 'white' is this kind of colour and so forth.

Now, suppose that we are in the plight of 'radical translation'. We are attempting to come to grips with the practices, including language, of a people who are completely alien to us, with whom we have nothing in common. We shall want to decide what they are doing and what they mean by their words. How are we to do this?

We need, as we have said, to interpret meaning against the background of belief, but we do not know what these people believe. How are we to establish what they believe? Through their actions and sayings. But we cannot identify these unless we know something about their beliefs. We seem to be in an impossible position, but there is a way out. It is, says Davidson, to hold belief and solve for meaning. In other words, we should suppose, pending evidence to the contrary, that a great many of the aliens' beliefs are the same as ours, and assume that they hold a great mass of true beliefs (i.e. ones which are the same as those we hold true). We are compelled, if we are to get anywhere with the work of translation, to adopt what Davidson, following Neil Wilson, called the 'principle of charity'. We shall simply have to assume that there is a broad background of shared beliefs common to us and the aliens against which any significantly different beliefs will show up.

What about the possibility, though, that we shall have thoroughly misinterpreted the aliens, that they have a different conceptual scheme from ours and that we have simply and wrongly imposed ours on them? As we noted above, if one does not suppose that language involves 'concepts' then one does not need to take arguments about alternative conceptual schemes seriously. Davidson amusingly remarks that he sees no difference between those who argue for many different conceptual schemes amongst human beings and those who argue for just one. Monotheists are just as much in the grip of religion as polytheists. The idea of total failure of translation, he says, makes little sense. If there was some pattern of alien behaviour from which we could not make any translation, why should we want to suppose that this was language behaviour in the first place? Putting it crudely, translatability is a criterion for something's being a language. As for partial failure of translation, well this only occurs in the context of substantial success in translation.

In addition, Davidson argues that the idea of conceptual schemes and of possible alternative ones derives from what he calls the 'third dogma' of empiricism, that there is a distinction between interpretive scheme and uninterpreted content. If we dispense with this distinction it may be that empiricism is so divested of dogmas that it is also deprived of distinctive content but we avoid the difficulties that arise in connection with different possible alternative schemes.

It seems, then, that Davidson is settling for translation which is reasonable rather than right, in the terms in which such things are argued about. We certainly cannot eliminate indeterminacy from translation. Remember that Davidson is no less a holist than Quine and no less concerned with the development of a system of translation for languages as wholes and the best we can hope for in support of any system will be (as Davidson himmself calls them) the 'thin bits of evidence' provided by people's verbal behaviour. What that evidence can show must, as we have just argued, very much depend upon a good deal of interpretive work for, of course, when we come to identify specific actions and sayings we shall not have to make some broad assumptions about commonality of belief but will have to make some pretty refined and differentiated attributions of belief to cases for which there cannot be a unique solution.

Reference and Necessity

Quine and Davidson stand amongst those who consider sentences the important unit of language. Those to whom we now turn our attention are prepared to question this and seek to return the argument to a discussion of how words and the world are related. They do so principally through the consideration of the problem of reference.

Hilary Putnam, who has played a very prominent part in this debate, sees the emphasis on sentences as counter-intuitive, and unhelpfully so. It goes against what we know about how language is learned and understood. We teach people words and not sentences; people ask for and are given the meaning of words, not sentences.

However, this is not simply a reversion to the classical positions, for Putnam, Saul Kripke and others have been thoroughly critical of the traditional theory of the relationship of reference.

In brief, the problem is how, when we use a word to refer to something, is it possible for us to single out the thing that we refer to? Suppose that someone says 'Socrates is wise'. He says something of someone, Socrates, but who is it that he is speaking about here? He is speaking of some human being, but which one? It should, by the way, be apparent that questions about reference are not a million miles from questions about truth and about analyticity. First, the truth of 'Socrates is wise' will depend on who Socrates is. Then, second, there are questions about whether any of the things we say of Socrates are necessarily true of him or whether they could be contingent. Can we truly say, for example, 'Socrates is wise but he could have been stupid'?

This latter kind of problem is given a particular sharpness by the problem of 'modal logic', that area of logic concerned with the analysis of notions of necessity and possibility, such as notions of must, might, could and so forth. The development of this has involved talk about 'possible worlds', a notion which has caused difficulty and controversy. In this world Napoleon retreated from Moscow, but logically it is possible that he might have gone to take that city. There is, in other words, a logically possible world in which Napoleon conquered Moscow. Necessity has come, therefore, to be construed as something which must be true in all possible worlds.

A key theory which occupied the field prior to these recent developments is one we shall call 'the theory of indirect reference', because it believed that our reference to something was made by way of some description of it. Thus, if we describe Socrates as the ancient Greek philosopher whose doings were recorded by Plato, then it is to the person who was the ancient Greek philosopher whose doings were recorded by Plato that we refer. What, however, if our beliefs about Socrates are wrong? On the indirect theory, if we do have mistaken beliefs about someone or something then we fail to refer when we use the expression. So, if we believe that apart from being a philosopher, Plato was a champion wrestler and we say 'Plato was a champion wrestler' we will not *actually* be referring to the real Plato, who was only a philosopher. The new theory, to show the contrast, can be called 'the theory of direct reference' (sometimes called 'the causal theory of reference'), though Hilary Putnam would prefer to call it 'the social cooperation plus contribution of the environment theory'. It puts forward a simple claim, that the connection between a name and that to which it refers is made by an act of bestowal, the giving of the name to whatever it refers. We can, thus, refer to Socrates because that is his name (ignoring problems and difficulties arising from translation etc). The name has been attached to the thing, the thing has been 'dubbed' with the name and this connection, once made, can be preserved and passed on through a chain of communication between users of the name. Those who give Socrates his name introduce him to other people by it, they in turn tell others about this person and so forth, each of them using the word to refer directly to the person who is called by that name.

Proper names and those of 'natural kinds' (such as cat, tiger, sheep) are, on this theory and in Kripke's terminology, 'rigid designators'. That is, they stand for the same person, thing or kind of thing in all possible worlds. Thus, though it is the case that Napoleon might, in some other possible world, have conquered Moscow, or in yet some other one never have gone there at all, it is also the case that it is *Napoleon* that we are talking about in each of these imagined worlds. It is *this particular man* whose actual and possible accomplishments we are talking about. The question is, what makes Napoleon the same man in all these cases? In effect, it is his flesh and blood, the genetically provided substance which comprised this particular human being. Napoleon could perhaps have had a different history and career and still have been the same man, but he could not have been this and born of different parents. The connection between the name Napoleon and the man was made by giving that name to this particular product of that particular genetic combination.

The same argument goes for natural kind terms. In some other possible world gold might look blue because of the conditions of light. But the point must be that if our comparison between this actual and some possible world is to be a comment on what gold might be, then it has to be the case that it is the same kind of stuff that we are talking about. Gold has to have the same physico-chemical constitution in other possible worlds as it has in this. The giving of a name to a natural kind is of course different to the giving of it to an individual, because the person who coins the name 'gold' or 'tiger' gives it to a sample or instance of the kind. Thus, someone who coins the term 'gold' attaches to it these chunks of gold in the first instance. But it is attached to them as samples of this kind of thing, this kind of substance. Thus, gold has to be the same stuff in different worlds, whatever makes it that kind of stuff.

We can see that the notion of 'essence' is being reintroduced into philosophical discourse, despite the fact that the attempt to locate essential characteristics has been notably unsuccessful (cf. particularly Wittgenstein, Chapter 8). Certainly the sorts of characteristics such as colour and texture and reaction to heating, which the coiners of the term may have used to single out the sample of gold and by which they may have identified all other samples, will not do as essential characteristics. We can imagine cases in which the appearance might be different, the reaction to heating altered because of changes in other conditions. These will not do to identify essential characteristics. What is essential is the nature of the stuff, the physico-chemical constitution of the material because when we talk about how gold might react to light, heat etc. in some other possible world we are talking about the behaviour of this kind of stuff and we cannot say that in some possible world gold might have had the physico-chemical constitution of water and still have been gold.

The direct theory, then, goes for origins and essence. What links a word and a person, thing or kind is some initial act of 'dubbing' of either individual or sample, and what the name is linked to is whatever it is that makes the individual or sample the kind of stuff it is, its essence. However, it could be objected that those who give the name 'gold' to an original sample of this stuff do not know what makes it that kind of stuff. They do not know what the physico-chemical constitution of gold, water etc. are. This is right, and is one of the challenging implications of the theory of direct reference, that scientists discover essences and in so doing they discover necessary relationships. They discover what it is that makes something what it is, what makes it what it has to be.

There is something of an ironic situation here. The proponents of this theory agree with Quine that we can have no knowledge stronger than science. However, Quine claimed that we cannot have any necessary truths, whereas these new theorists are claiming that one cannot have stronger knowledge than science because it discovers the very strongest kinds of truths, namely necessary ones.

Those who give a thing or kind its name in the first place are not aware of the physico-chemical constitution of the thing that they identify by it, but their capacity to single out other samples of it is dependent on the operation of the unknown laws of nature or the unknown constitution of the stuff. We can single out gold by its colour, texture, response to heat and so forth in our world just because the laws of nature provide that such substance reacts to light, heat etc.

in these characteristic ways. This perhaps makes it clear why Putnam thinks that the cumbersome name for the theory is the best, because it emphasises both the extent to which the use of a name depends upon the socially cooperative process of communication by which a name's use is passed on and preserved and also the extent to which the capacity for this cooperative process to work is dependent on the 'contribution of the environment', that is, the operation of its yet-to-be-discovered laws on its yet-to-be-discovered constitution. Science has, in important respects, found out at last what we have always meant by 'gold'.

The direct theory of reference goes along, then, with a realist view of science and offers, in Putnam's view at least, an answer to those like Kuhn and Feyerabend (cf. Chapter 10) who argue that there is no continuity between scientific theories. The latter argue this because they share the assumptions of the theory of indirect reference, supposing that reference is governed by our beliefs and ideas of what things are. Thus, if one person talks about electrons and has certain beliefs about what they are and another person talks about electrons and has very different beliefs, then they are referring to very different things. Thus, 'electron' in one theory is just different from 'electron' in another theory and so after a scientific revolution, even if the same terms have been retained, then different things are being talked about.

However, the direct theory eliminates this difficulty. If people before and after a revolution use the same words the fact that they had different beliefs is irrelevant because the beliefs do not 'fix the reference' of the term. Even though they had very different beliefs about the things they were talking about they were, none the less, talking about the same things — namely electrons. Putnam thinks one can go somewhat further in opposition to the Kuhn/Feyerabend emphasis on discontinuity in scientific history and reject their idea that in scientific history there is displacement of one theory by another incomparable one. In a mature science, he argues, there is convergence. He means by this that when a theory is replaced by a successor then it is the case that the displaced theory will not be counted wrong but as a limiting case of the successor theory: it will be incorporated into it.

Putnam is a realist, but he is not what he terms a 'metaphysical realist'. This is one who insists that the world exists wholly independently of our way of talking about it, the sort of realism that was associated with classical empiricism.

Putnam's account of reference, however, does not exclude but actively incorporates a connection between the nature of things and the way we talk of them. When we dub a sample of stuff 'water' then we do so with the intention of using the term generally for this kind of stuff, whatever makes it the kind of stuff it is. Given our intentions then 'water' cannot have been anything other than H_2O but in talking about what water has to be we have to link that to our intentions and practices in using the word. Putnam maintains metaphysical realism is the product of the deep conviction that there can be only one true description of the world, that which would be given in something *like* the terms that physics now uses. There might have to be alterations in our physics but no fundamental revision of the whole conception is expected or thought possible. The supposition is that causation is 'built into' nature itself, in that it is the character and constitution of things which makes them interact as they do.

However, it is just this idea of causation as a physical relationship that Putnam wants to question. He wants to suggest that though the determination of a causal connection has to do with our understanding of the nature of the character and constitution of things, the shape of a causal explanation is as much determined by the relevances of our search. That is, what counts as giving a causal explanation depends upon the background information that we have against which we shall, in the first place, find things puzzling and in terms of which, in the second, specify what it is about any occurrence that is to be explained and from which, in the third, we shall derive our standards against which sufficiency of information will be assessed. In the very simplest example, if there is a fire in our house and we ask for an explanation and are told there was oxygen in the house, we shall not be satisfied that the cause has been identified, though we shall not either be suggesting that there would have been a fire without oxygen. The availability of oxygen to make things burn is something we take for granted (is a background condition). We shall therefore want as 'the cause' of our fire something like the leaving of a lighted cigarette, the exposure of the electric wiring etc.

Body, Mind and Social Science

The fundamental tendencies of the kind of philosophy we have been outlining here would appear to be congenial to those who are concerned to emphasise the objectivity and realism of the social sciences. Certainly, Quine is inclined to suppose that the natural sciences tell us what there is and they tell us that there are only material things. He further takes the view that the natural sciences are seeking to identify structures that are given in nature, that they are describing features of the distribution of particles, forces etc. within the universe. These views, plus his conviction that there is only the one kind of knowledge — that of science — would seem to suggest that he would have to argue for the unity of natural and social science. And he does, in so far as he recommends and adopts behaviourist strategies in the examination of human doings, especially language.

However, appearances in this respect are misleading, for Quine's are dualist views about the natural sciences and the social studies. What the latter can generate does not, in crucial cases, comprise knowledge at all. It cannot because there is nothing in it to give us knowledge of, there is no 'fact of the matter' (to use one of his famous phrases) to be identified and to give a verdict on rival theories. The natural sciences need not necessarily have correctly identified them but they are dealing with different distributions of the matter in the universe. There is some fact which obtains independently of their disagreements about its nature.

We can take the case with translation, to see what is being suggested here. Two quite different systems of translation are compatible with the same pattern of behavioural dispositions and there is nothing to choose between them in terms of the distribution of matter. Even a complete knowledge of everything, right down to the finest mapping of the distribution of particles and physical forces would give us no basis for deciding between different translations since these could, as noted earlier on, be equivalently compatible with any corpus of data, no matter how comprehensive. What we can acquire through that kind of inquiry into human behaviour does not, then, in Quine's calculations count as knowledge.

Davidson follows Quine in assuming a basic 'materialist' stance. Human actions are identical with physical events. There are no disembodied actions or thoughts, therefore they must be some kind of physical occurrence. However, thoughts and actions are identical with physical events only in one sense, or under one description. Someone makes a move in chess. This is an event which is identical with a physical occurrence, that is a player picks up a piece of plastic with his hand and moves it across the board and puts it down again (or writes down some marks on paper, seals these in an envelope and transmits them via the mail, or yet again picks up the telephone receiver, dials and speaks to someone). However, whilst there is an identity between an action and some physical occurrence, it is not the case that we can have a lawlike relationship between physical occurrence and 'mental event', that is, action or thought. As the example of the chess move shows, the same move in chess can be embodied in very different kinds of events. Deciding which kind of action a particular event performs requires interpretation and is not to be established by the physical properties of the event itself but by their relationship to other, circumstancing occurrences. Whether a physical pulling of the trigger is a homicidal shot or an accident will depend on whether it resulted from a tripping up of the person holding the gun or a balanced, poised stance with a carefully sighted and directed shot.

Though there is an inseparable connection between a physical event and a mental one, there cannot be a regular, lawlike correspondence of the mental to the physical. The gap between them will never be closed; it is not a product of the contemporary paucity of our knowledge of the physiology of human beings. Even if we knew everything about how the human organism behaved as a physical system, although we should certainly have made great progress in psychology-as-physiology and should certainly have learned much from physiology that would be of benefit to psychology generally, we should not have reduced psychology entirely to physiology, for those areas of the discipline which have to do with 'intention', 'belief', 'wants' etc. will still have their role to play.

'Anomalous monism' is the name that Davidson gives his position: he is a monist, a believer that the universe contains only one substance, matter, and that therefore the mind is a material phenomenon. However, he believes that mental phenomena are anomalous to the laws of physical science, in that they cannot be systematically related to nor deduced from them. There can be no psycho-physical laws.

The idea that there is an identity and lawlike correspondence between mental and physical events has been one of the standby assumptions of materialist philosophers but the problem has always been to give any substance to such an assumption by identifying the physical (ideally brain located) occurrences which are mental events. Davidson is not alone in raising doubts that this will ever be possible.

Putnam has contributed importantly to the 'functional' theory of the mind, one which is intended to preserve the view that the mind is material but which will also free it from the unjustified assumption that one can identify physical and mental events with each other. The functional theory suggests that we look at 'mind' as form rather than substance and argues that the easiest way to see this is to draw on the analogy with computers and computer programmes. There is an important sense in which what a computer does is to carry out a set of physical operations such as transmissions of electronic signals etc. However, we should make a fundamental mistake if we were to think that by studying the electrical and mechanical behaviour of this computer we should have found out what physical occurrences constituted a computer programme. We know that the same programme can be 'realised' in very different ways, worked through on very different physical systems. Certainly if the programme is to be carried out then it must be carried out on some physical system but these systems do not all have to have anything like the same physical structure and properties. The computer programme is a 'functional' thing; it specifies a series of things to be done which are done by sequences of physical occurrence but it is not to be identified with any particular sequence. Likewise, we can look at the mind as a functional thing, something which has a certain kind of organisation which has, of course, to be embodied in some physical system, but which does not have to be identified with just one kind of physical system. Hence there has to be a relation of mind and brain, but not one such that certain kinds of brain events uniquely constitute certain kinds of mental phenomena.

It is this kind of functional argumentation, borrowed from students of mathematical computing, which encourages the hope that we can have thinking computers. Since the mmind is something other than the physical thing in which it is embodied, then there is nothing to stop us assuming that the physical construction of a computing machine which can realise the functional relationships which make up the mind is entirely possible.

Arguing that there is nothing to stop this raises the ire of John Searle who points out that though these people may think of themselves as materialists, or monists, they are in fact the dualists they want to avoid becoming; they believe that body and mind are distinct and separable and that the mind is capable of dissociation from human biology. Kripke certainly is overtly dualistic. Attempts to identify mental events (such as pains) with physical occurrences simply will not do. The word pain is attached to a certain kind of sensation; it is a rigid designator in picking out this kind of sensation in all possible worlds. What physical conditions might produce this kind of sensation may vary from world to world and we cannot therefore identify the sensation with the physical events which in *this* world give rise to it.

Quine, Putnam and Davidson, no less than any of the philosphers we review in this book, realise that the subject matter of the human sciences is quite different to that of the natural sciences. Certainly everyone agrees that there can be no easy and painless way of achieving explanatory and methodological unity, even those who are most in favour of it. Where the divergencies lie — and here is where most of the philosophical disputes have their origins — is in the weight that they wish to put on the differences, and particularly in the propriety of holding one as a model for the other. As we shall see this is of prime importance when evaluating the importance for the cultural sciences of recent debates in the philosophy of science. The eagerness with which the new realism has promoted and defended scientific knowledge has not blinded them to the importance of the difference between the social and natural sciences. Some, like Putnam, have concluded that 'verstehen' or something like it is indispensable for the understanding of human social life. Others, more inclined to Quine perhaps, have embarked upon a campaign to revive scientific realism in the social and cultural sciences.

Recommended Reading

W.V.O. Quine has published many books. The key ones for our discussion are *From a Logical Point of View* (Harvard University Press, 1953), *Ontological Relativity* (Columbia University Press, 1969) and *Word and Object* (Massachusetts Institute of Technology Press, 1960). The essays 'On what there is' and 'Two dogmas of empiricism' in *From a Logical Point of View* and 'Epistemology naturalised' and 'Ontological relativity' in *Ontological Relativity* are especially important. Not only does Quine write much. He is much written about. Alex Orenstein, *W.V.O. Quine* (Twayne, 1977) and Roger Gibson, *The Philosophy of W.V. Quine* (University of Florida Press, 1981) give clear expositions, as does Quine himself in the interview with Bryan Magee in the latter's *Men of Ideas* (BBC, 1978). This book also has a useful interview with Hilary Putnam on Philosophy of Science. Putnam's own essays are collected in three volumes, *Mathematics, Matter and Method* (1975), *Mind, Language and Reality* (1975) and *Realism and Reason* (1978), all published by Cambridge University Press, as is his *Reason, Truth and History* (1981). *Meaning and the Moral Sciences* (Routledge, 1978) gives some of Putnam's later views on the problems of social science. Donald Davidson's essays are collected in two volumes, both published by Oxford University Press: *Essays on Actions and Events* (1980) and *Inquiries into Truth and Meaning* (1984).

Saul Kripke's main statement is in 'Naming and Necessity' in G. Harman and D. Davidson (eds.), *Semantics of Natural Language* (Reidel, 1972) and published in book form by Blackwell, 1980. A short statement is in Ted Honderich and Myles Burnyeat (eds.), *Philosophy As It Is* (Penguin, 1979). A discussion of the 'indirect theory of reference' is provided by Nathan Salmon, *Reference and Essence* (Blackwell, 1982). John Searle's views on the mind–body problem are detailed in his Reith Lectures, *Minds, Brains and Science* (BBC, 1984). For applications to issues in the social sciences of some topics raised in this chapter see, for example, G. MacDonald and P. Pettit, *Semantics and Social Science* (Routledge, 1981), R. Harré and E. Madden, *Causal Powers* (Blackwell, 1975), R. Bhaskar, *A Realist Theory of Science* (Leeds Books, 1975), Andrew Tudor, *Beyond Empiricism* (Routledge, 1982).

8 WITTGENSTEIN: PHILOSOPHY AS THERAPY

For most students of the social sciences the first time they have any contact with the philosophy of Ludwig Wittgenstein is when they are introduced to Peter Winch's book *The Idea of A Social Science* and the papers which he wrote subsequently. Much of the discussion of Winch seems to indicate that if he and Wittgenstein are saying what they seem to be saying, then they are not just wrong, but absurd. If, as it appears, they want to defend beliefs in witches or to deny the heliocentric theory of the solar system, they must be asking us to give up soundly held rational beliefs. In this chapter, it will be our aim to show that these absurd conclusions are not ones which Wittgenstein and Winch want to press on us.

To think that they are is, in fact, to fail to appreciate the context in which Wittgenstein's work is placed as well as the specific grounds for the arguments he makes. Once we see that what puzzles Wittgenstein and Winch are questions formed in logic — and particularly the logical character of the distinction between philosophical matters and those of the natural and social sciences — all of the supposed absurdities disappear. Because the presumption that Wittgenstein's views do entail anti-rationalism has distorted all the discussion of his philosophy within the social sciences, we will start with this. We will show, first, what was at issue over the notorious case of witchcraft and its comparison with science, before going on to show how that argument is to be located more generally in Wittgenstein's philosphy.

Wittgenstein made a sharp distinction between philosophy and science. Sometimes he used 'science' to mean 'the sciences' but equally often he would use it in a much broader way to mean 'factual matters ' of all kinds, including but not restricted to, those of science. He insisted on the distinctness of philosophical work from any kind of empirical inquiry and maintained throughout that whatever philosophy was about — if, indeed, it was about anything — it was most emphatically not about factual matters, though these were of course a very prominent concern of science. Philosophy could not have anything to say that would disagree with what science, broadly construed, said. In so far as philosophy did ever say anything of a factual kind that could only be the sort of thing that everyone could agree with. It was no essential part of philosophy's task to make factual findings or assertions though this task would sometimes involve saying things about facts, but these should only be trivialities and truisms. He would sometimes say that philosophy must leave everything as it is, and it is just such things as the propositions of science that he would have in mind when saying it.

In the light of this thoroughgoing separation of factual and philosophical questions it should be clear that if Wittgenstein sticks to his own idea of philosophy he cannot have, at least as a philosopher, anything to say about the results of science, nor have anything to say for or against the theory that the earth goes round the sun, nor the other way about.

Wittgenstein cannot criticise science as science but he could take exception to and felt himself very far removed from a particular attitude toward science, a philosophical conception of the nature and importance of science which, he felt, both grossly exaggerated the importance and misunderstood then nature of the science which it so excessively valued.

If Wittgenstein and Winch do not endorse the conclusions that are so commonly believed to follow from what they say, then why are they repeatedly understood to have done so? There are, we think, some important sources of incomprehension and one has been indicated in the remarks that we have just made. The attitude toward science of which Wittgenstein was so sceptical is one which is characteristic of the thinking of many of the social sciences. In suggesting that we make something of a fetish out of science Wittgenstein and Winch are going very much against the current. They have, too, great difficulty in getting people to see the difference between their targets; an attack on a certain attitude toward science will be taken by those who hold that attitude as an attack upon science itself, as a suggestion that there is something wrong with science. We repeat, then, that neither Wittgenstein nor Winch seek to find fault with science but they do argue that there is something wrong in being overawed by it.

There are two other important sources of misunderstanding one of which bears directly on the issues raised above whilst the other, which does not connect to them so directly, does go very much against the grain of contemporary attitudes. This latter source, which we shall call 'reservations about generality' we shall come to after we have dealt with that prime source of difficulties, the true/false contrast. Both reservations are expressions of an unease which Wittgenstein came to feel over the programme of logic to which he himself had once been a prominent contributor. One of the most important things to remember about all of Wittgenstein's work is the preoccupation which he had with logical questions, logical form and logical relations.

The True/False Contrast

The contrast between the true and the false is one which seems to be absolutely basic and comprehensive. Everything which is said must be either the one, true, or the other, false. Reading Wittgenstein, or Winch, on such questions can make their writing seem quite baffling. Indeed, at times they sound as if they are saying the absurd things that have been attributed to them. When they talk about something like magic or witchcraft, they are reluctant to say that it is false and so, on the view just given, there is no other option but to understand them as saying that it must be true. Reciprocally, since science and witchcraft are in conflict and the latter is, apparently, being held to be true, then it cannot but be implied that the former, science, is being said to be false — unless of course some sort of relativist views are being put forward which will maintain that science is neither more, nor less true than witchcraft. If they are not understood as saying science is false, then Wittgenstein and Winch are likely to be read as arguing for relativist views.

All this would be so if the relevant contrast was between that which is true and that which is false. But in Wittgenstein's philosophy it is frequently not so. He is interested in a significantly different and prior distinction. It is between, on the one hand, that which is *capable* of being either true or false and, on the other, that which *cannot be* either true or false.

The connection to make here is with Frege's and Russell's views on meaning. Frege had defined meaning as reference and had equated it with truth value. This meant that some propositions — those of mathematics especially — which had no truth value were meaningless. Mathematical statements were neither true nor false. The logical problem was first to decide how to treat such statements and, second, to determine whether they were confined to mathematics.

Wittgenstein does not assume that everything which is said has the form of a factual statement, i.e. must be either true or false. He was interested in tracing the boundaries of factual discourse, of separating those statements which can say something true or false about how the world is from those which do not. It was a distinction which he characterised as being between those propositions which are meaningful (that is which can be true or false) and those which are meaningless (which cannot be either true or false). The boundary was, then, that which separated sense from non-sense. There was no simple way of marking out this boundary so that the different kinds of statements are recognisable 'on sight' because they can look very much like one another. Mistaking one for the other was, in Wittgenstein's view, a major cause of serious intellectual difficulties. It was a main part of Wittgenstein's objective to resolve these.

Wittgenstein's reluctance to say that witchcraft and magic are false does not, therefore, signify a corresponding desire to say that they are true. He is not to be forced into those alternatives. He wants to say that they are neither true nor false. They are neither more nor less true than science because that, too, is also the sort of thing that cannot be either true or false. This does not mean that a relativist position is being taken because such a position maintains what is here being denied, namely the view that magic and science *are* the sorts of things which can be said to be true or false. Relativism wants to say that the question of magic and science are to be judged true, because they are to be judged on their own terms. This is very, very far removed from arguing that questions of truth and falsity are wholly irrelevant and that the issues of truth and falsity do not arise at all. Since witchcraft cannot be true (or false), there is no question of one being more true or false than the other.

More will need to be said below on this, but a cautionary note should be sounded now. The above argument is not about scientific theories, but about the *institution* of science. A scientific theory can be true or false. The heliocentric theory is one or the other. But science itself is neither true nor false. It is, Wittgenstein and Winch both say, only within the institution of science that it makes sense to talk of the truth and falsity of scientific theories. Those who see Wittgenstein as insisting on the existence of witches or as denying the truth of the heliocentric theory of the solar system are overlooking his fastidious determination, his persistent insistence, that philosophy is constitutionally incapable of settling questions of this kind; scientific arguments do not settle the matter for believers in witchcraft. It is only because we first accept science that we accept the truth of the heliocentric *scientific* theory.

Reservations about Generality

From Wittgenstein's point of view, the response that many of his social science critics have made to what they take to be his views would look very like manifestations of the problem he is complaining about. Those critics are apt to react to Wittgenstein as if he had affronted them by proposing that description is better, more desirable, than explanation. Wittgenstein is seen as being prejudiced against explanation and invariably in favour of the description of instances.

The object of Wittgenstein's criticism is not generalisation as such but, again, an attitude to it, one which comprises a virtual fixation on it, which gives us an inappropriate 'craving' for generality: a conviction that anything other than generalisation is worthless and inferior to it, which leads naturally to a contempt for the particular case. It is not, then, for Wittgenstein, a matter of opposing generalisation but of attempting to correct the rather gross excesses which result from an obsession with it. Not all questions are best dealt with by generalisation and it is the case in philosophy that, on Wittgenstein's argument, the provision of generalisation is characteristically inappropriate. All that people think they want from a generalisation can be obtained from the careful description of particular cases.

The reason why we say that social science responses to Wittgenstein would manifest the problem should be apparent, because they would manifest the same unquestioning attachment to the idea of the invariable superiority of generalisation which is being put into question. However, they are misguided responses since Wittgenstein does not, in any case, question the legitimacy of generalisations in science.

The power of the demand for generalisation results from the fact that generalisation can often provide explanation, and so useful can generalisations be in explanation that some people are led to think that explanation and generalisation are indissolubly associated, if not identical. To explain is to show that something follows from a generalisation. Wittgenstein thought that the inappropriate insistence on generalisation resulted, in no small part, from the mistaken idea that all intellectual problems are settled by explanation, that whenever we are puzzled we are in need of some explanation. Since that is identified with generalisation, then it follows we are in need of some generalisation. Wittgenstein would not accept the identification of explanation and generalisation to begin with, but more importantly, he was of the view that it is often the case that our puzzles do not need an explanation for their solution.

Putting it extremely crudely, we can say that Wittgenstein thought that there were two quite different kinds of difficulties that we can have in understanding, expressed as two quite different kinds of puzzles that can trouble us. There are (a) those which are problems of ignorance and (b) those which are problems of confusion. As with the issue of the distinction between statements with and statements without sense discussed above, here too it is the case that the things being distinguished are not easily and readily discriminated; they can look very much like one another. Problems which are really those arising from confusion may very well be taken for problems resulting from ignorance, thereby leading people to seek for generalisations where these are neither effective nor necessary. Let us note a further connection between this distinction and the earlier one between sense and non-sense. One prominent basis for philosophical confusion is the mistaking of a statement which says nothing true or false for one that does — a confusion of non-sense with sense.

There are, then, two kinds of problem. There are those which arise because we need further information. There are things that we do not know and finding them out will resolve our puzzlement. However, there are other cases in which we find that something puzzles us, but where our puzzlement does not derive from a deficiency of knowledge. We already know all that we need to solve our problem but we cannot get a suitable view of the things that we do know. We have all the pieces but we cannot see how to put them together. Further pieces are not what is required and the introduction of them will make things more difficult and confused, not less. It is, to continue the puzzle analogy, only be sorting out the pieces and putting them together in the right combination that we shall have come to a solution.

The confusions originate very much in language, Wittgenstein suggests. We know our way about in our language and when we are speaking it in the ordinary way of things we have no difficulty with it. When we are making 'instinctive' use of the language we are right in our employment of it. Trouble begins when we start to reflect on language, to reflect on our use of words, for then we become self-conscious about something that is properly done in unselfconscious fashion. When we start to reflect on the language, then we begin to lose our way in it, to lose track of our place within it and of the relationship between its different parts. Eventually we find ourselves quite lost. We know our way about in the language but we have lost ourselves; we are not in a situation where we need further knowledge, new information, for we know what is necessary to find our way about in the language. What we need is to put ourselves in mind of what we know, to sort out the information that we already have and thus to get ourselves out of the difficulties we have got ourselves into.

It is the problems of philosophy that originate in confusions about language. These are not problems, therefore, that have to do with matters of fact, with the acquisition of knowledge, for they have instead to do with sorting out what is already available, with reminding people of things about their language with which they are quite familiar. Since these problems are distinct from the kind that science deals in, how is it possible for the things Wittgenstein has to say to have any importance for the social sciences?

Enter Winch

It is here that Peter Winch's contribution assumes its importance. The distinction between 'science' and 'philosophy' has not been drawn, let it be noted, in a way which is straightforwardly identified with disciplinary boundaries such that 'philosophy' is clearly one sort of pursuit and 'science' another. Philosophy and science, as we have spoken of them in this chapter, are distinguished by the kinds of problems that they have, whether these are factual or, as we shall for convenience now call them, 'conceptual' ones. The question can then be asked: are the key problems of the social sciences ones which result from ignorance of factual matters? Are they scientific in character or are they, rather, the sort that arise from confusions about our language? Winch argues that some of the central questions of the social sciences are philosophical rather than scientific, they are ones which result from us failing to take proper account of what we already know rather than ones which arise because we just do not know enough.

Putting it more bluntly than Winch would perhaps be prepared to, his argument is something like this: sociology is not concerned so much with finding out about society, which would be a factual inquiry, but it is engaged much more with the idea of a social science. The core question which sociologists are apt to ask themselves is 'what is the nature of sociology's subject matter?' or, put another way, 'what is the nature of social reality?' This might well look like a factual question but that it should do so would fit with the argument to this point. Questions which are not factual often look as if they are and are mistaken for factual ones. Rather than resulting in the enumeration of social facts, asking such questions produces discussion of the question 'what is it for something to be a social fact?' and it is this kind of question which, Winch claims, philosophy rather than science deals in. Physics may well collect abundant scientific facts but it does not ask the question 'what is it for something to be a scientific fact?' It is, rather, the philosopher who asks and attempts to answer that question.

Winch is not saying that sociologists never collect facts about society for, plainly, they often do. He is maintaining that some of the pre-eminent topics of sociological discourse do not involve collecting factual information and are much more the sort of questions philosophers ask than those with which science can be concerned. The attempt to tackle such questions under the impression that they are factual in character and therefore to be solved by new information is likely only to make the problems worse, not better. Or so Winch argues. This leads Winch to examine the problems that arise as a result of seeking to solve, through the inappropriate use of the means of science, a practice which is alien to our own society and ways of thinking. Take the magical practices of 'primitive people'. These are often deeply puzzling to us, they are strange and bizarre, they make no sense. We cannot see why people should engage in them.

Here, surely, is a problem which arises from ignorance, which results from our lack of knowledge about the nature of human societies and their constituent practices. Here if anywhere is the place in which generalisations will be needed, where a 'comparative sociology' can make a telling contribution. Winch does not think so. He sees it as leading to serious misunderstandings rather than contributing to greater insight.

Cutting a long, complex and subtle argument as short as we possibly can, we can say that Winch tries to persuade us that the creation of a comparative sociology requires the comparison of like with like and that the successful identification of appropriate comparisons obviates the need for the general scheme. In order to decide which institutions of one society — our own in many cases — to compare with those of another we shall need to be able to match those institutions, to say what kind of part they play in their respective societies. We will want, presumably, to compare two different institutions because they play much the same part in the societies in which they are found. However, if we are in a position to say what part each institution plays in the life of its society then we have already achieved a very good understanding of it. We will have already answered the question 'what part does an institution play in the life of those who enact it?' — which our comparative sociology was designed to answer for us.

Winch focuses, as Wittgenstein had done before him, on the question of 'primitive magic'. Their arguments, taken together, go something like the following. There is a tendency to find magic puzzling because it is assumed to be a kind of mistaken science. Magic is seen as having the role of explaining nature to people and therefore as involving — even arising from — a theory of nature. This theory of nature is very different from our own, which would explain why magic is alien to us but, since our theory of nature is right, and the theory involved in magic conflicts with ours, then that theory must be wrong. Primitives think, for example, that one can harm others just by wishing it, but we know that it is impossible to do physical harm by means of thoughts. Therefore their magic and witchcraft rest on mistaken premisses. The giving of this explanation does not, however, really resolve the puzzlement because the question then becomes: 'how can people believe in a theory of nature when it is quite obviously false?' Since their magic can't work what stops it from showing itself to be wholly ineffective? What stops these people from seeing the world in the right way.

Wittgenstein and Winch invite us to take stock. Is magic really like our science? Does it really have the role of explaining the course of nature? Does it play the same role in 'primitive society' as it does in ours? On what basis is it alleged to involve a 'theory of nature' which differs from our own? Examine what primitives do know about nature and we find that their grasp on it is, on the evidence provided by those who have reported on primitive magic, much the same as our own. It is not a matter of adding to the evidence that we already have, but of taking the evidence that is already available and arranging it differently. It shows that those people have a practical grasp on the world which is every bit as sound and empirical as our own — in fact it is very like our own. They know what time the sun rises and sets, what the sequence and rhythm of the seasons is, what is edible and what inedible, how to feed and clothe themselves, how to do damage to each other with quite physical means. Where does magic enter in? One place where is does so is where knowledge runs out. Not, notice, where *their* knowledge runs out, where they know less than we, as it were, but, where our knowledge runs out as well. The magic comes in where the possibility of knowledge runs out. Where there are things that can be asked that science does not, cannot, answer. For example, the question of why some people are subject to misfortune and others are not is one such place. Our science may tell us that there is nothing to explain here, but that is something quite other than giving us an explanation which is more correct than that which magic offers.

For this, and other reasons, it is disputed by Wittgenstein and Winch that magic plays anything like the part which a theory of nature plays in our lives. Their own 'theory of nature', their own empirical knowledge, plays much the same role in their lives as does our very similar 'theory of nature' in our lives. What part does magic play, then? It has much more to do with the allocation of blame, the taking of precautions, the making of decisions. What kind of institutions in our society would make better parallels with magic in that case? There are some which are of a magical or religious kind, such as — to name but one or two — the casting of horoscopes, the offering of prayers, the reading of omens, the possession of charms. Then there are those of a more secular sort, such as — to name but one or two — the courts, marriage guidance counsellors, stockbrokers, racing tipsters. It is not so tempting nor so easy to look on magic as a mistaken way of doing things comparable to filling in one's football coupons according to the birthdates of one's relatives or through the stabbing of the coupon with a pin. Nor is it at all easy to see how such practices embody any kind of 'theory of nature' either.

The important point in this connection, from the Wittgenstein/ Winch viewpoint, is that one comes to understand the magical practices of a primitive society better by examining them more closely and thoughtfully, by examining the way the facts about them relate to one another. After one has done that one is better placed to draw parallels with our own society. But the parallels are drawn on the basis of an understanding of the practice, not as a precondition for it.

Language and Reality

Having taken the implications of Wittgenstein's philosophy first, we can now turn to a consideration of the philosophy itself. In order to do this as coherently as possible within the restricted space available we shall present those views as if they centred on the problem of the relationship of language and reality. This, however, is something of a distortion, for Wittgenstein's most persistent and pervasive concern was with the nature of logic and philosophy. It is from that preoccupation that his interest in language derives. Wittgenstein's thought can be seen as being dominated by four terms: logic, language, thought, reality. It is his effort to clarify the relationship of these that gives rise to the question of the relationship of language to reality. We elect to concentrate on this question because it will be intelligible and interesting to social science students in a way that the understanding of logic will not.

Wittgenstein's work is divided into two main periods. The early, which goes from before the First World War through to the end of the nineteen twenties, and the late, which develops in the latter half of the nineteen thirties through to his death; both are linked by a period of transition. The *Tractatus Logico-Philosophicus* was the only book that he published in his lifetime and that crystallises his early thought, indicating the importance of logic in its title. The *Philosophical Investigations*, incomplete at his death in 1951, is the most developed formulation of the later position. Throughout his life Wittgenstein was an assiduous notetaker and it was from those notes, 'remarks' as he called them, that he would refine his published work. It is from the large corpus of remarks that most of the posthumously published work has been extracted.

The arguments in Wittgenstein's later work are often aimed, more or less directly, at his own earlier thinking which he came to see as embodying many of the classic confusions of philosophy. Though the *Investigations* provided a most severe critique of the *Tractatus* it is necessary to stress that Wittgenstein thought that there were vital elements of continuity between them.

In the *Tractatus* Wittgenstein put forward a theory, something that he aimed to avoid doing in the later work. The theory was intended to give a general account of the relationship of language to reality. How does language relate to the world? We say things and some of those things do relate to the world in that they say something true about how the world is. How is that possible? It might seem that if we want to understand the relationship of language and world then the way to do this is to understand what it takes to say something true. However, in order to say something true, we must say something; a saying can only be true if it has sense. Something without sense does not say anything either true or false (see Wittgenstein's distinction of sense and non-sense above, p. 179-80). Saying something with sense, then, comes before saying something true, involves saying something which *could* be true of the world. Therefore, in saying something which could be either true or false one is saying something which is *about* the world. There is, then, a relationship between language and reality which makes it possible for us to form propositions, to make statements which are about the world, saying something which is either true or false of it.

It is, as we indicated above, with the nature of this possibility that Wittgenstein is concerned: what is there about language and reality that makes it possible for statements in language to be about reality, whether true or false to it?

The argument of the *Tractatus* is complex, dense, highly technical, intricate to an extreme degree, wide-ranging. Its centre piece is the picture theory of meaning. This is meant to explain how language can be about reality. Wittgenstein holds that there is a correspondence of structures, that the structure of language and the structure of reality match each other. In an important sense, language and reality share the same structure, a logical structure which is also common to thought — giving the linkage of our four terms. Language and reality are structurally isomorphic. The structure of language corresponds to the structure of facts in the world in the way that the structure of a picture corresponds to the structure of that which it portrays — hence, a picture theory of meaning.

The idea is, then, that the structure of a sentence 'pictures' the structure of the facts as the structure of a portrait pictures its subject. This is a difficult idea to grasp. It is hard to conceive how a sentence can relate to a situation in the same way that a portrait relates to that which it portrays. However, it must be remembered first of all that the correspondence is one of structures and it is not the fact that a picture looks like its subject matter that provides the kind of relationship being talked about here. The picture portrays its subject because it embodies an organised system of representation and thus, in the same way, the grooves on a 'record' album 'picture' the music that the album contains. The elements which make up the picture or album are arranged in ways which match the organisation of the things they are to record.

It needs also to be recognised that Wittgenstein's idea of the nature of the correspondence is not simple but elaborate. The crucial element of correspondence is not to be found in the matching of our ordinary statements against commonplace situations, for these are complex things and the relevant correspondence comes at a much more basic level. The statements of our ordinary language can be broken down into their simplest components — into elementary propositions which cannot, themselves, be any further decomposed. This is the process of 'analysis' which exposes a statement's logical form. Likewise, situations can be 'analysed' into their basic elements, into those facts which cannot be further broken down. These are 'atomic facts.' It is at the level of elementary propositions and atomic facts that the possibility of correspondence between language and reality is established. Atomic facts consist of the arrangement of 'objects' in relationship and those objects are represented in language by names. There is, that is, another connection between language and reality than that provided by structural correspondence. It is that which is given by the fact that names stand for things. Propositions are made up of names in combinations, a view which, in general terms, is inspired by Frege's logical system. The way in which names are arranged in a true proposition matches the way objects are arranged in reality. The ways in which names can be arranged in propositions represents therefore the possible ways in which things can be arranged in situations.

It must be stressed that elementary propositions, atomic facts and objects are not the same things as our ordinary commonplace propositions, facts and objects. These commonplace things are compounds of the more elementary ones. If this means that the idea of what an elementary proposition, atomic fact or basic object is like is not at all clear to the reader this should not provide any source of anxiety for it was not clear to Wittgenstein either. He was arguing what the logical analysis of language *must* reveal if it was carried through. It was not incumbent on Wittgenstein to say anything further or more specific about what would be the results of carrying it through. To find that out, one would have to do the analysis.

The achievement of this exercise is, on Wittgenstein's argument, that it has circumscribed the limits of factual expression. It has shown how the limits of factual expression are related to the limits of language. This is why such importance has been set on the idea of possibility at various points in our argument. Wittgenstein is not interested in establishing what are the facts, but in determining what can be a fact, and something can only be a fact if it can be stated in a factual expression, one that can be either true or false. The possibility of facts must, then, fall within the boundaries of factual discourse. Thus, one can state a possible fact with 'there is a big dog in the next room'. This might be true or false, depending upon the situation, whether there was indeed a dog in the next room. Whether or not it is true depends upon the facts, whether or not there is a big dog in the next room.

Compare, now, 'my height is five foot seven and six foot two'. This does not state a possible fact, it does not say something that could be either true or false and therefore, in important ways, it does not say anything at all. It does not state a possible fact because it attributes two heights and I cannot have two. I can be either five foot seven or six foot two but I cannot be both at once.

We have said, Wittgenstein does not interfere with science. It might seem, though, that in what we have been saying about the limits of language and the limits of reality coinciding (*not* the limits of language setting the limits to reality) Wittgenstein is trying to pre-empt the business of science, part of which might be to determine what, for example, is physically possible. Nothing of this sort is involved. Wittgenstein is interested in the logical not the empirical limits to reality. Consider the case of height. A physical scientist might, for imaginary example, want to propose that it is not possible for a person to be taller than ten feet; our knowledge of genetics, anatomy, structural engineering and so forth can be called upon to explain that under normal gravitational conditions a human being's body would collapse from the strain of being so tall. Such might be the limits of possibility in an empirical sense, but Wittgenstein is not eager to have what he has to say hinge on facts like that. Thus, the point about height is that someone can't be two heights at once not because of any facts which affect their growth, dimensions etc. but because of the way we measure height. Our practice of measuring height is such that it allows only one height for a human at a time. It just doesn't work in such a way as to make two simultaneous heights something that can result. It *might* have been the case that our ways of measuring were different and that we did have two different heights for everyone — say, standing up and crouched down, but that isn't how we do it and so we cannot sensibly say 'my height is five foot seven and six foot two'.

It is in such ways that the logic of language marks out the limit of factual possibility.

Philosophical Investigations

Wittgenstein thought that the *Tractatus* was definitive, that he had shown where the limits of logic and language lay and so could give up philosophy. When it became apparent to him, as it did, that his 'picture theory' was not satisfactory then, since that theory was the best possible one, the conclusion to be drawn was that the problem was not to be dealt with by putting forward *any kind* of theory. Through comprehensive reconsideration of his earlier position

Wittgenstein came to the view that philosophy should be a kind of 'therapy'. As such, it should refrain from attempting to put forward theories and should, instead, attempt to remove philosophical puzzlement by showing that the problem was not a genuine one, only a product of confusion and, with the clearing up of the confusion, would evaporate.

We asserted above that the discontinuities between the *Tractatus* and the *Investigations* can conceal some important connections. The discrimination of sense from non-sense, for example, remains as important in the latter work as it was in its predecessor. So, too, does the fact that expressions which are non-sense can look very like those which have sense and that it is the confusion of the two which gives rise to philosophical problems.

The nature of the distinction between sense and non-sense is changed, however. In the *Tractatus* the distinction had been drawn between what we have called factual discourse and other kinds, a distinction which was due not only to the structure of language itself but also to the structure of reality and the nature of their relationship. In the later period, consequent upon the abandonment of the picture theory, the distinction between sense and non-sense is made entirely internal to language. It no longer depends on any correspondence with external reality but has to do with the failure of users of the language to accord with its patterns of proper use. Those things which are said that make sense do so because they involve the proper use of the words of the language. Those which do not, fail to do so because the words which comprise them are, somehow, being used improperly.

Though the *Tractatus* had explicitly recognised that language was a human practice and institution, the view that language was a product of the human organism and could therefore be neither more nor less complex than it had not figured very largely in the account that was there given. In the *Investigations* it assumes central significance. It is this that makes Wittgenstein's later work look as if it might be much closer to sociology than some other philosophies because it places major emphasis on the institutional and collective nature of language. It attempts to deal with the topic of the meaning of language by replacing the picture theory with what we shall call a methodological emphasis on the relation of use and meaning. It is quite common for people to talk of the *Investigations* as containing a 'use theory of meaning', which is all right if it is recognised that this does not refer to anything like a theory in the sense in which the 'picture theory' was one and is instead effectively a methodological doctrine.

The later work is, we said, critical of the earlier. Much of the *Investigations* focuses its attack on the idea that words get their meanings by standing for things. This was the idea which had been a cornerstone of the earlier doctrine and Wittgenstein attempted to undermine it from several very different angles. He did not want to maintain that words are never names because, quite plainly, they are, but he did want to attack the idea that the relationship between a name and what it stood for was the foundational basis for language. The capacity to make a link between a name and something in the world was one which could only originate within language itself and hence that connection of name and thing could not be foundational to language.

The idea that the meaning of a word was what it stood for was, then, the target of criticism. It is tempting to think that the meaning of a word is the thing(s) it stands for because it seems to fit: proper names like 'Ludwig Wittgenstein', for example, stand for the person and so it seems natural to think that the meaning of 'Wittgenstein' is the person so named. It seems natural to construe all the words of a language as if they operated in the same way as proper names. However, looked at slightly differently, even the case of proper names does not encourage the view that the meaning of a word is what it stands for. It seems very odd to say that the meaning of the word 'Ludwig Wittgenstein' is the man Ludwig Wittgenstein. It seems, that is, very odd to say of Ludwig Wittgenstein that he is the meaning of his name. But if the meaning of a word is not the thing for which it stands, then what is it? It is against the idea that meaning is any sort of thing that the doctrine of 'meaning as use' is put forward. Exactly the same point of departure is found in the work of Quine and Davidson in Chapter 7, but it leads in entirely different directions.

If someone accepts that the meaning of a word is not the thing for which it stands, then they may want to think that the meaning of the word might be something else — perhaps the idea that a person has in their head. The meaning of the word 'red' would, then, be the idea that we have in our heads of what 'red' is. This is, in Wittgenstein's view, just as bad as thinking that meaning is a thing. One only wants to take up the view that meaning is an idea because one wants to think that meaning is a kind of thing, and if it can't be an object, then what other kinds of things are there that it could be except for ideas?

The view that meaning consists of ideas can lead into the 'private language argument'. If the meaning of our word is the idea that is associated with it, then what is there that ensures that we mean the same thing by the same word? The meaning of 'red' may be the idea of red in our heads, but what ensures that the idea in the head of one of us is anything like the same as that in the head of others? Our ideas are inaccessible to the direct observation of others and so it is entirely possible that we should all have wildly incongruous ideas of what red is. We would then be speaking 'private languages', languages which were private in the sense of peculiar to each of us and which are also private in the sense of being inaccessible to any one other than their individual speaker. In order to undermine what Quine calls the 'idea idea', Wittgenstein devotes a central and crucial part of the *Investigations* to showing that the idea of a private language is completely incoherent, that it makes no sense to talk of such a thing. It is not the basis of his argument but it is a consequence of it that language is a public, collective thing, something that is passed from the community to the individual and not built up from individuals into a common thing.

The only way to get away from reacting to the rejection of both claims about meaning — that it is a thing, that it is an idea — by asking 'well, if it isn't either of those, then what other kind of thing could it be?' is to get away altogether from the assumption that meaning has to be some sort of thing. And it is to enable this that Wittgenstein encourages the examination of use.

Thinking of the problem in terms of use invites analogy (invites, in fact, more than one analogy) with the use of tools or instruments. If we ask about the use of a tool this does not seem anywhere so mysterious as the meaning of a word. To ask what the use of a tool is, is to ask to be told or shown what can be done with it, to have identified the tasks in which it can be employed and so on. And, of course, an important aspect of the analogy is that a given tool may have a very wide range of uses.

Of course, we want to use tools ourselves and we learn to do this by grasping techniques, by acquiring knacks, skills and so forth. In learning to use a screwdriver, for example, we will be shown how to hold it and handle it, how to stand, to apply pressure etc. It will often be enough to watch someone else employ the tool; watching what they do we can find out what the tool does and how we can make it do that ourselves. In order to learn to use the tool there is no need to 'grasp an idea' but only to emulate other people's actions and, pushing the analogy through, learning 'the meaning' of a word is learning what can be done with it, mastering the techniques for its deployment. In order to learn this one need do nothing very different from what is done when one learns to use a tool. One learns to emulate the actions of others, one picks up from witnessing their activities the techniques which they use to deploy the word.

Knowing what a word means, then, comes to be very much like knowing what a tool is for. If someone can handle the tool in the right way, can use a screwdriver to put in and take out screws for example, then we can say that they know what the use of the tool is. If someone can employ a word in the right way, can put words into arrangements that make sense and that are appropriate to the circumstances in which they are spoken then we can say that they know what the words mean — even if they are unable to say, of a particular word, what its meaning is.

What settles the question of what is 'the right way' or 'the right use'? What decides whether a use is right, is in accord with community standards? This is the way that we, in this community, use this tool or word and coming to use it in the right way is coming to use the word in the same way as the rest of us do. Why is driving on the left side the right way to drive? Because that, in our community, is the way we do it; it may be done differently elsewhere but here we do it in this way and not in some other. Likewise, why is it right to use, say, the word 'know' in this manner? Answer, because this is how we speak the language, this is the part the word plays in our language. The question of what a word means is, then, internal to the language of which it is a part, and the business of determining what it means is, then, a matter of seeing how it gets used, what its characteristic modes of employment are. It involves, in other words, a survey of the uses to which we, as ordinary speakers of the language, put a word when we make different kinds of statements.

The objective of such surveys is not informative. They do not enable us to find out something which we did not already know. The aim is therapeutic and the strategy is to remove our difficulties by reminding us of things with which we are already familiar, by enabling us to get a clearer view of matters about which we have become confused.

Wittgenstein draws our attention to the fact that the words which give us trouble in philosophy are words from our ordinary language — words like 'know', 'mind', 'body', 'true', 'perceive', which are at the heart of the central philosophical disputes. Wittgenstein is not making some point about the superiority or preferability of our ordinary language to technical or scientific terms but is, instead, pointing out that those words which are at the centre of philosophical controversy are not problematical because they are technical, but because we do not understand the technical context from which they are taken. These are words from common language and, therefore, as speakers we know how to use them. We know what they mean. If, therefore, they are giving us trouble it is because we are trying to make them do things they cannot do, are trying to use them for ends to which they are not suited. We have, at some point, gone off the rails of the language from which those words are taken and it is only by bringing back to our attention the ways in which the words are used when the language is working properly that we shall appreciate what the words will do and see that they will not, cannot do the things that we are asking them to do. Wittgenstein is not criticising the words of our ordinary language because they will not do the things that philosophers are asking them to do. His point is that if the therapy is effective then we shall be persuaded that the desire to set such tasks for the language is a result of our misunderstanding of it and that when we get a proper perspective on what we can sensibly say, then we shall find that what we thought was a problem was not really one at all.

Because Wittgenstein's later philosophy was much occupied with elucidating what we called his 'sociological' conceptions of meaning and language, his ideas have proved attractive to a few social scientists. They have found in his remarks a general theory of the relationship of meaning and language, concepts and social institutions which, they have felt, thoroughly demolishes the more orthodox views in philosophy. Armed with this theory some have rampaged through the classical questions of epistemology and the philosophy of science, seeking to replace the 'absolutist' view of certain knowledge and pure reason with a 'relativism' based in the sociology of knowledge. And, to be fair, some fairly recent developments, in the philosophy of science especially, have not been all that unsympathetic to this aim. However, from all that we have said in this chapter, it ought to be clear that such an interpretation of Wittgenstein is antithetical to the tenor of his later thought. He was, as we have seen, deeply suspicious of the craving for explanation and the demand for general theories. Trying to explain our present knowledge by relating it to social institutions is still trying to explain it. More than anything else, what Wittgenstein was trying to get us to see was just what sort of questions we can ask about meaning, language, knowledge and reality, and just where the differences lie between empirical questions to be answered by science and social science, and conceptual questions that are the province of philosophy. It was no part of his intention that the therapy he offered philosophy should give rise to the very symptoms it was supposed to cure.

Recommended Reading

The *Tractatus Logico-Philosophicus* (Routledge, 1961) and *Philosophical Investigations* (Blackwell, 1958) are the two main sources of Wittgenstein's different views. The *Tractatus* is very difficult and a good, clear introduction to it is provided by H.O. Mounce, *Wittgenstein's Tractatus: an introduction* (Blackwell, 1981). Expositions of Wittgenstein's thought can be found in A. Kenny, *Wittgenstein* (Penguin, 1975) and David Pears, *Wittgenstein* (Fontana, 1971). A more difficult exposition is Robert J. Fogelin, *Wittgenstein* (Routledge, 1976). Winch's views are presented in his *The Idea of a Social Science* (Routledge, 1958) and 'Understanding a Primitive Society', *American Philosophical Quarterly*, vol. I (1964), reprinted in Bryan Wilson's *Rationality* (Blackwell, 1970). A summary statement of his position can be found in 'Language Belief and Relativism' in H.D. Lewis (ed.), *Contemporary British Philosophy* (Allen and Unwin, 1976) and his *Ethics and Action* (Routledge, 1972). A recent collection of papers edited by two persistent critics of Winch and Wittgenstein is S. Lukes and M. Hollis (eds.) *Rationality and Relativism* (Blackwell, 1982). The most persistent critic of all is Ernest Gellner whose complaints about the whole style of philosophy inspired by Wittgenstein can be found in his *Words and Things* (Gollancz, 1959). They are directed most sharply against what he sees as the evils of Wittgenstein's influence in the social sciences in 'The New Idealism' in I. Lakatos and A. Musgrave (eds.), *Problems in the Philosophy of Science* (North Holland, 1968) and recently restated in 'Tractatus Socio-logicus' in S.C. Brown (ed.), *Objectivity and Cultural Divergence* (Macmillan, 1984). Attempts to discuss Wittgenstein's implications for social science may be found in Derek Phillips, *Wittgenstein and Scientific Knowledge* (Macmillan, 1977), David Bloor, *Wittgenstein, A Social Theory of Knowledge* (Macmillan, 1984) and Susan M. Easton, *Marxist Humanism and Wittgensteinian Social Philosophy* (Manchester University Press, 1983) and Stephen P. Turner, *Sociological Explanation and Translation* (Cambridge University Press, 1980).

9 ORDINARY LANGUAGE PHILOSOPHY

Like many other general labels, the title Ordinary Language Philosopher is often more of a hindrance than a help in identifying and characterising those to whom it is applied. In the first place, it seems to imply that what differentiates such philosophers from their contemporaries is that they are concerned with a whole new branch of philosophy, namely the philosophy of ordinary language, or that they conduct their philosophy solely in terms supplied by ordinary language, or both. This is misleading because, as we shall see, Ordinary Language Philosophy is concerned with standard and classical problems. The deliberate avoidance of formal notation is no more than a preference for certain gains which are, it is thought, made thereby. Second, the use of the general label suggests a commonality of line, a uniformity of theory and problems, which would be quite wrong. And yet the term does have some advantage. One thing that does link Ordinary Language Philosophers is an attitude towards philosophy itself, and particularly the goals it should aim for. They are extremely sceptical of all attempts to build large scale speculative systems based upon the universalising of categorial distinctions. They offer none themselves and are prone to think that philosophers would be more at home with the concrete and particular than they are with the general and abstract. The painstaking nature of their investigations and the patient accumulation of findings is in direct contrast to many other tendencies in recent philosophical history. The unity discerned in Ordinary Philosophy is mainly due to the fact that the two pre-eminent figures, Ryle and Austin, were contemporaries at Oxford. It is further encouraged by the preference which both shared for writing essays rather than books. Ryle produced only one book length work and several collections of papers. Austin published only a handful of lectures and papers. The limited output and the deliberate refraining from advocating general theories allows for the blurring of differences.

In spite of the size of the philosophical output, for a time in the late 1950s and early 1960s, Ryle and Austin wielded considerable influence in a number of Philosophy Departments both in Britain and in North America. Two reasons may be offered for this. To begin with, in their piecemeal, meticulous investigations Ryle and Austin seemed to have roughed out a novel approach to philosophy which looked as if it might eliminate many of the conventional problems, or at least render them more tractable. Second, and perhaps equally as important, was the effect of their personal styles. Austin in particular had a quite unique personal authority among his students. Both wrote their philosophy with a flair, wit and lightness of touch that is virtually unrivalled. They were serious philosophers but neither could ever be accused of being unnecessarily po-faced and solemn.

The verve of the writing combined with the inclination to propound only the most minimal claims for philosophy has given rise to the impression that Austin and Ryle are 'philosophers' philosophers', and so they have been somewhat neglected in other quarters. They do not seem to be concerned with the important questions of the age or with the timeless dilemmas of human existence. This has certainly been the view within the human sciences, where only a few small groups have paid any attention at all to their work. This is a pity. We ought not to mistake reticence for irrelevance. As we shall see, Ryle's notion of 'category mistakes' and their logical consequences could well have very important applications in psychology, sociology and elsewhere, while Austin's search for precision and clarity with regard to supposed distinctions such as part/whole, free/determined, general/ particular might have cut short much needless theoretical dispute in all the social sciences. A more positive reason for taking an interest in Ordinary Language Philosophy is that it is primarily concerned with the topic of the human sciences, human action, and its proper characterisation. What is it that makes something an action and not merely a piece of behaviour? What sorts of action are there? How are they defined and organised? If we were to take such an interest, it might occur to us that many of the models of human action that are advocated within the human sciences are wholly inadequate, having neither the flexibility nor the subtlety to fulfil the general applications claimed for them. As we have already hinted, in its own idiosyncratic way, Ordinary Language Philosophy might very well shake our confidence in the broad and apparently firm philosophical distinctions which are thought to be central to our endeavours; those between appearance and reality, subjectivity and objectivity, free will and determinism, and so on. It would not be all that unfair to say that it is Ryle and Austin's conclusion that much of the discussion of these distinctions and the questions to which they relate has been ham-fisted in the extreme. Since the human sciences are so dependent upon them, clarification and definition of what is at stake could only be beneficial. It might, for example, encourage us to avoid many of the pitfalls that we stumble into and help us to unravel the knots that we tie ourselves in when we try to escape.

We said at the beginning that Ordinary Language Philosophy is not a set of theories, nor even a uniform method, but an attitude. It is often thought that Ryle and Austin wished to defend the infallibility of commonsense and replace genuine philosophical definitions and concepts with those commonly used by the man in the street. Nothing could be wider of the mark. The interest in the stock or common use of concepts as they are to be seen in the things we might ordinarily say, arose out of a preoccupation which has been central to philosophy of every kind, namely the relationships that might be said to hold between our concepts and the world. Does the logical structure of our concepts match that of the world? Some philosophers felt that clear progress toward deciding this might be obtained if philosophical reflections were couched in a formal language, the logic of which operated according to predefined principles. The model often promoted was the branch of mathematical logic known as set theory. It was argued that the gains made if this were to be done would far outweigh any drawbacks formalism might have. For a start, definitional clarity would encourage the tracing out of all implications and presuppositions thereby going a long way towards preventing arguments slipping into paradox or contradiction. The demonstration of the power of formality was to be seen in the way that fresh light was thrown on classical problems. A second gain that was to be made was the proceduralising of philosophising itself. The central philosophical task became the translation of the problem into the appropriate notation. This had one important effect. It soon became clear that translation was not simply the application of a lexicon term by term. The *sense* of the expression as well as the *reference* of the terms had to be conveyed. Such sense was determined by looking to the context of use. The difference between sense and reference, that was outlined in the Introduction to this section, and the determination of meaning by looking to context became the cornerstones of nearly all later discussions. As we will see, in part, Ordinary Language Philosophy is distinguished by its particular interpretation of what 'looking to the context' might mean.

The major thrust of an important part of philosophy, then, has been towards formality and the introduction of mathematical logic. Not everyone followed this line. Some felt that the drawbacks acknowledged by those advocating formalism were far more substantial than often allowed. The requirements of translation into the relatively narrow confines of symbolic logic often stretched and distorted concepts in ways that went unnoticed. This could result in confusion, if not outright absurdity. For example, as Austin once pointed out, Frege's definition of a name should tell us why the name 'Julius Caesar' is not a number. But why should philosophy concern itself with silly questions? Such sentiments go back in British philosophy as far as Hume, at least, if not further. But probably the most well known of the more recent advocates of the importance of keeping one's philosophical feet on the ground is G.E.Moore. Lying behind this disquiet is the conviction that philosophy is not the name of a body of knowledge over which one gains technical mastery, but an activity. Philosophy's technical vocabulary is not applied to empirical statements in the way that science's is. Terms like cognition, perception, existential quantifier, material implication are elucidated by reference to other non-technical terms drawn from everyday life. We talk about what we know, feel, require, think, take to be implied or presupposed, and so on. In philosophy one does not gain knowledge of some set of special things or philosophical objects existing in the world but of how we use our concepts to deal with the world. Since philosophy makes use of ordinary concepts in this way, some philosophers felt that rather than seeking formality and translation, we ought to give attention to those terms and their relationships in their natural settings. We ought to try to get to know what we are ordinarily doing when we use them. Looking at how such ordinary terms are used would, it was felt, reveal their underlying or *informal logic*. This knowledge would enable us to see how and when formal and informal logic meshed. The way to reveal this informal logic was through the examination of cases. There was another reason for turning to ordinary concepts and language. The proceduralising of philosophical questions began to look as if it would reduce, perhaps even eliminate, the purely philosophical issues involved in favour of the logical. We might become more concerned with why and how failures in the standard techniques occurred than with the philosophical points to be made.

The turn towards the consideration of ordinary concepts as they are on view in the things we say marks a distinct departure from what was becoming the dominant strain in philosophy. Its guiding rationale can be summarised like this. Central to all philosophy is the aim of defining what sorts of things there are in the world and how they are to be described and related. What can be said to be true, good, real, solid, imaginary? In answering these questions, philosophy has tended to want to demarcate the qualities which characterise Truth, Goodness, Reality and Imagination etc. It is these qualities which inhere in good deeds, true statements, real objects and imaginary fears. Philosophers like Ryle and Austin wish to break with this approach. All talk of examining essential qualities seems to end up as talk about what we might say in certain circumstances. That is to say, the search for essences ends as talk about particular cases. This being so, they thought, we might as well suspend the assumption that there are essential distinctions which inhere in nature independently of our concepts and direct our attention to those which are institutionalised in our language and the concepts it expresses. The examination of these distinctions will reveal their informal logic and the rules (their logical grammar) by which they are used.

Such examination can only take place on a case by case basis. Each has to be examined on its own because we have suspended the assumption that some essential quality or qualities can define them. Both Ryle and Austin accept that philosophy should aim for generality; it is how that is to be arrived at that is at issue. If one adopts the attitude that generalisation must follow from the consideration and comparison of cases, then with Ryle and Austin, one is likely to find that most philosophical theories fail. In fact, they cannot even meet the simplest of tests, namely the translation back into the ordinary terms from which the formalised, logical formulae were derived! Why does the existence of external objects cause such perplexity? What is so odd about a stick appearing to bend in water? Who would deny that they can tell when a person is angry or excited? What is so difficult about an object having two names? The consequence of pointing out that these and many other hallowed examples and difficulties might be predicated upon the distorted, perhaps even inept, use of ordinary concepts is a sort of stealthy desecration. Problems tend to be eliminated rather than accumulated. This too probably contributed to the popularity of Ryle and Austin. They seemed to be saying that, when viewed with an unprejudiced eye, many philosophical questions and puzzles seem not so much venerable as myth-eaten.

Gilbert Ryle

'Ask not what the conclusions are', Ryle advises writers of

philosophical texts and summaries, 'but look for what the big worry was'. Summaries of conclusions do not convey the point of philosophy or philosophising. They eliminate the essential feature, the formulation, consideration and appraisal of *arguments*. The discoveries that genuine philosophers make — and Ryle was not averse to speaking of philosophical discoveries — are not sets of conclusions reached, points of termination, but the routes by which they are attained. What we have here is a distinctive version of the view of philosophy that we outlined just now. Unlike the sciences, philosophy does not provide new information about the world. There are no philosophical objects to scrutinise. To think that there are, that if science is the study of the physical world and its objects, then philosophy is the study of the mental world and its objects — that is ideas — has been a recurrent mistake.

> Philosophical problems are problems of a special sort; they are not problems of an ordinary sort about special entities. (*Collected Papers*, p. vii)

What is special about philosophy's problems is that they are concerned with processes of reasoning, not the objects that we reason about. This might seem a bit strained, but what Ryle is getting at here is the way that philosophical problems are never *solved* but rather *restated* in a different form. This restating involves trying to get clear what was muddled, and untangling what was knotty and confused. It is the finding of a novel way to bring clarity to some question that constitutes a philosophical discovery. The best discoveries show how whole heaps of confusion, whole thickets of thorny questions can be straightened out and cleared. Seen in this way, it should be fairly clear that Ryle is far from advocating a single 'proper' method for philosophy. A new approach, like his own, he thought, might make some things go smoothly now whereas before they were stuck. But this being the case, they will only get stuck somewhere else. Disputation, perplexity and uncertainty are the core of philosophy. In this sense, Ryle is of a very different temper to Austin. As we will see, Austin felt that in his own preferred corner of philosophy at least he was laying down the possibility of real and permanent progress by bringing order and system. At some time in the future, the possibility was that whole classes of philosophical questions would be taken over by sciences of one kind or another. Ryle, on the other hand, doubted that anything could or should remain settled for long. He certainly did not think that matters were ever *finally* resolved.

So, what is Ryle's big worry? Luckily enough, Ryle himself has given us some indication. While not particularly attracted to nor adept at the notational complexities of modern symbolic logic, Ryle was convinced that the developments made by logicians in the past hundred years or so would, or ought to have, a significant impact upon philosophy, even in those areas where it might seem that logical issues were remote such as the philosophy of mind. The gains that were to be made, however, would not be without hiccoughs and difficulties. He saw his own role as one of facilitating the 'transactions' between logic and philosophy, a sort of broker whose task it was to indicate what was on offer and of interest, just what kind of repackaging of issues would be necessary and what the costs might be. Part of this role was the obligation to point up just what the transactions told us about the similarities and differences between logic and philosophy. At heart, the big worry was that philosophy might be swamped by logic. We suggested at the beginning of this chapter that he and Austin were part of a reaction against the overformalising of philosophical questions. The primary reason for this was not a rejection of formality itself, but the feeling that the search for formal expression in logical form often meant that the informal logic of concepts and the part it plays in philosophy was downgraded and ignored. Philosophy, as opposed to logic, ought to be preoccupied with the informal logic of our concepts. Where the downgrading occurred, Ryle felt, there appeared to be a real danger that philosophers might end up talking one or other species of nonsense. Exposing just when and how this might come about was to be Ryle's life's work.

To gain a preliminary view of the way that Ryle saw this issue, we will go fairly slowly through one of his earlier and justly celebrated papers, *Systematically Misleading Expressions*. Having grasped the general approach we will then turn to two clusters of problems to which Ryle returned again and again, the apparent irreconcilability between some ways of thinking, especially science and common-sense, and the peculiarity of some of the philosophical foundations of psychology.

Philosophers are not much interested in particular facts such as 'the speed of light in a vacuum is 186,281.7 miles/sec' or in particular meanings like one of the meanings of 'geometer' is 'a species of caterpillar'. They carry out what are sometimes called 'second order' investigations. They want to know what it is about statements like those given that makes them factual or meaningful. What is the relationship between a state of affairs and the factual proposition which describes it, or between a word and its meaning? In undertaking such investigations philosophers have to abstract and generalise. They do so by looking to the formal properties of the statements they collect together. The difficulties begin when they look *only* for formal features and hence fail to pay attention to the informal logic of the concepts — such as 'meaningful' and 'factual' — which they invoke. This can happen when the formal syntactical similarities of statements and expressions are taken as a firm guide for their logical character. When this happens, formal logic and informal logic get out of tune. It could happen, for example, if *all* factual statements are taken to have the same logical character and be about the same sorts of objects. This might lead us to think that because 'the speed of light is 186,281.7 miles/sec is a fact' has the same syntactic structure as 'the magpie is a bird' then 'facts' and 'birds' are the same sorts of things, namely describable objects in the world. Ryle's suggestion in *Systematically Misleading Expressions* is that just this sort of blunder has occurred time and time again in philosophy and has given rise to quite a few pseudo-philosophical problems.

Take the sentence 'Seb Coe is Olympic 1500-metre champion'. This records a fact about an individual, Seb Coe. We might be inclined to say that there must be some sort of relationship between that individual and the sentence which underpins its factual and meaningful character. We might then go on to say that all factual and meaningful statements stand in the same relationship to the objects or states of affairs they describe. However, were we to do this, we would soon run into trouble. What would we want to say about the sentence 'the Centaur does not exist'? This is true, meaningful and records, we might say, a fact. But 'the Centaur does not exist' cannot be about the Centaur in the same way that 'Seb Coe is Olympic 1500-metre chanpion' is about Seb Coe, or can it? The Centaur does not exist and Coe does. If we say that being Olympic champion is a feature or quality of Coe and not existing is a quality of the Centaur and the two sentences describe the possession of these qualities factually, then we have a contradiction. How can 'not existing' be a quality of something which does not exist? How can anything which does not exist have *any* qualities? To get round this, philosophers have resorted to saying that there are two sorts of objects in the world: bicycles, trees, people and other objects, and non-subsisting objects like Centaurs, unicorns, square circles. The phrase 'the Centaur' refers to a non-subsisting object in exactly the same way that 'Seb Coe' refers to Seb Coe. As we saw in the Introduction, even while they were propounding and defending this solution, many philosophers were unhappy with it. With the development of symbolic logic at the end of the nineteenth century, it looked as if a way might have been found to eliminate the need for non-existing subsistents. The logical analysis of the sentences in which such terms occurred would reveal the ontology to be unnecessary. This logical analysis consisted in the translation of such sentences into others which would then display their logical form. Thus we might 'unpack' 'Seb Coe is Olympic 1500-metre champion' into 'There is someone who is both Seb Coe and Olympic 1500-metre champion'. 'The Centaur does not exist' becomes 'there is nothing that is both half-man and half-horse and which exists'. The importance of this is that the unpacked sentence now does not imply anything about *any thing* which does or might exist.

The root of the difficulty we faced was the way that 'the Centaur does not exist' seemed to commit us to the existence of certain sorts of things because it looked to be about those things. It has, says Ryle, a 'quasi-ontological' character. It is not the negative which is causing the problem but the fact that we are dealing with an existential proposition. All existential propositions look as if they have the same sort of logical character and appear to commit us to accepting that they describe the existence of things. But they do not; they are systematically misleading. This does not mean that they do not function perfectly well in the situations where they are ordinarily used. It is only when they are transported into philosophy and logic that things go awry.

Why? Take the sentence 'this pen is red'. This commits us to accepting that this pen is an object in the world because if it is true it says something about this pen, namely that it is red. And if it is false it also says something about this pen, namely that it is not red. Now look at the case of 'Seb Coe exists'. This is an implication of the truth of the sentence 'Seb Coe is Olympic 1500-metre champion'. In Ryle's view, it would be misleading to think that this was about Seb Coe in the same way, that is, that it records a fact which might be true or false and which is parallel to 'this pen is red'. But this cannot be so for while everything looks fine if we accept that 'Seb Coe exists' is true, what about if it is false? If it is false then there is nothing for the sentence to be about. We have the difficulty with non-existent subsistents and the proposed solution of logical analysis only because we have been misled by the syntactic similarities of existential propositions to others. But existence is not like redness or solidity. It is not a quality which something can possess. The consequence of accepting Ryle's line of thinking is an increasing scepticism towards those branches of philosophy such as hermeneutics and phenomenology that have set themselves the task of elaborating and defending metaphysical schemes containing terms such as Being, Reality, Objectivity and examining the status of different orders of Being, Reality and Objectivity. Given Ryle's point of view, they are churning out systematically misleading expressions in the guise of philosophy. Any investigative discipline based upon them is similarly systematically misleading or misled.

Having dismissed the necessity for attempting to rid philosophy of non-existing subsistents and having hinted that the study of Being, Reality, Number and so on may be manufacturing metaphysical monstrosities, Ryle turns his attention towards the idea of universals. When someone says 'honesty is the best policy', this appears to be the same sort of expression as 'John is the best swimmer'. The appearance of similarity has led some philosophers to talk of there being two sorts of things in the world; universals such as beauty, truth, honesty and the like, and particulars such as this beautiful picture, this true statement and this honest person. But this is to be misled. The character of the muddle we are in can be glimpsed if we ask what it is that 'honesty' is supposed to be referring to in the sentence 'honesty is the best policy'. Is honesty the name of something separate from the things that a person does like paying for goods bought, returning items borrowed and so on? Honesty is not a separate line of action to be adopted alongside returning tools and paying bus fares. It is a characterisation of those lines of action. Thus if we unpack 'honesty is the best policy', honesty is not the name of something. Ryle feels that the implication of this is that any debate about the supposed existence of universals and exactly what sort of existence they might have is pointless. Justice, progress, equality, freedom are not the names of a certain sort of object, the characteristics of which are on display in their particular manifestations. These particulars do not have *essential* characteristics, features of the universal which they share, and to search for them is misconceived.

The third sort of misleading expression which Ryle attacks is that which he calls 'quasi-referential'. The problems which they have created are very much more familiar. For example, a great deal of philosophical energy has been expended on the sentence 'the present king of France is bald'. This is perfectly intelligible; the phrase 'the present king of France' has sense but no reference. How can this be? 'The present king of France is bald' looks rather like 'Paris is the capital of France', where 'Paris' is the name of the capital of France. But if that is the case, whom is 'the present king of France' naming? To whom does it refer? Before we rush to logic to seek an analysis, Ryle advises us to consider sentences of this sort, 'Neil Kinnock is not Prime Minister' and '17859 is not the largest integer'. These appear to be syntactically similar but they are not logically the same. The sentence 'the Prime Minister is not Neil Kinnock' is true; 'the largest integer is not 17859' is neither true nor false. There is nothing which could be the largest integer and so the term 'the largest integer' is not a name nor a description. It does not refer at all. Ryle asserts that we have to keep in mind in our philosophical discussions just when 'the . . .' expressions refer and when they do not. Many terms of location like 'the top of the tree', 'the centre of the storm' do not refer to particular things or items but to relative positions; they are attributional. Some of the difficulties raised in the philosophy of mathematics and science, for instance, might be less daunting if terms like path, space, region, value, magnitude, time and so on were treated as relative rather than referential.

What Ryle is insisting we accept is that not every sentence which appears to describe or refer actually does do so. If we don't see this, we can be lured into asking all sorts of misconceived questions. If someone were to say 'the idea occurred to me in the bath' or 'the thought flashed through my mind', we might want to reflect philosophically on what sorts of things ideas were, whereabouts in us they could occur and how long this occurrence might last. We might ask what sorts of things thoughts and minds are so that one can pass through the other. Is the relation like a current in a circuit? Similarly, to take Frege's famous case, if we fail to see just how misleading 'the meaning of "Hesperus" is identical with the meaning of "Phosphoros"' is, we will fret for a long time over what sorts of things meanings could be and how they might relate to the terms just given.

Two features of Ryle's philosophy ought to be apparent by now. First, there is the firm conviction that the examination of the grammar of concepts is a genuine and pressing philosophical task. It is a concern with informal logic and should be carried out in as perspicious a manner as possible. Second, many of the internal squabbles and confusions in philosophy owe their origins to failures to see how misleading the most ordinary of expressions can be if they are translated into philosophical discourse without reflection. They are not designed for that use and unless exercised with care will play havoc with our arguments. These two join in the work of unravelling some of the knots and tangles that philosophers have tied themselves into. We will look at just two of those with which Ryle occupied himself: what he called *dilemmas* and the logical grammar of *the concept of mind*.

A dilemma in philosophy appears when we find ourselves drawn in conflicting directions by rival ways of thinking and talking, neither of which is decisively and obviously superior. The opposing arguments look as if they should refute one another, and yet neither does. We are stuck and do not know which way to go. Here are a few of the sorts of dilemmas Ryle has in mind:

(1) You are seated at a desk reading. All around you are familiar objects. Out of the window you can see other equally familiar objects. They have a solidity, a reality, which is wholly indubitable. From your shelves you take a text in physics. Pretty soon you learn that physics has shown that ordinary solid objects are no more than whirling conglomerates of elementary particles held together by various electromagnetic forces. They only appear to be solid; really they are otherwise. You put your apparently solid coffee cup down on an apparently solid table. Your apparently solid jaw drops. Here we are pulled two ways at once. If a cup or a table are not solid, we do not know what is. And yet we do not want to deny the progress and achievements of physics. What do we say?

(2) Your eldest child is growing apace. He can now wear your shoes and clothes and pretty soon will be as tall as you. But, before he can be as tall as you, he will have to grow half the difference in your heights. He will then have to grow half the remainder and half the remainder of that and so on. It seems that there will always be an amount, no matter how infinitesimal, still left to be grown. He gets closer and closer to your height but never quite catches you up. Although you might find this quite cheering, it looks odd. We know children outgrow their parents and yet the logic of the measurement system seems to imply that they don't or can't.

(3) Here is a third. We all decide to meet for a drink next Friday. We discuss arrangements between ourselves and agree that Friday is the best time. We have made a choice. Now, if we do meet on Friday then it is true on Saturday morning that we met on the day before. Since truth cannot be time dependent, it must also have been true last Christmas that we would meet next Friday. And if that is the case, then it was true in 100 B.C. that we will meet for a drink next Friday. Faced with this, we might want to say that it is already fixed in advance

that we will meet next Friday, for we were not alive in 100 B.C. to affect the decision. We have no choice in the matter. What appear to be free actions are in fact determined. And yet we want to say that we did make a choice; nothing was fixed until we made the arrangements.

Ryle argues that what is going on here is the muddling up of 'technical' and 'untechnical' concepts because of the failure to pay sufficient attention to the role of informal logic. If we think about the cases put to us, we should soon see that what appear to be competitive ways of thinking are, in actual fact, only alternate ones. They are, or could be, quietly coexisting and the image of rivalry is a misconstrual. As we shall see, such a line will have considerable implications for the supposed boundary disputes and arguments over which explanations are 'more basic' in the human sciences.

Let us see how Ryle might untangle the meeting for a drink example. We can then look more briefly at the other two. What seems to be being said is that if it was true in 100 BC that we will meet for a drink next Friday, then this is exactly the same as the truth of the statement that we met on Friday uttered on Saturday morning. There is, to use the terms, no distinction between anterior and posterior truths. But 'we will meet next Friday' is not a statement about a state of affairs that exists; it is not a proposition which can be true or false. It is a prediction. Predictions cannot be true nor false; they can be well or ill founded, correct or incorrect. The truth or falsity of a proposition about an event is a verdict that can be arrived at only after the event. It is not a quality which can be displayed in advance. Our meeting next Friday makes the proposition true. The truth of the proposition does not make us meet next Friday. The connection between events and propositions cannot be causal, with propositions causing events; but neither is it logical. The truth of the proposition does not entail that we meet. Truths are the consequences of other truths. The truth of the proposition on Saturday morning entails the proposition that 'if in 100 B.C. some one had said "if they meet on Friday . . . then it will be true on Saturday morning that they met" ' will be true. The statement 'they will meet' would have been neither true nor false. It is only because the connection between propositions is seen as a causal one that the correctness of the prediction somehow determines the events it predicts. Causal connections hold between objects and events, not propositions. We will only succumb to what Ryle calls the fatalistic argument if we do not see that the ordinary words 'can', 'must', 'cause', 'effect' have uses in ordinary life which ramify and soon get out of control if we are not careful when we use them in philosophy.

The two other dilemmas can be reduced in much the same way. Consider the case of the growing child. As we outlined it, the problem in hand seems rather like that faced by a mother who has to divide a cake equally among her children. She could use a rule which says 'give each child the same sized portion'. Or, she could use a rule which allots to each a slice commensurate with their position in the age ranking. On this rule, perhaps, the oldest child would get half of the cake, the next oldest would receive half of what was left and so on. There would always be a portion of the cake, albeit not very much, left to divide among the remaining children. Clearly, we treated the growing child in terms of a rule such as the latter. But what has an infinite character here is neither the cake nor the difference in the heights but the number of times we can apply the division rule. We can keep dividing *ad infinitum* because the number series is infinite. There is no largest integer and hence there is no smallest fraction. The physical process of growing cannot be subjected to recursive division. We only have the dilemma when we take that principle out of its natural setting in arithmetic and try to apply it where it does not fit, namely to physical processes like growth.

The example of physics ought now to present very few problems. It looks like we have a flat contradiction between commonsense and physics. But Ryle asks us to remember that we have little or no bother in accepting that the sciences have specialised equipment and vocabulary; we do not normally use potentiometers, electron microscopes and cyclotrons. We do not normally talk of volts, quarks and creep fracture. What we have also to remember is that science also uses perfectly ordinary words in specialised ways, and this is what is happening when the physicist and we seem to be at odds over chairs, tables and cups. Think of the statement of income and expenditure that an accountant might give for a small business. We might find items like salaries with figures allocated, but no indication of what the people did to earn their salary; we might see miscellaneous travel, but have no idea from where to where the journeys were taken nor with what purpose. What does the allocation of the sum for the purchase of the microcomputer tell us about the reports written by using the word-processing package it runs? These matters would be irrelevant to the accountant. They look for a match between real expenditure and items claimed; assets and those owned. The owner and employees of the business have entirely different interests. These would be expressed in the descriptions or theories they would offer. There is no overarching, single, ultimate interest that we could take in the firm, no unique description that could be given. In the same way, the struggle between commonsense and science, or between religion and science, or between psychology and many of the human sciences is really only a sham. They offer the descriptions they do based upon the interests which they have; we can only make the conflict between them appear to stick if we set those interests up as conflicting. But they do not have to be. We should be very careful in ensuring that two different technical disciplines really are describing things in the same way before we advertise their rivalry. This is a very important point to grasp because we may easily be led into thinking that because, say, sociology is about people and so is psychology, if their accounts differ either they must be reconciled or one must be right and the other wrong. If sociology and psychology are not describing people in the same sort of way, how can they be rivals?

The use of psychology as an example was calculated. In the human sciences there has been a long-running and bruising dispute over the role that psychology ought to play. Is it the foundational discipline? Or is it merely one of a number of approaches? Some of the disquiet that is felt about psychology stems from the sorts of directions that accommodation with psychology would require us to follow. Several philosophical theories have been devoted to just this, but none have been particularly successful. In Ryle's *The Concept of Mind* we find an examination of some of the contributory reasons for this state of affairs. There, he shows how his own distinctive philosophy bears upon those covered in Part One. Ever since the Enlightenment, and perhaps even earlier, philosophical psychology has been preoccupied with the relationships between mind and body, the mental and the physical. That these terms designated a distinction between two orders of things was taken as foundational. In characteristic style, Ryle takes exception to the use of the distinction. It is based upon a mistake, and the predication of both the philosophy of mind and psychology upon it is nothing less than a monumental blunder. The distinction embodies what he calls with deliberate abuse, the Cartesian myth. His aim is to demythologise the concept of mind.

What are the tenets of the Cartesian myth? We all know that the world is made up of physical objects and processes. Bicycles are ridden, trees lose their leaves, window-sills rot. We explain these processes by causally relating certain processes with their effects. We know, or can find out, the nature of the forces enabling the bicycle to roll along, the combinations of light, soil chemistry and temperature which produces leaf fall and so on. In addition to these processes and objects, we also know that other things go on which may or may not be correlated with physical manifestations. A special category of these involve ourselves. We can show anger, or bottle it up and act as if nothing is the matter. We can count the days of the week in our heads or on our fingers. Ever since Descartes, some philosophers have wanted to treat these activities as parallel to the physical processes of bicycle riding, leaf-fall and window-sill rot. They are causal, but the causes are to be found in another dimension, as the science fiction writers might say. We are not simply physical objects; we are physical objects plus something else. We are objects with minds and what characterises our actions of holding our anger and our tongues is the involvement of our intellects or wills.

Now, after Newton's revolution in physics, it was thought, erroneously as it happens, that it would eventually be possible to explain all events in the physical universe via a mechanical model — the clockwork interaction of objects exerting forces upon one another. If this was the case, there seemed no reason why the same approach should not be applied to non-physical events such as those which involve our minds. A 'para-mechanical' model could be used with 'mental events' as well. It was thought that psychology would provide the descriptions and causal explanations of these events and particularly would demonstrate the causal interactions between mental processes and physical ones, between minds and bodies. Mental events are special because their operations are not directly open to public scrutiny. We cannot directly examine a person's thoughts, desires, wishes and feelings. They are hidden from view in the mind. The body/mind distinction segregates two different sorts of entities which interact. The physical body is a machine which is motivated (the term is deliberate) by the mind. It is our minds which cause us to make the sounds we do or control our temper. The external signs of shouting and waving and the physical correlates and effects of the mental activities of being angry or counting.

One implication of the privacy of mental phenomena is the presumption that we and we alone have privileged and direct access to them. Only I know my true thought, hatreds and wishes. The mind is defined as an inscrutable presence, the ghost, in the machine that is our bodies. Alongside any physical action of ours is the mental action which impels it. Before we wave, we must wish to wave; before we count, we know the arithmetical sequence.

For Ryle, the whole of this conventional psychology rests on one gigantic mistake, and its effects have percolated through all of the human sciences. The mistake is the pushing together of two different categories of things and processes, their concatenation in philosophical propositions and arguments. The result is a logical howler, a category mistake. The notion of a category mistake is the technical wedge which Ryle pushes into the mind/body distinction. By hammering away at it with different mental concepts — knowledge, volition, sensation, imagination, intelligence — eventually the distinction fractures. This does not mean that Ryle reduces the mental to the physical, that he insists we cannot talk of our having a mental life and only of our behaviour and brain processes. Rather it is the way that the two are set up as contrast classes which is at issue. Treating them in this way is what constitutes a category mistake.

So, what is a category mistake? Here is a Rylean type of example. Some friends come to stay. You show them around your new house. At the end of the tour, one of your visitors turns to you and says 'We have seen where you sleep, where the baby sleeps and where the older children sleep, but tell me where does the family sleep?' To ask this question is to mistake the family for something over and above the parents and the children, an additional entity that is just like them. It is a category mistake, for a family just is the parents and their children.

The category mistake on which philosophical talk of minds and bodies rests is, at root, a tendency to employ an episodic characterisation of our mental lives. Such mental acts are treated as *events* occurring in the mind. It is only because this characterisation is taken for granted that we worry where and when they occur and how long they last. We talk of mental events as if they were essentially no different to physical ones. We say the meal took an hour to cook, the children played football in the garden, the telegram arrived at 5 pm. To extend this episodic treatment to mental events leads to absurdity. Do we say someone understood the calculus between 9 and 9.30, that he knew the date of his wedding anniversary in the garden but not in the kitchen? You can have a bruise on the shin, but where do you have an idea? In the head? This surely is only a metaphor because what the neurologist can point to are brain states and neuron firings, not the ideas you have. In contrast to the episodic view, Ryle suggests that we use mental verbs to describe *dispositions*, tendencies to act in certain ways, not to describe events that are going on somewhere. If one is reading attentively or counting accurately, one is not performing a physical act of moving the eyes over the words *and* a mental act of paying attention; one is not pointing and being aware of what one is doing. No self-monitoring needs to be taking place at all.

Some dispositional verbs are polymorphous, as Ryle calls them, and others are not. That is to say, some are amenable to precise descriptions of the activity they describe, others are not. You might say that a bricklayer does some fairly specific things, like laying bricks; but what specific things does teaching involve? Teaching, unlike bricklaying, is a polymorphous concept. Teachers do lots of different things and not all teachers need do the same things. Thinking, planning, solving, understanding are all polymorphous in that doing them does not involve some precise and fixed action of the mind. We can do them out loud, silently, on paper, in conversation, some spontaneously and some thoughtfully. In addition, some of these mental verbs are not process verbs at all but mark achievements. They are like defeating and finishing, not like fishing and writing. We cannot ask how long someone was finishing (except in an extended and peculiar sense), so we do not ask how long they were understanding, grasping or solving a problem.

With the notion of the episodic description of mental events as a category mistake, Ryle cuts a great swathe through the philosophy of mind. If we look at the concept of knowledge, for instance, straightaway we see that we use the verb 'to know' not just about propositional knowledge (knowledge that such and such is the case) but also dispositional (knowledge how to do such and such). To treat both of these as associated with the same mental activity requires us to reduce the one to the other. This is what the philosophy of mind has been tempted to try to do. It suggests that knowing how to play chess, the favourite example, we know the rules of chess (that pawns capture diagonally, that rooks move in straight lines) and the criteria when to apply these rules (which pieces are pawns and rooks). The problem with this assimilation is that it is regressive. To know how to apply the rules of chess won't we need to know rules and criteria about rules, and hence rules and criteria about the rules of rules? In any case, knowing how to swim, play the piano or make shadow figures on the wall doesn't seem to require us to be able to list sets of propositions about these things. We can do all of these things with little or no knowledge of a theoretical sort. We might want to say that such propositional knowledge is to be found at a deeper level, although that geological image is a little mystifying. Linguists have struggled for years to assimilate the knowledge of how to speak grammatically to knowledge of propositions concerning the grammar which underlies how we speak. They have not met much success and at least one group of them have written the whole issue off by defining grammar as innate.

The importance of the dispositional view is not that we stop employing mental predicates but that it stops us treating them as all of a piece. People do mental arithmetic; they also count and add up with pencil and paper, on an abacus or even with a computer. People can reason in silent contemplation but also in conversation with friends or by drawing pictures. The thinking of thoughts, the reasoning, does not have to be treated as an occult activity going on alongside or prior to speaking or drawing.

As with knowledge, so with another of the specifically mental concepts, volition. This is a technical term covering wishing, willing, wanting, trying, and was 'invented' to provide the causal connection between the mental and the physical. It is by exercising our will that we raise our hand in greeting, control our tempers or kick the cat. However, Ryle argues that the whole catalogue of volitional concepts rests upon a false dichotomising of the terms 'voluntary' and 'involuntary' when applied to actions. It is said that some actions such as blushing, sneezing or blinking are involuntary or automatic while the rest are voluntary. What characterises a voluntary action is the exercise of our will, which makes it both morally appraisable and the expression of our mental life. In Ryle's view, this juxtaposing misses the whole character of our ordinary uses of voluntary and involuntary. I might try to poison next door's dog by putting out slug pellets, but do I try to move the pen when I write? What has my will got to do with the latter automatic action? What of actions that are habitual or conventional? Do I wish to return a greeting when I respond to someone else's 'hello'? Or do I just do it? Ryle argues that the question of the voluntariness or otherwise of an action arises only when something fishy has occurred, where there has been a lapse or violation in expectations. Such cases cannot be generalised to all actions. The purpose of stretching the concepts was to create enough space for the exercise of free will and so fend off the threats of materialism and mechanism. But these two hobgoblins need only be feared if we allow them the toe-hold upon the mental which they require, namely the contradistinction between the voluntary and the involuntary as part of the larger class of distinctions, namely those between mind and matter.

At first sight, it is easy to suppose, as many have done, that in dismantling the mind/body distinction Ryle has no alternative but to adopt behaviourism of one sort or another. This is to jump to the conclusion that if Ryle is being polemical — and he is — *against* a theory of the mind, it must be because he is arguing, albeit if tacitly, *for* some other one. This is not the case. Ryle wants to put a stop to wholesale generalisations, fixed frameworks and stipulative definitions. His case is that the instance of the oppositions of mind and body, widely adopted in the philosophy of mind, shows that such generalisations do not stand up to sustained examination. Throughout the rest of his life, Ryle continued to worry away at what exactly there was to be said about thinking, speculating, learning, and what exactly *le penseur* was doing. He does not advocate behaviourism, or any other programme, because to his mind they are all equally defective, if in differing ways. The behaviourist, for example, will not allow a describable difference to be described between someone waiting for a bus and someone sheltering from the rain. They go through the same physical motions, namely standing immobile in the bus-shelter. But waiting and sheltering are not the same, and a 'thick description' of the activities would reveal it. The dissatisfaction with all settled schemas as they stand is reflected in Ryle's view of the psychological sciences. What is generally called psychology is, for him, a peculiar and rather restricted research programme which, as we have already indicated, would have to be placed alongside linguistics, sociology, psychiatry and literary criticism. Abandoning the Cartesian myth will mean the abandonment 'of the idea that there is a locked door and a still to be discovered key' (*The Concept of Mind*, p. 302) which it is psychology's task to find. Under the rubric of Cartesianism, psychologists have studied facial and other physical movements, verbal responses and manipulative skills in the belief that these were the outward sign of inward processes. In so doing they have restricted themselves to some not very interesting and rather uninformative data, often in the confused belief that they are thereby being more scientific. He does not want to stop those who are interested in these things from practising their arts, but to try to wean psychology from the conviction that this is *all* that it is allowed to study. The data normally used by policemen, stockbrokers, teachers, judges and social workers is all psychological, as is that of the historian who interprets the motives for signing a treaty or declaring a war and the architect who plans a building that is both pleasing to look at and work in.

If we give up the idea that psychology is about something that the other human studies are not about, and if give up, therewith, the idea that psychologists work on data from which the other studies are debarred, what is the *differentia* between psychology and these other studies? (*The Concept of Mind*, p. 304)

The answer, of course, is that there is none. But this should not bother us, for the doctrine that all of the physical world is explainable by theories in physics leaves no room for Mendel or Darwin to offer their distinctive theories, just as it leaves no room alongside psychology for economics, librarianship or marketing. The two-worlds dogma is also a two-sciences dogma, the single science of the physical and that of the mental. If we drop the distinction then there is no need to force psychological explanations into the strait-jacket of causalism, thereby rendering them not just implausible but absurd.

Although Ryle's aim was to sensitise philosophers and others to the nuances of the informal logic of our ordinary concepts, his work has not proved all that easy to accommodate within the social sciences. In part this is because the major implication of what he has to say must be that many of the treasured distinctions, such as that between the mind and the body, are simply inadequate. This point has been repeatedly made by Jeff Coulter, among others, with regard to the aims and ambitions of cognitive science and psychoanalysis, but with little effect. Ryle's influence has been rather more strongly felt in anthropology where it has been mediated through the writing of Clifford Geertz. Geertz has made particular use of the idea of 'thick description' in bringing out the important part which interpretive understanding must play in anthropological accounts. It is not enough to give a résumé of functions and causes; a detailed description of the ambitions, motivations, desires and so on of the participants is a *sine qua non* of any adequate understanding of a way of life. In some ways the social and cultural sciences have been able to insulate themselves from Ryle's philosophy. Austin, on the other hand, was for a while extremely influential in a very delimited sphere.

J.L. Austin

Ryle gives considerable attention to the larger issues of method and the scope of philosophy as he sees it. He is at considerable pains to locate his interests and approach. Austin is not. He gives only a passing explanation of his objectives in two places. In *A Plea for*

Excuses he indicates something of how he goes about attacking a particular problem and in *Ifs and Cans* he connects what he has to say with other discussions of free will to be found in moral and ethical philosophy. The rest of the time the links remain allusive, hidden in puns, asides, jokes and revamped examples. He is well aware that, as a consequence, many will find his work trivial and irrelevant. But he is inclined to think that, as they do not share his attitudes and priorities, they would probably miss his point anyway. To take an example; many philosophers are interested in how to make moral judgements. To achieve this they look for criteria by which to distinguish the description of an activity from its appraisal. They need these so that their appraisals can be firmly based. In Austin's view, if after the examination of cases it turns out that the distinction between appraisal and description is by no means as clear-cut as might be thought, this has obvious implications for moral philosophy. The moral philosophers looking for firm guidelines on how to make the distinction, on the other hand, are apt to find him baffling. He says he is talking about their problems, about what is good and what is right but to them he doesn't seem to be doing so.

Part of this, of course, has to do with the self-effacing style that Austin adopts. But also, it is a result of the approach. If philosophy wishes to sharpen up our perception of the complexities of human action, then one way of doing this would be to sharpen up our understanding of the ways in which we talk about such action. If we prise words off the world we will get a better view of both them and the world. Or at least that is Austin's view. The philosopher can do this either by falling back on his own individual resources and ingenuity — the examples he can dream up and the distinctions he can invent — or he can use those already available to him and enshrined in common, ordinary discourse. The latter have a distinct advantage over the former in that they have stood the test of time. They have proved their usefulness. There is a need for care though. Not every question shows itself immediately amenable to this kind of handling, nor are significant results obtained every time. But enough progress has been made, in Austin's opinion, to warrant holding a modicum of hope for the settling of issues in some parts of philosophy. But there are also snags and obstacles, not however of the kind usually thought of. First, it is not being suggested, for example, that symmetry with ordinary usage is the criterion for the acceptability of philosophical distinctions. Rather, where such symmetry is absent, we should be offered clear and defensible reasons for it. Ordinary language has the first word not the last. This is an attitude which many of Austin's colleagues have remarked was present even before his philosophy took the distinctive turn that it eventually did. Second, although usage does differ, such differences are by no means as deep-seated or prevalent as might be at first imagined. Often they reflect real differences in cases or, what is much the same, perceptions and definitions, and not a mismatching of concepts.

Austin's favourite philosopher was Aristotle. Both share the same tendency towards dealing with questions by classification and taxonomies. Austin would begin by drawing up a list of the terms and concepts closely associated with the issue at stake. If we are interested in perception, then the list might include see, hear, feel, sense, watch, tune in, notice and so on. Then, as many synonyms as possible are collected by reference to dictionaries, thesauruses, disciplines with a technical interest in the topic (psychology, in this case perhaps) and anywhere else that we might think relevant. Austin's own favourite was Case Law. Once the collection has been compiled, it is arranged into types, classes and taxonomies.

> With these sources, and with the aid of imagination, it will go hard if we cannot arrive at the meanings of large numbers of expressions and at the understanding and classification of large numbers of 'actions'. Then we shall comprehend clearly much that was, before, only made use of *ad hoc*. Definition, I would add explanatory definition, should stand high among our aims: it is not enough to show how clever we are to show how obscure everything is. Clarity too, I know, has been said to be not enough: but perhaps it will be time to go into that when we are within measurable distance of achieving clarity on some matter. (*Philosophical Papers*, p. 189)

Using this method, Austin sought to bring clarity to a range of philosophical problems. To look at them all would require so much truncation and summarising that we would do Austin a grave disservice. The insight and power of his work lie in the particularities. Perhaps as much as any other philosopher, and more than most, Austin has to be read in the original. What we will do is to set out Austin's reflections on two themes that have bedevilled the human sciences, namely, the old and trusted opposition between free will and determination (one of the paradoxes we discussed with regard to Ryle) and the identification of types of action.

One approach to the mare's nest of problems in moral philosophy has been to separate those actions where the individual is deemed to be free from constraint and those where he is not. The former are to be treated as morally different from the latter. For example, we may abdicate responsibility by saying that we were acting under orders or under threat. In *A Plea for Excuses* Austin looks at the fundamental distinction between freedom and constraint. In philosophical discussions the question of freedom has tended to be raised somewhat negatively. In his opinion, philosophers have tended to define freedom as 'not unfreedom'. In general, claims about the limitations put on freedom of action arise in the consideration of non-normal cases, when someone would have normally acted otherwise but for the constraining conditions, whatever they were. It is clear, then, that one place where the issue of moral evaluation is visible in ordinary life is when the question of responsibility for an action arises, and hence when attempts are made to slough off, avoid, deny and duck such responsibility by making the action excusable. It is Austin's conclusion that more progress in moral philosophy might have been made if less attention had been paid to the range and types of constraint under which actions are performed, and more to the allocation of responsibility.

The method is as follows. First, excuses are segregated from justifications. Both are offered when someone is accused of something untoward. Justifications claim that the circumstances made it permissible: excuses insist that more should be taken into account. The two are of course interrelated and overlapping.

> You dropped the tea tray: Certainly, but an emotional storm was about to break out: or, Yes, but there was a wasp. In each case, the defence, very soundly, insists on a fuller description of the event in its context; but the first is a justification, the second an excuse. (*Philosophical Papers*, p. 176)

In turn, each of these classes is separated from others such as palliation, provocation and extenuation. This is done by examining the fine detail of occasions when each might be offered and found acceptable. If we were to work our way through such cases, Austin thinks that we would have to accept several conclusions, all of which hinge on the breakdown of what seem to be simple, obvious and unimpeachable distinctions. We would find that some straightforward negations such as voluntary and involuntary do not seem to be used oppositionally. I might not want to describe my flicking a switch to turn on the radio as an involuntary action, but it would only be under certain special circumstances that I would want to call it voluntary either. Again, not all modifications of actions are equally applicable in all circumstances. I can unwittingly indicate that I know more than I let on about a crime, but can I unwittingly confess to it? If we do look at how different concepts act in association or are kept apart, how modifications are made and descriptions phrased, we will soon be convinced that simple, generalised distinctions are by no means as useful for describing actions as we might have thought. We will have got to the inner workings of the machinery of action. We will also have become sensitive to the 'trailing clouds of etymology' which, as we have already seen with Ryle, philosophers are prone to overlook. For example, the original use of cause and effect has spilled over into philosophy giving rise to the arguments over free will and determinism. Once we are aware of this, we can discount it.

The consideration of excuses also indicates just how ordinary usage is limited and undergoing change, as well as what philosophy can offer by way of help. Austin offers two examples of the extension of technical distinctions in the human sciences to ordinary life: compulsive behaviour and displacement behaviour. Both have been noted and described by psychiatrists and psychologists. Here is an intriguing question for ethics. Does defining some behaviour as compulsive or displacing take it outside the scope of moral evaluation? If so, can any action be so defined, or only limited classes? Under what circumstances might an action be so described? Can you be a compulsive divorcee as well as a compulsive gambler? Can you displace affection as well as aggression?

Three Ways of Spilling Ink takes up the question of responsibility by looking at the logical grammar of volitional concepts such as intentional, purposeful and deliberate. These terms are central because, on the conventional view, it is the application of them to certain actions that makes them morally appraisable. Austin, as usual, launches a two-pronged attack. He assembles and examines an array of cases wherein the different terms apply, and where alternatives would be inappropriate. We might ask our daughter's beau what his intentions are, but hardly what his purposes are, and we know what his desires are! He can have honourable intentions; what would honourable purposes be? We might say that George killed the golden goose intentionally, thereby indicating that he meant to do it. If we say he killed it deliberately, we meant with and after deliberation.

In doing the deed George might achieve his purpose; he could not achieve his intention. The taxonomy is built up by surveying and marking what we would say about the actions of intending, deliberating and purposing, the modifications that can be effected on them and relationships they stand in. What is the significance of the fact that we do something *on* purpose but *with* intent? These observations lead Austin to suggest that ascribing an intention is a way of structuring a set of activities so that we can see that 'all along they intended to . . .', while purposes are aims that can be achieved. But none of the terms govern the meanings of their 'negatives'. 'Voluntary' and 'intentional' do not 'wear the trousers' for involuntary and unintentional. Anyway, what exactly are the negatives of deliberate and purposeful? The gradation of descriptions of actions and their appraisal cannot be reduced to the stark contrast between 'free will' and 'determination'. Things are never that simple.

In *How to Do Things with Words* the range of Austin's virtuosity is on show and the innovations for which he is most well known are made. In what follows we will endeavour to give the essentials of the argument while knowing full well that we will do him less than justice.

Let us consider, once again, the notorious sentence 'the present king of France is bald'. When examining this and the other familiar examples 'here is a hand', 'Scott is the author of Waverley', philosophers have primarily been occupied with the logical character of propositions. They have worried about what makes them true or false, meaningful or meaningless. Do we have to posit non-existent subsistents? Are descriptions names? Does saying 'here is a hand' imply that I know here is a hand, and does that presuppose that I believe I have a hand? If so, is 'I have a hand, and I believe it' a tautology? These and other considerations focus on what might be called the logic of statements and disregard the logic of the actions performed in making the statements. Conventional philosophical logic has broadened the notion of context to the whole sentence or expression, but has not included the action the expression accomplishes. Like Ryle, Austin suggests that focusing on the propositional character of expressions alone can be misleading or limiting, for not everything that looks like a statement actually is a statement, and not all propositions are cast in propositional form. The saying of 'I name this ship Britannia' ia naming the ship, not a proposition or description of the action. 'I promise to pay the bearer on demand' is an act of promising, not a description of an intention or a proposition about some future action. Rather than having truth conditions, entailments and presuppositions, such *performative utterances* are only successful when the required felicity conditions are fulfilled. These conditions govern the informal, conventional logic of performance of the actions. *How to Do Things with Words* is given over to sketching out this logic.

Austin begins by making and considering the distinction between the acts of promising, swearing, betting and the performative of stating something. These latter are *constative actions*. Many of the philosophical difficulties brought out by the examination of constatives such as those of entailment, implication and presupposition, only arise because the contextual conditions normally considered with regard to activities are ignored or processed out. Mood, tone of voice, occasion are context dependent and so not formalisable. And yet these are precisely the resources that we use to grasp the meaning of utterances, including constative ones in ordinary life. We can usually tell when 'the plates are hot' is a warning or a description etc. In Austin's eyes, logic is cutting itself off from the means of solving its own self-imposed problems. As ever, he finds this to be both significant and not very widely recognised.

However, the distinction between performative and constative is not really a useful one. It breaks down too easily. So Austin goes off on another tack. He identifies three differing aspects of utterances, what he calls the locutionary, illocutionary and prelocutionary. This marks his real technical innovation and is used as follows.

(1) The locutionary aspect is the use of words simply to convey certain meanings: 'the plates are hot' simply as a description of the plates.

(2) The illocutionary force is the conventional action accomplished in saying 'the plates are hot' as a description or a warning.

(3) The perlocutionary aspect is the effect or consequence so achieved. In warning you, I prevent you from burning yourself.

The difference between these three marks the difference between what is *done* and what is *said*. Once that is on the philosophical agenda, the next obvious task is the elaboration of more and more other performatives and the delineation of their felicity conditions.

Austin makes no bones about the preliminary nature of the list of performatives given and the need to refine and amend them. Many subsequent discussions have tried to update or wreck one or some of them. Two things do become quite clear. First, the scheme allows Austin 'to play Old Harry' with a number of hallowed philosophical distinctions, in particular what he calls the true/false and fact/value fetishes. If one can promise 'falsely', does that mean one can promise 'truly'? Are these the same as saying that a promise is true or false, correct or incorrect? What of fact and value? Is a finding always the report of a fact? Or can it sometimes be an appraisal? What about denial, refutation and speculation? Once doubts have been raised and the complexities appreciated then it will be apparent that the analysis of performative utterances — speech acts as they became known — might show how the beginnings of a science of human action could be laid down as well as indicating how to get a grip on some slippery philosophical issues.

As it turned out, Austin's influence was largely limited to speech act theory. Within philosophy this soon dropped out of vogue. Consideration of the minutiae of cases and the provision of taxonomies of concepts are still to be found, as in the work of A.R. White, but the real impact was felt elsewhere. This was in the application of John Searle's extension of speech act theory to problems in linguistics. Consideration of performative characteristics was suggested as a way of dealing with semantic ambiguity, as when 'who's there?' might be analysed as a question or a challenge. Linguists sought to elaborate performative rules of implication to show how a sentence like 'what I say now is false', while meaningful, is a paradox. The irony is that the machinery brought in to make possible this type of analysis is that provided by modern symbolic logic. Socio-linguistics — and in particular Conversation Analysis — has been influenced by the phenomenon of performative utterances and the structural connections between sequences of such actions rather than by the philosophy. Discourse analysts have found similar uses for the term by looking for the rules by which meanings are located and determined within the conversation as a whole, and by its social context.

In an entirely different part of the sociological universe, Habermas has been developing a theory of communicative competence which as we have seen in Chapter 3 is an attempt to provide a hermeneutic philosophy of social life. Speech acts have been identified as the elementary unit of linguistic communication. The conditions surrounding 'the ideal speech act' of communicative action and of theoretical discourse differ. They require different competences. In the communicative action of ordinary life there are background determinations of comprehensibility, truthfulness, veracity, etc. which are taken for granted. In theoretical discourse, it is the argumentation itself which convinces. Where such ideal conditions do not obtain, we have the entry of human interests and the possibility of ideology. The discussion of Habermas in Chapter 3 shows how this is all connected to his critical theory of social life.

Austin's influence has been primarily in linguistics, and even there it is on the wane. But at least it was in an area to which he himself felt attracted. He did make a direct contribution to developments in sociolinguistics and semantics. Ryle can draw little if any such comfort. In spite of the energetic promotion of his views by Coulter and others, his views on the logical problems in the philosophy of mind, thought and language seem not to have percolated through to psychology and those others who take a professional interest in such matters. More importantly, the indisputable character of the foundational categorical distinctions remains intact, and indeed revered in the human sciences. It would be a rethinking of these that Austin and Ryle would probably prefer to have as their legacy.

Recommended Reading

The best general collection of work available is Richard Rorty, *The Linguistic Turn* (University of Chicago Press, 1967). Two other collections are Colin Lyas, *Philosophy and Linguistics* (Macmillan, 1971) and the two-part series *Logic and Language* edited by A. Flew and published by Blackwell, series I in 1966 and series II in 1968. Apart from Ryle's *Collected Papers* (Hutchinson, 1971), some of which are devoted to exegetical exercises in Greek philosophy, the three most important writings are *The Concept of Mind* (Penguin, 1973), *Dilemmas* (Cambridge University Press, 1954) and *On Thinking* (Blackwell, 1979). A set of appraisals is to be found in O.P. Wood and G. Pitcher (eds.), *Ryle* (Macmillan, 1971). A serious exposition is contained in W. Lyons, *Gilbert Ryle* (Harvester, 1980). A very recent presentation of Ryle's views is A. Palmer, 'Ryle Cogitans', *Philosophy*, vol. 59, (1984), Austin's work is nearly all contained in three places: his *Philosophical Papers* (Oxford University Press, 1970), *Sense and Sensibilia* (Oxford University Press, 1962) and *How to Do Things with Words* (Oxford University Press, 1976). Two collections on Austin give useful guidelines: K.T. Fann (ed.) *A Symposium of John Austin* (Routledge, 1969) and Isiah Berlin (ed.) *J.L. Austin* (Clarendon, 1973). The major extension of speech act theory is John Searle's *Speech Acts* (Cambridge University Press, 1969). Stanley Cavell's *Must We Mean What We Say* (Scribner, 1969) is also worth consulting. An exemplary contemporary example of work carried out in the Austinian style is A.R. White 'Shooting, Killing and Fatally Wounding', *Proceedings of the Aristotelian Society* (1979-80). The application of Ryle's philosophy to the human sciences has largely been through attacks on cognitive science by Jeff Coulter such as his *The Social Construction of Mind* (Macmillan, 1979) and *Rethinking Cognitive Theory* (Macmillan, 1983), and Clifford Geertz's use of the notion of 'thick description' in the paper of that name in his *The Interpretation of Cultures* (Hutchinson, 1975). Austin's work received wide attention in linguistics. A summary of the use to which it was put can be seen in J. Lyons, *Language, Meaning and Context* (Fontana, 1981). Another more technical account is in S. Levinson, *Pragmatics* (Cambridge University Press, 1983). Applications to the areas of socio-linguistics are W. Labov and D. Fanshell *Therapeutic Discourse* (Academic Press, 1977) and Roy Turner's 'Words Utterances and Activities' in his *Ethnomethodology* (Penguin, 1974).

PART THREE

10 THE PHILOSOPHY OF SCIENCE

In essence, the philosophical questions asked about the social sciences are all to do with their distinctiveness. Does the fact that their subject matter differs so markedly from that of the natural sciences mean that the forms of theory, methods and the attitudes we take towards them have to be different too? In a sense, we could say that discussions of the social sciences have taken place in the shadow of the natural ones. Time and again, decisions over whether to have general causal laws, what sorts of objects social sciences have to posit, how best to ensure a fit between theory and data, are taken in light of what is felt to be the case for the natural sciences. The aspirations we can have for the social sciences seem to have been defined by the epistemology, ontology and methodology of the natural sciences. As we have seen in our previous discussions, it has proved extremely difficult to break out of the compulsion to make implicit if not explicit comparisons with science all the time. In fact, it is the attempt to break with this mentality which makes philosophers such as Wittgenstein and Derrida so difficult for social scientists. The comparison with science is, then, almost built into the social sciences' self-identity. It forms the most important, if not the only theme unifying discussions of the history of theory and the character of contemporary theoretical pluralism. The comparison, and its centrality in conceptions of disciplinary identity, can be seen in the special emphasis that is given to methodological training in the social sciences. Newcomers to the subject do not learn facts about social science, as is the case in the natural sciences. They are given courses in methods.

This comparison with the natural sciences often proceeds through an acquaintance with the philosophy of science. If we can establish clearly exactly what the character of theory, method and so on are in science, we should — or so it is thought — be better able to determine the claims to scientific status which the social sciences can make. A difficulty now arises. Such discussions are usually couched in terms of a consideration of the history of science or, even more often, the history of one or two special sciences, physics, astronomy or chemistry, with little or no attention being given to why these sciences should be thought to be philosophically significant. Their history has been taken as definitive of all scientific theory and method. We will

229

try to keep these two aspects separate although, as we will see, many philosophers do not. They tend to look to the history of science to tell us what the nature of scientific knowledge is, as well as what it is about science that enables or encourages us to give its conclusions so much weight. Since these questions have dominated much of the consideration of the philosophy of science in the social sciences, we will spend most time with them. We will see that discussion about the nature of theory, the nature of method and the logic to be applied to both are all closely intertwined. At the end of this chapter, though, we will also introduce a different consideration, one which is concerned not with scientific theory but with scientific experimentation and observation and what they can tell us that is of philosophical interest. In all of this we will confine ourselves deliberately to introductory matters, to finding our way around in the arguments. In addition, we will set aside those questions which can be raised with regard to any body of knowledge. How do concepts and data relate? What is the relation between theoretical knowledge and empirical knowledge? The answers that might be given have been systematically alluded to in all of the various chapters that have preceeded this. The greater part of our discussion will reflect the emphasis that has been given to settling the form of theory and method — that is *methodology* — in the philosophy of science.

There is a second reason for taking this line through the debates. Incontestably, the most important influence on all discussions of the philosophy of the social sciences since the 1950s has been the work of Sir Karl Popper. Popper's 'falsificationism' has, for many, been the only topic which they are familiar with within the philosophy of science. 'Falsificationism' is a methodological doctrine and while it does have very strong and clear connections to the 'evolutionary epistemology' which Popper espouses, these connections are not usually examined in any detail.

This chapter, then, follows the normal tradition. We have made Popper's contribution the fulcrum around which the others will turn. We will begin by sketching the background to Popper's methodology, the sorts of questions which it was designed to answer. We will then examine 'falsificationism' in some detail together with the explanatory strategy with which it is associated. From there we will go on to look at the responses that philosophers and philosophically inspired historians of science have made to Popper's suggestions. We will end with a look at how the whole question of methodology has been largely circumvented by recent developments.

The Classical Background: Inductivism

To most non-philosophers, and perhaps to most non-scientists as well, it is indisputable that science makes discoveries about the world. In itself, though, this assertion doesn't take us very far. If they were to be pushed a little harder, it is likely that most people would say that (a) science accumulates well attested facts, and the addition of new facts does not affect the factual status of those we already have; (b) from the list of facts we have, it is possible to formulate or infer an entirely novel fact, a true general law; such laws express and summarise collections of known simple facts; and (c) the confidence we can have in a theory depends upon the number of confirmatory instances of it which we have to hand. A general or universal law is accepted because all of the cases which we have so far examined are in accordance with it. On this view, scientific theorising is the combination of these three elements and is grounded in the logico-experimental techniques which all the best sciences use. Other sciences are forced to use approximations to these techniques which are more or less satisfactory.

A crucial element in inductivism — and it is this which allows it to be harnessed to the techniques of experimentalism — is the prediction of novel facts; wholly new instances are derived on the basis of the ones which are already known. Such predictions enable experiments to be designed and a certain form of logic to be invoked in order to test the generalisations being offered. One convenient way of summarising the whole methodology is to see it as an interconnected set of steps.

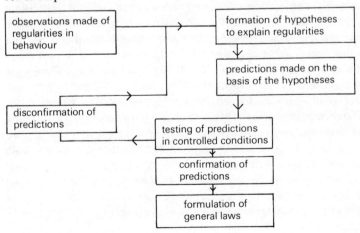

One example that is often cited to show how science proceeds in this inductive way is the discovery of Neptune. Ever since it was first observed it had been noticed that the orbit of Uranus was eccentric. This eccentricity was relatively stable and regular. Drawing upon Newton's celestial mechanics, John Adams and Urbain Leverrier separately came to the conclusion that the eccentricity could only be explained by hypothesising the existence of a further planet of a particular size orbiting beyond Uranus. Whenever this planet passed close to Uranus its mass exerted a gravitational pull and it was this which explained the eccentricity in Uranus' perihelion. Adams and Leverrier calculated the mass of the planet and exactly when and where to look for it. In 1846, John Galle focused his telescope on that spot and found the planet Adams and Leverrier had predicted. It has since been named Neptune. This discovery provided yet another instance of the confirmation of Newton's theories.

The discovery of Neptune displays all of the elements to be found in inductive reasoning and the use of logico-experimentalist techniques. It is premissed on a principle of universal causality, where every observable event, the eccentricity of the perihelion in this case, has a knowable cause. This cause is the conjunction of prior sets of conditions and the relationship which holds between them. In the example we have the close approximation of the two celestial bodies and the universality of gravitational effects. The task of scientific theory, on the inductivist view, is to identify the causal conditions and to generalise them into causal laws. This identification is achieved by what are called the 'method of agreement' and the 'method of difference'. The method of agreement enjoins the investigator to examine the antecedent conditions to two identical events. If there is a common condition among the two clusters, then this is the cause. If there are many, then they must be varied under controlled conditions so that their causal contribution can be evaluated. The method of difference is the reverse of this. If two clusters of conditions are identical save in one respect and they result in different events, then what is different in the conditions is the essential cause of the difference in outcomes. This is the *logic* of logico-experimentalism. All that experimental sophistication adds is greater and greater control over the conditions being studied and hence greater precision in the predictions being made.

If inductivism is the methodology of science, then the implication for the human sciences is quite clear. As far as possible they will have to model themselves on this methodology and forge investigative techniques that correspond to logico-experimentalism. They will have to search for generalisations concerning efficient causation by means of precise prediction and observation. Because of the practical and ethical problems of running experiments on human beings, in many cases this has meant that the social sciences have had to rely upon techniques of sampling and inferential statistics. In psychology, though, it has been deemed possible to match the natural science inductive method fairly closely. Of all the social sciences, experimentalism has been taken furthest there — though at what cost has been a prominent theme in some of the previous chapters, where we have seen that those that have resisted the introduction of the natural science model within the social sciences have done so precisely because the principle of universal causality did not capture the essential feature of human social and cultural life. This was held to be interpretive and subjective and not causal and objective. The consequences seen to follow from this difference have been explored at length already.

Despite its grip on the popular imagination and the long shadow that it cast over debates in the social sciences, several serious objections to the plausibility of inductivism as the methodology of science have been raised. One of them owes its origins to an argument which David Hume propounded in the eighteenth century. It has been rerun in different guises in modern times. The sceptical argument associated with Hume can take two forms, one epistemological and the other logical. The former asks what guarantees our certainty about scientific knowledge. How do we know we have identified the real causes? How do we delimit the conditions to be examined? How do we relate the theoretical conceptions we use, such as, say, valency and chemical bonding with the actual way that compounds are stuck together? These questions raise the grounds of knowledge, how theories are arrived at and test conditions shaped up. As we saw in the Introduction to Part One, they can be raised about any body of knowledge, not just science, and even today still cause puzzlement and irritation to philosophers. The second form of the sceptical question concerns the adequacy of inductivism as a logical or rational reconstruction of what science does in fact do. If science actually does tell us truths about the world, can it possibly do so in the way that inductivism suggests? One version of the logical question asks about the extension of claims made about some members of a set to all members of that set. This is one way of characterising Hume's own particular contribution. The other version asks about the truth status of any single general law in the light of scientific history. This is known as the successor theory problem. As we will see in a moment, Popper's 'falsificationism' was designed to solve both Hume's problem and the successor theory problem.

Let us take Hume's logical problem first. Essentially the argument is this. What are the grounds for supposing that the regularities we have observed so far for a class of phenomena are generalisable to all members of the class? We may have been testing the proposition 'all sulphur burns with a yellow flame' for some time, and so far every sample of sulphur we have set fire to has satisfied the generalisation. We may feel fairly confident that the next sample will do so too. We may even feel that it is bound to burn with a yellow flame. But our compulsion to say that it is bound to burn with a yellow flame is not a logical one. It is based upon a supposition of symmetry between all future cases and those which we have examined so far. Our willingness to bridge the logical gap between 'some' and 'all' is, for Hume, an understandable habit of mind. Putting it in logical terms, we can say that we cannot extend the quantification from 'some' to 'all' and be certain we have preserved the truth of the proposition. The move is not truth-preserving of itself.

It ought to be clear by now that it is not the truth of scientific propositions that is at issue, but the strategy for arriving at them. It could well be that 'all sulphur burns with a yellow flame' is perfectly true. However, if it were to be arrived at by induction then, on Hume's argument, its truth could not be guaranteed. The method of reasoning does not guarantee the preservation of truth. The symmetry between the two classes, and hence the proposition, is achieved by the assumption that the world will continue in exactly the same way that it has up until now. That assumption is itself unsecured and unsecurable. It is important to see that the argument is not saying that science is illogical or invalid. All it is saying is that, whatever else it is, the logico-experimental method of science cannot be deductively valid. And, if deductive validity is used as the criterion of truth, then we are not able to guarantee that scientific generalisations are true. Their truth is contingent and not necessary. Things could have been otherwise.

One common response when faced with arguments like this is to point to science's achievements. We have put men into space; we can cure deadly diseases; we can even control the most powerful of natural forces. Surely that shows science is right? Unfortunately all this amounts to is an attempt to justify induction inductively. Looking at the vast range of things that science has got right so far, assuming always that it got them right by use of induction, does not allow us to step from *some* scientific generalisations to *all* such generalisations and their truth. The inductive method might have been successful in the past, but that is no guarantee for the future.

Inductivists, of course, recognise the naïvety of arguing like this. They have often suggested that the past success of science simply makes it highly probable that it will be successful in the future. This involves redefining scientific generalisations as 'probability statements', with the number of confirmatory instances laying down the degree of probability. Well known and well tested laws, such as Boyle's Law and Ohm's Law, have probabilities that are so close to 1 (all probabilities lie between ± 1) as to make no realistic difference. This doesn't actually get us out of the problem, though. Hume's argument not only blocks generalisations to *all* future cases, quantifying upwards; we might say, it blocks it to any *particular* case, quantifying downwards. We cannot guarantee in advance of setting fire to it that this sample of sulphur will burn with a yellow flame. We may guess that it will; we may even presume that it will. But that is precisely Hume's point.

The worry over the validity of inductive logic has never really gone away. Logicians have attempted many different strategies to resolve the problem or to escape from it. In the end, most of them come down to a 'justification in the circumstances' argument. It would simply be illogical not to accept strong inductive inference.

The issue over successor theories is of a different kind entirely. If scientific generalisations are true, leaving aside for a moment how they are arrived at, what are we to make of the considerable changes that have taken place in the history of scientific thought? Galileo and Newton formulated some of the most thoroughly tested laws in physics. They took the strain of more than 150 years of application, prediction and confirmation. And yet, after 1915 and the General Theory of Relativity, their universal status had collapsed. They were found to be descriptive of a small part of the universe, what we might call middle-sized, middle-range objects and events. Their theories are not applicable at the intergalactic and subatomic levels. Einstein's theory did not prove Newton and Galileo wrong, merely limited. But, as we saw with the discovery of Neptune, the method is supposed to give universal generalisations. How do we handle the fact of disconfirmation? If a theory is confirmed by all the observations we make up to a certain point, say 1914, the use of inductivism allows us to say that it is generalisable and hence true or, at least, highly probable. Does it become untrue in 1915? Can truth be time-dependent? The range of facts that the theory was supposed to cover has not changed, merely our organisation of them. As the later discussion will show, the successor theory problem has proven very contentious in arguments over the significance of the history of science for its philosophy. Attempts to clear it up nearly always lead away from methodology and back into epistemology.

A last, and latterly quite significant, objection to inductivism takes issue with the supposed determinate relation between a theory and the domain of facts to which it is applied. In particular, it raises the question of the definitiveness of disconfirmation. The guarantee of inductivism was that failed generalisations must be discarded. One of the implications of the views that Quine and other modern realists have been developing is the notion of an underdetermination of a theory by the facts. The web of propositions within which the theory is located can always be adjusted to accommodate novel facts and apparent disconfirmation. In Chapter 7 we referred to this as the 'Duhem–Quine Thesis'. This is not a nefarious practice we are being invited to engage in; a point is being made about logical compulsion. In the face of disconfirmation we are not given only one alternative, namely rejecting the theory. We can make adjustments in the logical relations between this set of theoretical propositions and others, and so make an accommodation between it and the facts, without violating the canons of logic. The Duhem–Quine hypothesis leads to the conclusion that the central element in the logic of inductivism, the compulsion to reject theories in the face of disconfirmation, is itself unsecured.

Popper's Methodological Falsificationism

What we have been discussing so far is what we might call the attempt to justify the truth of scientific hypotheses and generalisations. Popper's philosophy of science begins by accepting that inductivism cannot give us such justification. It is also directed towards identifying what it is that is distinctive about scientific method, since quite clearly not all of the knowledge which we have about the world can be said to be scientific. To make the distinction between the different sorts of knowledge which our experience gives us of the world, Popper has to develop a criterion for distinguishing what he calls 'pseudo-science' or 'metaphysics' from proper science. This sentiment is one which Popper shares with the Logical Positivists, though for him the criterion is rooted in the methods which the sciences use and not in the meaningful character of scientific statements (cf. Introduction to Part Two). Inductivism cannot provide such a criterion. To see why, take the case of astrology. Astrologers spend a great deal of their time studying the movements of the stars and the planets and relating these movements to individual biographies. On the basis of their observations they make predictions, sometimes quite precise ones. These predictions may be substantiated. If they are, does that make astrology a science? Were we to look to inductivism for a criterion of scientificity, then it would seem that it would. This is intolerable, thought Popper. Astrology, along with psychoanalysis, Marxism and many other pseudo-sciences are examples of metaphysics, not bona fide science. But why? What is it that demarcates psuedo-science from proper science?

The 'demarcation criterion', as Popper calls it, is contained in a simple but quite devastating proposal. Science does not seek the confirmation of its predictions, and hence generalisation, but their falsification. Scientific theories state the conditions under which they will count themselves as having failed. It is this specification of the conditions of failure internal to a theory and the method by which those conditions are tested for that distinguishes science from metaphysics. Science is critical; pseudo-science is not.

By this one move, Popper transforms the way in which one can talk about the logic of science. The object is no longer the inference of generalisations from confirmatory instances. Rather, it is the search for disconfirmation and rejection of conjectural hypotheses. Scientific history is not the story of an accumulating body of true generalisations but the heaping up of conjectures which, as yet, have not been refuted. The introduction of falsification allows Popper to introduce a subsidiary criterion for the evaluation of bona fide scientific theories. Using the probability calculus, Popper argues that the best theories make very precise predictions which are therefore much more likely to fail. Good theories are, then, improbable ones. Often this can even be summarised in one crucial experiment the failure of which would count, for the theorist, as grounds for the rejection of the theory.

The example to which Popper often refers to illustrate the degree of falsifiability of good theories is General Relativity Theory. One of the predictions which this theory makes is that light will bend when it passes through a gravitational field. Einstein calculated that light passing close to the surface of the sun would be bent by the gravitational pull of the sun through an arc of 1.73 seconds. Clearly this means that if one could measure the distance between two stars at night, when the sun is absent, and during the day when it is present, and if the light from one of them passed close to the sun, it would appear as if the distance between them had changed. In 1919, a lunar eclipse of the sun allowed such an experiment to be carried out. The results corroborated Einstein's prediction. This does not mean that we can now say that General Relativity Theory is true, simply that this crucial experiment did not refute it. As Popper says in *The Logic of Scientific Discoveries*:

> I think that we shall have to get accustomed to the idea that we must not look upon science as a 'body of knowledge' but rather as a system of hypotheses; that is as a system of guesses or anticipations which in principle cannot be justified, but which we work with as long as they stand up to tests, and of which we are never justified in saying that we know that they are 'true' or 'more or less certain' or even 'probable'. (p. 317)

One of the most discussed features of falsificationism is the critical, competitive character that it ascribes to science. However, this is not, as many of Popper's critics seem to think, an argument in its favour but simply an extraneous feature it just happens to have. The strong arguments in support of falsificationism are all logical in character. The first is the asymmetry between the falsification and verification of certain classes of propositions. If we say that all mammals are viviparous then the discovery of the duck-billed platypus falsifies the generalisation. The duck-billed platypus lays eggs and yet suckles its young. No number of observations of mammals other than the platypus would verify the proposition though, as long as there is a possibility that we have not examined all possible mammals. The same cannot be said of existential statements such as 'there is an egg-laying mammal'. This proposition *is* verifiable. On the other hand, analytic propositions such as 'bachelors are unmarried men' are neither verifiable nor falsifiable. They are true by definition. The falsification criterion, therefore, is to be applied only to a restricted range of propositions. But in these cases it gives us a logically simple way of determining their status and so we should prefer it. In taking this attitude Popper is clearly in sympathy with the whole tenor of developments in Logic that we outlined in the Introduction to Part Two.

The second strong argument which Popper offers is based upon the distinction between falsifiability-in-principle and the actual practice of science. Scientific theories state in principle the grounds on which they would be refuted. It does not matter whether at any particular moment in scientific history we can actually reproduce the test conditions and so run the crucial experiment. Neither does it matter that, at any time, we might not find the countervailing observations compelling because we have good reasons to make adjustments to the web of propositions by offering auxiliary hypotheses. The fact that such adjustments are logically possible does not affect the point that it is falsifiability-in-principle that demarcates science from pseudo-science. What Popper is doing here is taking the line about verification and applying it to falsification. Just as verification is never inductively possible, neither is falsification. We may not be able to achieve falsification, but scientific theories have to state the grounds on which they would count themselves as being falsified. The Duhem–Quine thesis with regard to verification or falsification of propositions has been taken by some philosophers to have very different implications from those which Popper finds in it. We will return to it at the end of this chapter.

Exactly what is this notion of 'falsification' that Popper is promoting? It is quite clear that it is not some form of empiricism. He is not demanding that all we have to do is 'look at the facts' or make some reference to 'how things are'. He is quite happy to accept that facts and how things are are theory-dependent. The method which science uses, according to Popper, is the critical appraisal of the plurality of theories and hypotheses which are, at any moment, in competition with one another. It is by trial and error that science learns which to use and which to discard. The only function of any kind of empirical reference must be to ensure that 'the struggle for survival' among theories takes place and that the best fitted survive longest. The longer a theory survives the greater its 'verisimilitude', its approximation to a description of how things are. This gaining of knowledge by trial and error and the mutation of theories in response to attempts to apply and test them are an extension of what Popper calls his 'evolutionary epistemology'. Science accumulates knowledge and the ability to adapt to the world in an extremely sophisticated but in essence no different way to all forms of life. The continuity which Popper sees between the knowledge gained by science and other human institutions and the adaptations of lower forms of life has, naturally, been a point of much dispute.

Unfortunately we do not have the space to take it up here.

The ability of scientific theories to withstand tests is what Popper regards as their 'corroboration'. This is directly related to the degree of improbability of their predictions. Strong theories like General Relativity Theory enable very precise predictions across a wide range of test conditions. All of these conditions have a high level of empirical content. The higher the content, the more precise the predictions; the more often the theory has been tested, the less likely that the theory will withstand testing next time. The introduction of the improbability of corroboration allows Popper to be more specific about the criteria used for ranking scientific theories. The best theories minimise the number of auxiliary hypotheses they require to just those which enable empirical testing and accept those hypotheses which entail precise predictions.

The link between this falsificationist rational reconstruction of the logic of science and the actual history of science is through Popper's evolutionary epistemology. Science, like every form of knowledge, proceeds by mutation, trial and error. Because corroboration is probabilistic, it runs the risk of throwing away a sound theory prematurely as well as holding on to an unsound one far beyond its useful life. There are two reasons for this. First of all, ever since Kant we have had to accept that there can be no independent gauge of the verisimilitude of a theory. We cannot step outside of theory to look at the world directly. Second, non-logical criteria are involved in the actual selection and promotion of specific scientific theories. Such non-logical criteria are the fit between the theory and the tradition within a discipline, or the relative appeal of certain lines of inquiry over others, and the like. However, although these non-logical features are always part and parcel of the actual, empirical history of science, for Popper they are not definitive of its logic.

As Popper himself saw, the implication of falsificationism for the social sciences is enormous. Many known and trusted theories — Marxism, psychoanalysis, behaviourism — simply do not match up to the theoretical requirements that falsification entails. They do not express *testable* hypotheses; they do not make *precise* predictions; they do not state the grounds on which they would count themselves as refuted. In all cases, at least in Popper's eyes, what social scientific theories are offering are sets of organising categories, ways of looking at social life, not scientific theories. Popper's attack on the scientific claims of historical materialism is well known; his views on psychoanalysis are equally dismissive. Take the suggestion that a phenomenon like an 'involuntary' slip of the tongue is actually an expression of tensions in an individual's psyche. Where, asks Popper, does Freud state the conditions on which such slips would not count as this kind of expression? Where does he say what he will require for the theory to fail? Popper's answer is, of course, that he never does. Instead, what *The Psychopathology of Everyday Life* does is to show us in a dazzling piece of intellectual ingenuity just how we can replicate Freud's analysis with any phenomena from our own lives. Such analyses may certainly be brilliant, insightful and deeply helpful to those on behalf of whom they are carried out. But they are not scientific; they are metaphysics. To make the social sciences come into line with the natural science logic of falsificationism it will be necessary to develop a whole new research methodology. At its centre will be a concern for what he calls 'the situational logic' of human action. Elements in specific situations which affect individuals' desires, motives, perceptions, knowledge and aspirations will have to be filled out by accounts of the institutions of the surrounding society and how they interact. Such reconstructions of action are inevitably false simply because they are logical reconstructions. The task is to reduce what we might think of as their 'error margin'. Exactly how this might proceed is more than a little obscure. Certainly none of those who have enthusiastically supported the introduction of Popperian views into the social sciences have been able to demonstrate what decisive difference it might make to the research they do, as opposed to the sorts of claims they feel they can make on its behalf.

As we said right at the beginning, there is no doubt that Popper is one of the foremost figures in the philosophy of science. Accordingly his views have been the object of much discussion and dispute. One set of reservations has to do with the adequacy of Popper's picture of science as a description of how it actually carries on. When looked at as an historical institution, science does not always appear to be imbued with the critical spirit, the pluralism and so on that Popper claims for it. There are periods when very little serious and far-reaching criticism of the major theories is to be found. We will come back to this question when we discuss Kuhn, Lakatos and Feyerabend a little later on.

A second set of reservations concerns the point of Popper's criterion. Is it meant to be descriptive or prescriptive? If it is the former, then the difficulties we have just mentioned will be important. If it is the latter, then what do we do if its use not only rules out famous theories in the social sciences but requires us to demote, or at least drastically reformulate, well-known and trusted theories in the natural sciences as well? Such a situation could well arise because of the very narrow definition of what a theory is and what it is for that Popper uses. It must be predictivist; it cannot simply be a heuristic. But if that is the case, while the prominent theories of mathematical physics might pass the test, many other scientific theories such as those of Darwin, E.O. Wilson and many more will not.

The third set of reservations take issue with the gap between the idealisation of falsificationism and the 'working logic' of science. As a description of science it is overly rational. It is far too concerned with purely logical characteristics. The theory pays little or no attention to the reasons scientists have for accepting or rejecting particular hypotheses, the grounds they have for being convinced or otherwise and the lines which they might draw between what is scientific and what is not. This failure is unimportant as long as Popper's criterion is supposed to describe the logic of science. It matters a great deal if it is being invoked, as it has been, to enable us to distinguish 'proper science' from other things, and so affect how science is done. Part of this ommission is an underplaying of the commitment that scientists have to getting hypotheses confirmed. It also leaves out of account entirely the amount of scientific work done on purely taxonomic topics.

Apart from these objections to falsificationism as a description of science's methodology, a number of reservations have been expressed about the 'evolutionary epistemology' upon which it is based. We said at the start that we would not delve into these very deeply because they would take us far away from our present concerns. It is also the case that the 'evolutionary epistemology' has not proved all that popular with philosophers, let alone social scientists. However, it ought to be said that even if one could substantiate the claim that this epistemology is incoherent, as many have claimed they can, this would not of itself mean that falsificationism as the logic of science had been refuted. All it would mean is that Popperians would need a wholly different platform from which to make the claims they do about science — which is simply to say falsification might still be correct, but not for the reasons which Popper offers.

We have seen that the keystone in Popper's theory is the testing of predictions. But the most obvious question to ask is how we are to lay our hands on testable predictions. Which predictions are to be scrutinised and where do we get them from? To answer this question Popper falls back on a well-known procedure for producing deductively valid predictions which can stand as tests of the theories or hypotheses from which they are drawn. This procedure is called the 'Covering Law' or 'Deductive Nomological' method. It was first used to describe the logical character of acceptable scientific explanations. It tries to show how scientific explanations work *as* explanations.

The Deductive Nomological Scheme

Probably the best thing to do is to begin with an example. You turn on the tap in the bathroom and warm water flows out. The question 'why does the water run?' is an explanation-seeking question. So is the question 'why are you washing your hands?' and 'why do you need warm water?' But they do not seek the same sort of explanation. 'Why does the water run?' asks about the physical properties of the hot water system and might be answered by saying that the hot water tank is connected to a cold water reservoir in the roof. This 'header tank' is large enough to enable a fair volume of water to be stored in it. The mass of this water exerts a gravitational force on the hot tank because it is above it. If the hot tap is opened, this force is released and the water flows out. The explanation is a story about the *antecedent conditions* which cause the water to flow. But how does it work as an explanation? How do we know it is a true explanation? What the Deductive Nomological Scheme is, is precisely that; a logical scheme which shows how explanations can be correctly and validly derived.

The tap is opened; the water flows. According to the most widely used form of explanation scheme, that explanation is the outcome of an argument premissed in two sets of propositions, those concerning the initial conditions of the hot water system and those concerning general laws under which those conditions can be subsumed. In fact the scheme consists of an ordered pair of propositional sets, those containing initial conditions and general laws, the *explanans*, and those appearing in the explanation seeking questions, the *explanandum*. The proposition contained in our question was, of course 'the hot water flows'. If we apply the scheme to our example we get:

Explanans

C_1 .... C_n statements about initial conditions; the volume of water in the tank, the openness of the system etc.

L_1 .... L_n general laws about the fluidity, effects of gravity upon liquids etc.

Explanandum

E   the hot water flows.

This scheme is called a deductive nomological one because of two of its characteristics. The inference is deductive — that is demonstrative — and so truth preserving. It has exactly the same form as the classical syllogism we introduced in the Introduction to Part Two. The truth of E is provided in virtue of the truth of the propositions in C_1 .... C_n and L_1 ...... L_n. If these are true, then E *must* be true. The scheme is nomological because it contains statements about laws.

The deductive nomological scheme will provide true explanations as long as the following conditions are met:

(1) The propositions in E must be logically deducible from the combination of C and L.

(2) The laws in L must be universal and necessary for the explanation. E cannot be entailed by propositions concerning specific events. This is summarised by a slogan 'no entailment by specific statements' or NES.

(3) C must be observable or empirically verifiable.

(4) C and L must be true.

We can say two things about the scheme right away. Used retrospectively it provides explanations. Used prospectively it gives predictions. The precise specifications of the conditions to be incorporated in C — by means of some criterion such as that given by Popper — allows for the testing of the proposed universal or general laws. If they are true, then E will result. If not, then the prediction will fail. All that happens to the scheme in Popper's use is that the statements in L become hypotheses or conjectures, and the point is to find the conditions under which they will fail.

The second thing to say is that the scheme can be used with regard to all sorts of explanations. All scientific explanations, including those of the social sciences, ought to be amenable to framing in its terms. The only differences between social science and most natural science explanations will be in the knowledge that we have to hand about the conditions and laws which are relevant. The scheme produces *explanation sketches* and not full blown explanations in that case. These weaker explanations have to be filled out. One such explanation sketch is Gresham's law which says that the appearance of bad money will drive good money from the market. If people do not trust the medium of exchange they will go elsewhere. This has to be filled out by accounts of the peculiar nature of money markets, the primacy of exchange value over use value for money together with the psychological preferences we might have for liquidity.

Although the deductive nomological scheme is often felt to be the paragon of explanation-giving schemes, it is not in fact capable of providing us with all of the explanations we will find in science. This is because some of those explanations are probabilistic and not nomological. A sudden frost in June may make it highly likely that our strawberry plants will be killed off. But that doesn't mean they have to be. We might be lucky and they might survive. The explanation scheme involved here goes like this:

Explanans
  (1) There is a high probability that frost in June will kill strawberry plants.
  (2) These plants are not protected from frost ⌐
      _____   ⌉ highly probable.
Explanandum |
  (3) Our plants are killed. ◄⌐

Such deductive probabilistic explanations are of a different order to deductive nomological ones. They do not constitute a deductively valid argument because the relationship is not one of entailment from the truth of propositions but the likelihood of one event following others. The connection is not logical but statistical. It is the frequency with which frost kills strawberry plants which makes it likely it will happen again on this occasion. The uncertainty does not relate to the evidence but to the fit between the actual event and the expected event. This problem over the goodness of fit between the actual event and the expected event gives rise to a host of problems with regard to deductive probabilistic explanations that do not occur with deductive nomological ones. These are mostly to do with what, in statistical terms, are called Type 1 and Type 2 errors, that is the possibility of accepting a false explanation or rejecting a true one simply because the test conditions were highly unlikely. We might come to the conclusion that strawberry plants are frost resistant because on this occasion our plants did not die. But if we did so, the fact that we were just lucky will have led us to accept a false hypothesis. Another aspect of this relates to the security of the statements in the explanans. We have seen in our discussion of Popper that the failure of actual frequencies to match expected frequencies is not a *logical* ground for refutation, just as their correspondence is not a *logical* ground for confirmation. That some ravens are black does not confirm that all ravens are black; neither does the failure to discover egg-laying mammals refute the proposition that no mammals are egg-laying. The difficulties here have been addressed by resorting to the techniques of probability theory.

However, the most pointed objection to all deductive schemes is that, in the end, they are not explanations of anything. The combination of conditions and laws does not explain why the water flows. To do that, reference has to be made to specific causal mechanisms, such as the average surface tension of water, the causal properties of fluids and so on. These are not present in the scheme. We could enumerate all of the relevant conditions, and all of the general laws, and still have no idea why the event happened. Why does water flow in the way that it does? We have no idea, that is, why the conditions are subsumed under the law. Without knowledge of why the conditions fall under the law we will have no means of distinguishing specious from effective explanations. To keep with our gardening theme we might frame the following explanation scheme:

(1) Plants which are talked to are healthier than those that are not.

(2) We regularly go out and talk to the marigolds and geraniums.

(3) Our geraniums and marigolds are healthier than other plants.

Now if (1) and (2) are true then (3) will be true, and so the explanans will have 'explained' why our marigolds and geraniums are healthier than those of our next door neighbours, who hate gardening. But we would hardly accept the propositions in (1) and (2) as an explanation of the health of our plants. We would want to know why talking to plants worked. What it was about the nature of human discourse that made it therapeutic for plants? Is it just a knack we have? Will it work only for these plants? To provide enough detail to be able to make the connection between explanans and explanandum, we will have to describe the unique situation that we and our flowers are in, thus violating the NES requirement.

Another serious objection to the deductive scheme is that it does not work for all scientific theories. Functional theories, of which there are many in science, cannot be fitted into it. If this is so then since the social sciences make extensive use of functional explanations, we will have come across a serious stumbling block to the matching of explanation schemes in the natural and social sciences and hence the possibility of assimilation. Defenders of the deductive scheme, however, argue that the functional explanations of a phenomenon, even in the social sciences, can be cast in the deductive scheme. This can be achieved by putting certain supplementary premises in place. Even so the explanans remains not very enlightening; the explanations we get are not very good ones. To show how the proposal works, let us take a famous functionalist explanation from sociology about the distribution of power and wealth in society. In essence this argument says that the unequal distribution of wealth and power in our society is necessary because it encourages the most talented to take the most important roles in society since these are the ones to which wealth and power are attached. This explanation could be re-written as follows:

> i (the unequal distribution of wealth and power) is a persistent feature of a system of relations s (our society) and because this s is in conditions c_1 .... c_n (talent is not evenly distributed, some roles are more important than others etc.), the trait i has the effect of satisfying some need or functional requirement n of s which is necessary for the effective working of s (the fitting of the most talented to the most important roles).

The structure of the explanation can be formalised like this:

(1) At some time, t, s functions adequately in c.
(2) s functions adequately only if n is satisfied.
(3) If i is present, n would be satisfied.
(4) At t, i is present in s.

The trouble is all functional explanations include propositions concerning functional equivalence. Other sets of institutionalised practices could have the same effect as i. Proposition (3), then, is an open statement and not of the form 'only if i is present would n be satisfied'. We could imagine how we could slot people into roles on the basis of their birthdays or by centralised intelligence tests or whatever. We could define those people born in June as the most talented, or those people who have a measured IQ of 120 and above, and direct them into the top jobs. It follows that no functional theory can ever be predicated upon a theorem of functional indispensability. If the scope of the conditions were to be tightened up to exclude functional alternatives, we would be left with a tautology. Our society runs the way it does because it runs the way it does. To avoid all of this, we have to amend the propositions (3) and (4).

(3a) I is the class of empirically sufficient conditions (i_1 .... i_n) to produce n in s under the circumstances of c. I is not an empty class.

(4a) One of the items in I is present in s at t.

Yet again this is not much use as an explanation because it is not very specific. In addition to all of this, the propositions (2) and (3) require a general hypothesis concerning the self-regulation of systems. This runs into problems concerning empirical testability. Under what circumstances would we count a set of relations as a *system* if it was not self-regulating? Certainly it is hard to imagine empirical hypotheses which enable us to test the generalisation. As a consequence, even for those who would like to defend their scientific status, functional explanations — in that they are a combination of universal functionality and vague test conditions — are not all that prepossessing.

The combination of falsificationism and the deductive schema offers a fairly strong methodological programme both for science and the social sciences, always providing that the latter can match up to the demands set. Its appeal is founded on the claim that it describes both the logic of science's method as well as that of scientific explanations. The latter claim may be true only of a limited number of scientific explanations, and even there the deductive scheme doesn't really tell us why such explanations do explain. The former claim asks us to accept that the logical reconstruction which Popper sets out is a reasonable fit for what goes on in science. But should we? Is it entirely clear that science's method is one of falsification? It is to arguments about what the history of science can tell us about the logic it actually uses that we now turn.

Thomas Kuhn: Normal and Revolutionary Science

Popper's claim that falsificationism is definitive of scientific method but not of its history is somewhat weakened by his tendency to treat science as the epitome of evolutionary epistemology. That being the case, if human knowledge does proceed by means of trial and error, mutation and natural selection, then this ought to be on view in the history of the foremost branch of human knowledge, namely science. This is not to say that there has to be a continuity of criticism, but the pattern ought to be visible. In a seminal work which examines scientific history since roughly the seventeenth century, *The Structure of Scientific Revolutions*, Kuhn argues that such philosophic conclusions are not borne out by the historical facts. Instead of a logic of criticism, he says, the sciences have a logic of conformity and conservatism. The periods of upheaval and general mêlée are very brief and few. They are separated by periods of almost uniform attachment to general frameworks or *paradigms*. Normal science is conformist and conservative. Revolutionary science occurs in the upheavals.

What is distinctive about Kuhn's approach is that he calls upon philosophical views of the nature of knowledge in order to treat science as a particular social institution. Scientists are members of a scientific community. Science is a way of life. His account of normal and revolutionary science is, then, a history of stability, homogeneity and continuity as well as one of conflict, disruption, fissions and change. What holds the scientific community together at a point of stability and calm is the sharing of a set of basic ideas — the paradigm. What separates one stable state from a later stable state is the difference between the paradigms. In its broadest outline, this sociological and historical approach is often felt to have much in common with some of the ideas of Foucault and Wittgenstein who both drew attention to the fact that knowledge is held within a community. Indeed, Kuhn makes reference to these two but the detail of his arguments is quite distinct from theirs.

In taking this 'sociological' approach to science, Kuhn is able to pick out two distinct things. First of all, he can point to the importance that maintaining the boundaries of science has for science. The paradigm is invoked to rule things in and out. Second, he can point up how much it is socialisation into the acceptance and use of a paradigm which produces quiescence and conformity. It is only when, for whatever reasons, scientists begin to question the paradigm that a revolution becomes imminent.

It is clear, then, that the concept of a 'scientific paradigm' is crucial in Kuhn's thinking. But what exactly does it describe? Kuhn seems to have three different functions which it might perform. It could act as a general metaphysical framework, what earlier in Chapter 3 we called a 'Weltanschauung', which specifies the character of the world we live in and the relationships between the objects and processes on view in it. It is precisely differences of this sort that Winch was trying to alert us to in his discussion of witchcraft (cf. Chapter 8). Second, it can act as a disciplinary matrix, drawing the boundaries for what work in a particular discipline is to look like at a particular time. After Mendel, the biology of inheritance looks quite different to what had gone on before. Post-Chomskyean linguistics is utterly at odds with the relatively non-formal descriptivism that characterised investigations of grammar prior to Chomsky's development of Transformational Grammar. Closely associated with this is the third use of the term. Here a paradigm defines a classical or exemplary breakthrough, a series of experiments or body of studies which became models for work being done. Skinner's experiments with pigeons have such a status in psychology, while Durkheim's account of suicide was definitive of studies in this and related areas for very nearly half a century.

Whatever the precise way in which the term is deployed, paradigms seem to have the following features:

(1) A shared set of symbols and media of communicative reference. In most cases this is achieved through forms of mathematisation and measurement, the application of a narrow range of analytic techniques, the appeal to standard cases and the use of a standard format for reporting.

(2) A shared set of metaphysical commitments such as the universality of causation, the atomic theory of matter, the dualism of mind and matter, the reality of 'social facts', the 'unreality' of parapsychology and 'action at a distance', and so on. This element will become crucial to what we can say about changes in paradigms.

(3) A shared set of values and criteria for judgement such as the priority of prediction over description, the importance of objective method, replication, value neutrality and the like.

Becoming a member of the scientific community at any particular period in history means learning to use the criteria and standards enshrined in the paradigm unquestioningly and without hesitation. The affinity which this 'paradigmatic' approach might have with Foucault's ought to be obvious. By introducing the notion of a hidden distribution of power in which established ideas and commitments are used to prevent publication in journals, to direct funding away from, to campaign against and ridicule alternative theories we would have an account of 'force' in science. In our own times the cases of creationist biology and parapsychology and alternative medicine are very pertinent.

In the Kuhnian version, the development of science takes a standard form. Out of the ferment that occurs during the break-up of an established paradigm, one new framework gradually emerges. This is popularised and adopted. The new framework has novel and different standards of measurement, new topics methods, concepts and problems. Most of all, it enables new observations to be made. Scientists see things differently. In exploring this paradigm troublesome cases arise which give odd results and even disconfirmations. Because of the hold which the paradigm has, these troubles are set to one side. They are puzzles to be returned to when methods improve, the theory develops or we know more. The anomalies gradually heap up until they become intolerable. Everyone becomes convinced of the inadequacy of the existing paradigm and the search for a new one starts. The revolution begins once more.

In this explanation of scientific development, priority is given to non-scientific, psychological factors. The change in paradigms amounts to a gestalt switch which is always easiest for the young and uncommitted to make. The defenders of the old paradigm fight a rearguard action but either retire or fade away. The point about calling the paradigm shift a gestalt switch is to deny the possibility of holding to or working within both paradigms at once. They are *incommensurable*. Kuhn's discussion of incommensurability is somewhat vague, but two things at least can be said. The switch in paradigms is a *post hoc* rationalisation of what has happened. In some cases, the importance of a piece of research, for instance Crick and Watson's celebrated discovery of DNA's double helix structure, may be picked up fairly quickly. But it only comes to have paradigmatic status when it is clear what such cases have made available and how they set the pattern and standards for later work. They have to become 'text-book' examples. Because the gestalt switch provides us with a new way of seeing 'the same things', the relationships posited by the discipline will change. We will move from a mechanical universe to one where relations are probabilistic, or from treating insanity as 'possession' to treating it as 'illness'. Unfortunately, it is here that the problems arise for the notion of a paradigm switch. Kuhn talks of it in terms more associated with religious conversion than scientific argument and conviction. Some have felt, therefore, that in his eyes scientific progress becomes essentially irrational. Naturally this has worried those like the Popperians who would want to defend science as the paragon of rationality in our society. There is also the problem of defining scientific progress at all. Under the notion of incommensurability, there are no common standards to mark off progress between the paradigms. Everything has changed. When Lavoisier discovered oxygen and so refuted the phlogiston theory of combustion, the universe was different for science; there was no longer a possible entity called phlogiston. If we can have no theory-independent view of the world and if the movement from one paradigm to another is a wholesale incommensurable change then, on Kuhn's argument, all we can say about the history of science is that it is a history of changes. We cannot claim it is progressing towards the truth.

At this point we have come face to face with the way in which philosophy gets wound into the history of science. How do we choose between competing paradigms? Popper and the rationalists say we have logical grounds, those given by falsification. Kuhn argues, or seems to argue, that we do not choose rationally. The choice is determined by non-rational, extrascientific factors such as the distribution of scientific power, the nature of psychological commitment and so on. Certainly we do not choose by reference to 'the facts' because what will count as 'the facts' to be referred to will have changed. Exactly what sort of view this must lead Kuhn to adopt concerning the epistemological status of scientific theories is not clear. His conventionalism runs directly into the problem of radical translation as that was formulated by Quine (cf. Chapter 7). It leaves us asking, 'how can the terms in one paradigm be translated into those of another? How can the 'objects' described under one theory be redescribed under another? how do we know when we have been successful?'

Since Kuhn is not attempting to do anything other than describe the history of science, his views have very little implication for the social sciences except perhaps in terms of how one might proceed to write their history. Some have said that all of the social sciences are still awaiting their Newtons, Boyles, Keplers and Galileos, the founders of accepted paradigms. Others claim that recently we have seen nothing but one paradigm shift after another. Whatever conclusion one comes to, it is clear that, in Kuhn's view, one does not have to model the social sciences on natural science.

As we have drawn them, the differences between Popper and Kuhn resolve into a dispute over the character of scientific logic. For Popper this logic is critical and internal. For Kuhn it is neither. However, even as a general historical scheme, Kuhn's account has proved too broad and insensitive. When it is applied to cases, it tends to collapse. The periods of revolution grow in size while those of settled 'normality' contract. In the end, it seems that the processes of normal science are those of innovation and mutation within generalised 'research programmes'. This suggestion that the logic of scientific history might be best conceived as the progression and competition of research programmes is Imre Lakatos' contribution to the debate.

Imre Lakatos: the Methodology of Research Programmes

One way of taking Kuhn's suggestions about paradigm shifts in science is to say that they deny the possibility of progress in scientific knowledge. We do not know more today than we did in 1500; we know differently. To Lakatos, such a view is absurd. Human knowledge — scientific, mathematical, social, philosophic, whatever — is growing. This growth of knowledge can be exemplified in the development of chemistry from alchemy, non-Euclidian geometries from planar ones, and so on. But noticing and itemising this growth is not as important as characterising it. If we can say what the growth of scientific knowledge consists in, we may have a way of distinguishing the rational accumulation of knowledge in science from irrationalism. This could be important if we want to use science as the criterion for rationalism. Thus for Lakatos what is needed is a rational reconstruction of scientific history and not the meaningless comparison of scientific theorising with some hard and fast schema designed to obtain 'truth-in-the-abstract'. This rational reconstruction Lakatos calls 'the internal history' of science. It is what discussions of scientific methodology ought to be about. It is important to see that Lakatos is trying to reconstruct the history of science, not formulate its proper methodology. Many of the commentaries seem to have missed this point since they usually end up by saying that following Lakatos' dicta would be bad methodology. Lakatos is not saying what we can and can't do in science; only what, from the history of science, we can say scientists have done.

The key notion of Lakatos is not, as it is for Popper and Kuhn, the scientific theory, but the research programme. The history of science is the history of developing, competing and stagnating research programmes. The line to be drawn between science and pseudo-science — and Lakatos does follow Popper in this much — will not be in terms of theories but research programmes. The need to look beyond theories for a demarcation criterion is because falsificationism, while the best criterion with regard to theories, does not take into account the tenacity with which theories persist in spite of disconfirmation. This tenacity was at the heart of Kuhn's view of normal science. However, Kuhn's account, because of the commitment to incommensurability, is far too relativist for Lakatos' taste. If we accept incommensurability, we will never be able to tell pseudo-science from real science. Against Kuhn, then, Lakatos wants to say that science *is* a rationally accumulating body of knowledge; against Popper, he claims it does not progress solely by trial and error. Theories are held on to long after the 'crucial experiment' has been devised and carried out because the import that this experiment was *actually* crucial is a *post hoc* affair. That this experiment was crucial only emerges after what Lakatos calls 'the problem shift' has occurred. Prior to the problem shift, as Kuhn pointed out, the findings of the experiment can be treated as anomalous and so discounted or explained away.

What exactly is a 'research programme'? Getting a list of them is easy. Lakatos names the gravitational theory of Newton, the relativity theory of Einstein, Marxism, Freudianism. From elsewhere in the social sciences, we might add Chomskyean linguistics, Skinnerean behaviourism, Keynesianism, and many others. As 'research programmes' all of these had the same features:

(1) A 'hard core' of definitive propositions; Newton's 3 laws of dynamics and the law of gravitation; Marx's theory of value formation and surplus value creation; Freud's theory of personality development.

(2) A 'protective belt' of auxiliary hypotheses which connect the definitions to the domain of facts which they explain. Thus Freud's theory is spelled out through the stages of development of the id, ego and superego, the theories of fixation, sublimation and distortion, and psychopathology etc. These allow explanations for psychoses, neuroses, slips of the tongue, the character of dreams and so on. The

theories of alienation, diminishing return to capital and revolution play the same role for Marxism.

Given the scope of the list, it is important to see how Lakatos will distinguish science from pseudo-science, since, for Popperians, at least two of our examples are pseudo-sciences, namely Marxism and Freudianism. As is the case with the Popperians, the criterion is prediction. A scientific research programme is continuously predicting novel scientific facts, or facts which have been ruled to be impossible by other research programmes. The classic instance is the bending of light by gravity. This was a wholly novel consequence of Relativity Theory. In Lakatos' view, what makes Freudianism and Marxism pseudo-scientific is that they do not predict novel facts. Further, whatever predictions they might make — and it is not all that clear that Freud did make predictions — have failed. Be that as it may, the notion of novel fact prediction is not all that straightforward. Using it as a criterion, it is not easy to say whether Keynesian economics is or is not scientific, nor whether investigations of population dynamics are either. On Popper's strict view, though, neither would count as science.

The role of the research programme is heuristic. It lays out which problems are worth attacking and how to approach them. This can be both positive, by indicating fruitful problems and uncertainties, and negative, listing the problems to be avoided. The negative aspect is where the dynamism in research programmes is to be found. Change is found here because problem-shifts have their origin there. When a problem which has been avoided is taken on and solved then a problem-shift is under way. Durkheim's study of suicide to which we referred earlier is a case in point. In it, he showed that one could use the logic of the natural sciences as Mill had defined it, that is the method of agreement and difference, without being committed to a reduction of sociological explanations to psychological ones. The problem of the relationship between sociological and psychological explanations had been largely avoided by sociologists. Durkheim offered an answer. The study of suicide, which applied the methods he advocated, could be regarded as the 'normalisation' of the problem-shift.

As all research programmes have positive and negative functions, it is important to tell which is which. In doing so, we will be able to determine when a science is progressing, cumulating knowledge, and when it is not. Lakatos offers a simple rule of thumb. If the theory is running ahead of the facts, that is predicting new facts, then it is progressive. This is the case even though the facts it predicts may turn out to be disconfirmed. If a constant patching up of the theory in the light of the facts is going on, and Lakatos, like Popper, says this is what is happening in Marxism and Freudianism, then the theory is degenerating or stagnant.

What Lakatos has sought to do is to accommodate the rationalist concern with the logic of methodology with the actual history of science. This is a rationalist history, a logical reconstruction of science. This apparently 'irrational' tendency to persist with a disconfirmed research programme, which for Kuhn and Popper are indications of non-rational factors in science, has been transformed into the perfectly understandable delaying of judgement upon a theory until the research programme it has initiated has had time to mature. Such a line of argument is an internal feature of science's logic, not external to it. This does not mean that there can be no distinction between internal history and an external one, the history of its progress and the relation of that progress to other contemporary events. All it does mean is that the line between the two cannot be stipulated in advance and must be decided on a case by case basis. Internal history cannot be treated as if it were hermetically sealed off from external history. The degree of the relationship between scientific reasoning and historical factors is, then, a crucial point of issue. If Lakatos were to accept that the relation was one of determination then he would have opted for an epistemology which was thoroughly relativist in character. Knowledge is determined by historical circumstance. If he wants to argue that it is non-determinate, then what is the relationship between science's internal and external history? It was this question that Paul Feyerabend suggested had to be answered by looking at science *in* history. Once we do that, we will no longer feel quite so confident that science, or anything else, is a paragon of rationalism.

Paul Feyerabend: Science in its Place

Of all the philosophers whom we will be discussing in this chapter, Feyerabend's style is the most distinctive. He is trenchant, witty, dismissive and often extremely amusing. However, we should not let his clowning cause us to miss or underestimate the serious point that Feyerabend makes. He argues that *any* appeal to rationalist standards to evaluate science and scientific progress is bound to be self-justificatory. For us, science embodies those standards. We and science have a commitment to what Feyerabend calls 'dogmatic Reason'. The philosophy which Feyerabend propounds for science is but one aspect of a multifaceted epistemology and moral and political philosophy which Feyerabend has put together from the Logical Positivists, Wittgenstein, Popper and forms of artistic expression such as Dadaism.

The attitude to science which this philosophy gives Feyerabend is very clear cut. It involves the following set of steps.

(1) The appeal to rational, critical debate as a method for solving theoretical problems is a part of an intellectual tradition which has its origins in and is closely associated with one form of civilisation. As such, it is culturally specific and cannot be taken as the measure and standard of all intellectual activities. We only think it is superior to resorting to armed force, the examinations of entrails, or magic because it is *our* way of doing things. Because we appeal to reason on most matters, such appeals are taken by us to be 'objectively' superior. They are part of what Wittgenstein called our 'form of life'.

(2) The consequence of adopting the position in (1) is a kind of reasoned relativism. We cannot say that, in preference to superstitious practices, reason is the way to gain certain knowledge. Our preference for rationalism is, actually, a preference for our own culture and the role reason has in it.

(3) Intellectual traditions have their own ways of attracting adherents and keeping them within the fold. With rationalism these techniques are universal education and the professionalisation of knowledge. This has led to a situation where scientists, for instance, are indoctrinated with a particular view of what counts as science. They are systematically prevented from allowing their imaginations free rein. As a consequence we have trained incompetence — what Saul Bellow called 'high IQ morons'.

(4) When investigators come face to face with another tradition, as in the case of astrology, folk medicine, parapsychology, most invoke the dogma of rationalism in order to find such traditions 'inferior' to science and so 'false'. The best we can hope for is that they use a strategy of pragmatism, selecting what they can from both sides.

(5) Science is a social institution located in specific moral,

political and social contexts. As a social institution, it has to interact with other institutions. Inevitably these interactions lead to changes of direction, modification and adjustment that cannot be described in line with one methodological rule. If such a rule had to be proposed, it would be 'Anything goes', which is to say, there is no rule. Close attention to the detail of the history of scientific changes show this to be the case. The rationalists see such changes as progressive and uniform because they are in the grip of an obsession.

The cases which Feyerabend considers at length are drawn from the history of astronomy in the sixteenth and seventeenth centuries. Galileo's invention of the telescope finally broke the hold of Ptolemaic astronomy and vindicated Copernicus. But, says Feyerabend, if we want to say that the theoretical shift is progressive, this is not because the Copernican astronomers were more rational than the Ptolemaic, but simply that the standards had changed. The discoveries and theories have to be set alongside other beliefs and knowledge. Copernicus was convinced of his theory despite all the known facts. These facts had to be reconstructed in the light of his theory. This was done by neutralising and so overcoming the two most important objections to it, the 'tower argument' (why, if the earth moved, did a heavy object not fall at an angle rather than in a straight line when dropped from a high place?) and the argument from scripture. Both were taken equally seriously by scientists of the day. The second was dealt with by refusing to give a literal reading to the pertinent parts of the Bible while allowing such a reading for others. The first was handled by reintroducing into science outmoded theories which happened to suit the need. Copernicus called into play some, but not all, of Aristotle's theories, namely those which depended upon mathematical harmony in the universe against the 'facts' as we could see them. Such defences are not obviously any more rational than the arguments of Copernicus' opponents. Some people were attracted to the Copernican theory and so convinced by his arguments; others were not.

What eventually led to the general acceptance of Copernicus' theories was the propagandising genius of Galileo. The use of the telescope persuaded people to accept the heliocentric theory of the solar system. To do this they had to reconstruct 'the facts' as they knew them. The 'tower theory' was not finally laid to rest until Galileo invented a whole new theory of motion just to account for the phenomenon of free fall in terms of the Copernican theory.

Feyerabend's conclusion from the examination of this and similar cases is that scientific change and progress is really the conversion from one myth or set of myths to another. These myths comprise wholesale metaphysics. Such conversions do not take place simply through appeals to reason, argument, the evidence or method but rely on self interest, ideology and the attitudes of other social institutions in the surrounding society. Given this contextuality, science can have no claim to superiority over any other form of knowledge. It should be given a place alongside other forms of knowledge. It is this conclusion that enables Feyerabend to connect the philosophy of science with moral and political philosophy. To continue with the image, we have made an idol of science, we enforce worship at its shrine and extract a tithe on its behalf. We refuse to allow claims on behalf of forms of knowledge that run counter to those of science. The dogma of reason has given us big science and we bow the knee to expert opinion.

The reaction to Feyerabend has been mostly of two types. Philosophers have deplored his irreverence and have tried to counter his relativism. In so doing they have had to appeal to the superiority of reasoned argument to justify reasoned argument in science. Feyerabend remains unmoved. Some social scientists have adopted his philosophy of science because of its debunking nature. They have had even more scorn poured on them than the philosophers. Feyerabend is not offering an alternative methodology, just another theory to turn into a dogma. *He is against method.* Others, for example Habermas, have found in Feyerabend's scepticism arguments which are in sympathy with their own if not quite what they would have said. But Feyerabend does not want to stop science. He wants to put an end to all the pretentious talk about it. He does not want to offer a blueprint, merely to observe that if the recent and not so recent past is anything to go by, we cannot know in advance which ideas will prove fertile and which will not. Reactionary ideas might be just as useful as progressive ones. There is no independent rule for determining which is which. There might be a moral rule; but that is an entirely different matter from claiming that science is the embodiment of rational criticism.

Let us summarise what has been said so far. The central problem for the philosophy of science has traditionally been taken to be the logical or rational character of scientific theory. Do such theories give certain knowledge? Are they universal laws? If not, why not? We saw that this began as an epistemological problem, but in its inductivist form it soon ran into persistent and ineradicable difficulties. To circumvent these, Popper refined the whole issue in methodological terms. It was scientific methodology which was rational not necessarily its theory. Once this transformation had been effected, a link was forged between the logic of scientific methodology and its history. No matter what precise form the historical contextualising took, it always seemed to lead further and further away from any conception of science as 'pure reason' in practice. Scientific theories did not progress rationally. They were largely incommensurable.

While not everyone would accept the relativist and, in Feyerabend's case, anarchist conclusions that incommensurability seemed to imply, none the less it is fairly plain that epistemological and methodological considerations pure and simple are not sufficient to account for changes in scientific theory. This conclusion has recently been reinforced by the promulgation of Quine's version of the 'indeterminacy thesis' (cf. Chapter 8). This holds that any given theory is underdetermined by the facts and, hence, that any number of theories can be invoked to explain the same 'facts' or 'data'. Each would be made up of a slightly different web of propositions. For Quine, the implication of this view is the need to 'naturalise' epistemology by reducing it to a science of knowledge such as psychology and, presumably, ultimately the physiology of the brain. The laws of cognition and brain function will tell us why we accept and hold just those theories that we do.

Others have not felt the need to be drawn in quite this direction. Building upon what Mary Hesse has called a 'network model' of knowledge which is very similar to Quine's, they have laid great emphasis upon the contribution which the sociology of knowledge might make to explanation here. The nature of the internal logical structure of the network is an epistemological matter, they suggest, but the overall shape and constituents of the model are socially determined. Social, political and moral attitudes determine which propositions are left in and which excluded from the network. If one adopts this view, the philosophy of science becomes a sub-branch of the history of ideas. Studies carried out using this approach have, for example, tried to show how developments such as Boyle's atomic theory of matter, and with it the origins of chemistry, share the same corpuscular philosophy that motivated his opinions in social and political matters. This philosophy matches Boyle's social interests. Others have brought out the close relationship between innovations in statistical theory and the social and political theories of eugenics. It is the conviction of protagonists of this whole approach that the combination of epistemology and the social history of ideas makes a full blown 'science of knowledge' possible. Naturally, there are those who would disagree.

The views that we have discussed so far have, by and large, been centred on scientific theory. Even Imre Lakatos' notion of a 'research programme' follows this trend in that the programme is a compendium of methods of measurement, techniques and researchable problems all held together by a general, theoretical framework. But is scientific theory and its rationality the only point of entry we can make? What sorts of arguments arise and what issues are we led into if we begin from some other aspect of scientific activity? Do these look as if they will lead away from rather than into the entrenched positions we have examined up till now?

Let us go back to the closeness of fit that we noted between the questions of incommensurability and radical translation. Both of these had their origins in what Quine calls the 'underdetermination of theory by the facts'. The theory, the web of propositions for a language, the paradigm, can be adjusted to accommodate what are apparent counterfactuals. The difficulty which radical translation and incommensurability give us is how to express the concepts of one theory or paradigm in the terms of another *and preserve truth*. The solution which both Quine and Kuhn offer us is one which Quine calls 'semantic ascent'. One cannot fix the continuity of properties of objects as between theories, but one can fix the continuity of the truth of propositions. This can be done because the unit of meaning, and hence of truth for Quine, is the whole language. What we are offered, therefore, is the notion of a proposition being 'true in a language' or 'true in a conceptual framework'. To take Kuhn's famous case, the properties of phlogiston as they were described in pre-Lavoisier chemistry are not translatable, one for one, into the properties of oxygen in post-Lavoisier chemistry. In this sense the theories are incommensurable. But the *truth* of statements or propositions made about phlogiston in pre-Lavoisier chemistry is commensurable with the *truth* of propositions made about oxygen in post-Lavoisier chemistry. Truth has become internal to a theory.

As Quine clearly saw, this raises the question of ontology. Each paradigm or network will have its own objects and properties. In pre-Lavoisier chemistry there was an object called phlogiston, post-Lavoisier there was not. What are we to say about the relationship between these ontologies? When we examined Quine's view in Chapter 7, we saw that in logic there were no compelling reasons why one should choose one ontology over another, other than the rule of thumb summarised in Ockham's Razor. We can have a luxuriant ontology or we can have a simplified one but on the whole we should prefer the simplified. The question can now be asked 'How do we get a simplified ontology for science?' Is such a thing even possible? Clearly there are two things that we cannot do. We cannot attempt to look at 'how things are' to tell us which ontology to go for because that would be to succumb to naïve realism and empiricism. Neither can we take the other popular course, namely looking to theory, since to do that would bring us face to face with the incompatibility of theories once more. What philosophers have done instead is to turn to scientific investigation, experimentation, observation and measurement to see what ontological commitments they seem to involve. Theory and theoretical unity is only approached as it bears upon, or is derived from, experiment and observation. To use Ian Hacking's phrase, what such a philosophy is interested in is not how scientists *represent* the world in theories but how they *intervene* in it to investigate and observe it.

Let us take a couple of cases just to see what is involved here. Among botanists, the single-celled form of life called *Euglena* is classified as a plant because it photosynthesises. Anything which photosynthesises is, for them, a plant. To the zoologist, however, *Euglena* is an animal. It has a kind of proto-gut and moves about freely. What are we supposed to say *Euglena* is 'really'? Clearly there is no answer here. For scientists, *Euglena* is not 'really' anything. It displays properties belonging to two entirely distinct kingdoms. The situation is, if anything, even worse with some of the slime moulds. These ought to be fungi, since they reproduce by emitting spores, and yet they flow around like amoeba and digest food by engulfing it. One thing we could do, of course, is to invest a whole new kingdom to go alongside what we once thought were the exclusive categories of plants and animals, say plants-cum-animals, but that would entail multiplying the categories in the ontology. And it is not just botanists and zoologists who have these problems. High energy physics keeps replacing one set of 'basic constituents' like molecules and nuclei with atoms, protons and neutrons which in turn are replaced by electrons and quarks, mesons, bosons, muons, leptons etc. etc. Indeed, any science could tell the same story.

One way that we could try to cope with what turns out to be a ramifying ontology rather than a simplifying one is to take the same line with 'realism-for-ontologies' that we have for 'realism-for-theories'. Realism-for-theories only causes us problems when we try to make a fit between the theory and how the world is independent of the theory, for we have no way of fixing how the world is independent of some theory of it. In the light of this philosophers have tended to talk of realism-within-the-theory or what Hilary Putnam calls 'internal realism' (cf. Chapter 7). Propositions are true within a theory or true for a given language. We can cope with the diversity of observations made, things seen, properties displayed if, instead of thinking of ontologies as somehow matching how the world really is organised, we see them as taxonomies that allow us to make experiments and investigations and enable us to give organised descriptions of what we find. Just as we don't have to have a unified theory so we don't have to have a unified ontology. In what is a lovely contrast Nancy Cartwright compares the attitudes of those who seek unity and harmony with those who do not.

> Pierre Duhem distinguished two kinds of thinkers: the deep but narrow minds of the French, and the broad but shallow minds of the English. The French mind sees things in an elegant, unified way. It takes Newton's three laws of motion and turns them into the beautiful Lagrangian mathematics of mechanics. The English mind, says Duhem, is an exact contrast. It engineers bits of gears, and pulleys, and keeps the strings from tangling up. It holds a thousand different details all at once, without imposing much abstract order or organisation. (*How the Laws of Physics Lie*, p. 19)

It would seem, as far as we can tell from the sorts of descriptions provided by the various sciences, that if we were to put it in creationist terms, God has the untidy mind of the English.

What does this view lead us to say about scientific theory? First and foremost, the theories provided by the various disciplines within science are 'phenomenological', but in a very precise sense of that term. They are descriptions of what has been observed, measured, affected and brought about, the phenomena of studies, experiments and investigations. Such 'phenomenological laws' are discontinuous with each other because they are the outcome of many different sets of premises and interests. They reflect what, in Chapter 3, we called alternative theoretical attitudes and relevances. Chemistry does not have 'the same' problems as physics, nor does it want to carry out 'the same' studies. Neither do botany and zoology. Although the 'phenomenological laws' are correct within their domains, they do not add up to or reduce to a theoretical unity. Any attempt to unify them by translating their terms and descriptions into more 'fundamental' ones is bound to distort them. This will happen because the concepts being invoked can only be approximations to those applied in the original theories. As a consequence, any attempt to produce a set of 'fundamental laws' will result in 'lies'. Different orders of observation, measurement and phenomena do not reduce without residue to one another. If we accept this argument, then the philosophical view of science that we are likely to adopt is one which says that science is committed to 'multiple realities' and not the philosophical myth of a single, unified description of how things really are. These 'multiple realities' are available in the theories and descriptions given within the different disciplines.

Does this view of science have any implications for the human and social sciences? In one way, the answer has to be an unequivocal 'No!' and that *is* the implication. Since all the emphasis is being laid upon the disunity of science there seems to be little point in trying to unite the human sciences and the natural ones. Once theory has been pushed into the background we can forget about the requirement for conformity with some supposed canons of theorising or method. Certainly practising scientists don't have those worries. What they are concerned about is solving their scientific problems, making the observations and mounting the investigations which they see as important and fruitful. All they require of one another is that they should know what they are doing and pursue their own lines of interest with methods appropriate to them. Now if it is the case — and from all that has been said up to now in this book it seems to be — if the phenomena in which the social and cultural sciences are interested have properties which require distinctive methods of investigation and theorising, then so be it. Providing those engaged in such sciences know what they are doing and meet the strictures which they lay upon themselves, then there is no need to feel bound by any philosophically inspired stipulations. Certainly there is no need to try to emulate any 'natural science model' of theory and investigation, for, it seems, no such unified model exists.

Recommended Reading

Rom Harré's *The Philosophies of Science* (Oxford University Press, 1972) is still as good a basic introduction as one can find. Readings on the early debates can be found in J. Kockelmans, *Philosophy of Science* (Collier Macmillan, 1968) while Stephen Toulmin's *Foresight and Understanding* (Hutchinson, 1961) offers a different slant. Popper provides the best introduction to his own thought in *Objective Knowledge* (Oxford University Press, 1972) with *The Logic of Scientific Discovery* really being for the specialist. The application of his ideas to social and human science is sketched out in *The Poverty of Historicism* (Routledge, 1961). Bryan Magee's *Popper* (Fontana, 1973) is the place to start if you have no knowledge at all of this field. The hypothetico-deductive system is set out in C.G. Hempel 'The Function of General Laws in History' in P. Gardiner (ed.), *Theories of History* (Free Press, 1959). A more recent elaboration and examination is P. Achinstein, *The Nature of Explanation* (Oxford University Press, 1983). Kuhn's original argument is contained in *The Structure of Scientific Revolutions* (University of Chicago Press, 1970) and supplemented by the essays in *The Essential Tension* (University of Chicago Press, 1977). The confrontation between Popper and Kuhn can be found in I. Lakatos and A. Musgrave (eds.), *Criticism and the Growth of Knowledge* (Cambridge University Press, 1970). Imre Lakatos' work is available in his *Collected Papers*, vols I and II (Cambridge University Press, 1978, 1984). The countercase by Feyerabend can be seen in *Against Method* (Verso, 1978) and *Science in a Free Society* (Verso, 1978). Ian Hacking's collection *Scientific Revolutions* (Oxford University Press, 1981) contains a small but wide ranging set of relevant essays especially Larry Laudan's 'A Problem Solving Approach to Scientific Progress'. Hacking also provides the most readable introduction to recent discussion of realism in science in *Representing and Intervening* (Cambridge University Press, 1983). This should be tackled before approaching Nancy Cartwright's *How the Laws of Physics Lie* (Clarendon, 1983). Michael Dummet's 'Common Sense and Physics' provides a neat summary of the various positions adopted in G.F. MacDonald, *Perception and Identity* (Macmillan, 1979). A reasonable place to start with Putnam's view of science is 'The Corroboration of Theories' in Ted Honderich and M. Burryeat (eds.), *Philosophy As It Is* (Penguin, 1979) before moving on to *Reason, Truth and History* (Cambridge University Press, 1981) and *Mind, Language and Philosophy* (Cambridge University Press, 1979). Some help with the content of these discussions is to be gained from O. Hanfling, 'Scientific Realism and Ordinary Usage', *Philosophical Investigations*, vol 7 (July 1984).

POSTSCRIPT

The major aim of this book is to introduce a range of arguments and positions currently adopted in philosophy to those who have little or no familiarity with them. In doing so, we hope to enable readers to get their philosophical bearings and begin to find their own way about what, to outsiders, often appears to be formidably difficult terrain. To keep our task manageable, we have concentrated more or less exclusively on philosophers and philosophies which we felt would be of direct relevance to students of the human sciences.

In addition to this major aim, we have to admit to a second, one which is less informative and more pedagogic. In providing the introduction we have, we want to encourage readers away from two distinct outlooks with regard to philosophy which we have noticed are quite widespread among those who first encounter it, particularly in the social sciences. For want of better formulations, we have dubbed these outlooks 'the balance sheet mentality' and 'the search for the magic formula'. While it is quite understandable why students especially should have these general views, in our opinion they are a considerable handicap when trying to grasp the nature of philosophising as an activity. And, after all, philosophising is what philosophers do.

What then are 'the balance sheet mentality' and 'the search for the magic formula'? Both are associated with a more pervasive attitude common among many disciplines; the desire to have unity, consensus and a general agreement on a single frame of reference into which all positions are to be fitted. As part of this outlook, the balance sheet mentality asks 'Where we are up to?' 'What have we achieved?' 'What does all the argument and disputation come to *now*?' 'What's the bottom line?' When no answers are forthcoming, or at least no straightforward ones, those possessing the balance sheet mentality are apt to be nonplussed and dismissive. But, as we have tried to show, philosophical arguments are not like bills and invoices. They do not always total up as contributions to a larger sum. Philosophers are not accumulating good arguments and valid inferences as physicists are discovering and listing new elementary particles. We must be careful here, though. Some philosophers think that this is just what they should be doing and would dearly love to rid philosophy of its more inconclusive tendencies. And, of course, that of itself is part of a larger debate over the nature of philosophy. In any event, what seems to happen, whether we approve of it or not, is that arguments go on and on and round and round (which is not the same as being circular) with 'progress' being measured by the increasing subtlety with which positions are stated, the ingenuity with which connections are made to hitherto unrelated questions and, as in the case of modal logic of late, the application of whole new technical vocabularies to standard, not to say staid and rather dull issues, thereby enlivening them. Any attempt to produce a global statement of debits and credits, profits and losses for an enterprise such as this seems to be singularly inappropriate.

Given that philosophical questions are rarely 'settled once and for all', but more often set aside in preference for others which seem more interesting, fertile, or engaging, there seems to be little point in looking to philosophy for fixed and certain solutions to the problems which beset the foundations of any empirical discipline. Yet this is precisely what those searching for the magic formula are seeking. They would like a general set of principles, a list of epistemological and methodological instructions for how to achieve certain and guaranteed knowledge in their field of interest. With regard to the human sciences, many have felt, as we have seen, that such instructions might be had if we were to adopt what was termed the 'natural science model'. They then turned to philosophy to tell them what those instructions would consist of. The trouble is it is by no means clear what philosophers think the 'natural science model' might be nor even on what grounds we should accept or reject it. Although individual philosophers do have clear and forceful arguments for the positions which they advocate, philosophy as a whole does not favour this or that option. In the end, it is a matter of grappling with the specifics of the arguments and cases, and of making up our own minds. The drawing out of the realisation that making your own mind up is what philosophising is about — and hence what is involved in accepting or rejecting a set of considered arguments — is our third aim. It is not enough simply to dislike a set of conclusions or to be out of sympathy with a set of premises. Sound arguments are required if a position is to be overturned.

The balance sheet mentality and the search for the magic formula are expressions of what we regard as unrealistic expectations which many newcomers hold of philosophy. Yet, as we said, these expectations are understandable. Philosophers, themselves, have a great deal of difficulty conveying to others what they regard as the nature of philosophy. In a recent, influential study Richard Rorty suggests that perhaps the best analogy may be with a conversation: philosophy is the conversation of mankind. Conversations are a distinctive form of social activity. They are not engaged in for a point, other than just taking part; no conclusions are necessarily reached. Each participant offers himself and his views as his contribution. Topics change, sometimes coherently, sometimes randomly; they are taken up, broken off and returned to with hardly any conscious effort. Most of all, what Rorty's image catches is the openness and pluralism of philosophy. Each contribution has something to offer and something distinctive worth hearing. After all, a conversation is not a monologue; neither is it a ritual chant.

Recommended Reading

Richard Rorty's *Philosophy and The Mirror of Nature* (Blackwell, 1980) and *The Consequences of Pragmatism* (Harvester, 1982) provide general introductions to his view of the history of philosophy and its current state.

INDEX